Time-conscious Psychological Therapy

Counsellors and psychotherapists are divided about the morality and efficacy of short-term psychotherapy and counselling – this book offers a way through the controversy by giving back the central position to consumers of psychotherapy.

The model of psychotherapy described in the book is based on flexible adjustment to the individual client's development. It shows how a carefully structured, stage-based series of therapeutic relationships can be rewarding for both client and therapist. At each stage a clearly stated commitment is entered into by both parties in which the length of time and breadth of focus of the encounter are mutually agreed. The process can involve a series of relationships with different practitioners. It is adaptable to the client's needs at any one time and well-suited to work settings where constraints of time and money raise dilemmas for practitioners about the ethics of treatment.

Enlivened by progressive case examples, this is a book for practitioners of all psychological therapies who are looking for a rigorous but flexible approach to empowering their clients.

Jenifer Elton Wilson is a chartered counselling psychologist, a UKCP registered psychotherapist and Senior Counsellor at the University of the West of England, Bristol.

This book is dedicated to all the clients and practitioners 'in search of psychological evolution' from whom I have learnt my craft

Time-conscious
Psychological Therapy

A life stage to go through

Jenifer Elton Wilson

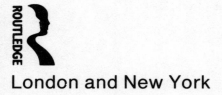

London and New York

First published 1996
by Routledge
11 New Fetter Lane, London EC4P 4EE

Simultaneously published in the USA and Canada
by Routledge
29 West 35th Street, New York, NY 10001

© 1996 Jenifer Elton Wilson

Typeset in Times by Datix International Limited, Bungay, Suffolk

Printed and bound in Great Britain by Clays Ltd, St Ives plc

British Library Cataloguing in Publication Data
A catalogue record for this book is available from the British
Library

Library of Congress Cataloging in Publication Data
A catalog record for this book has been requested

ISBN 0–415–11457–8
    0–415–11458–6 (pbk)

Every effort has been made to obtain permission for the lines
by Portia Nelson originally published in *Repeat After Me*.
The publisher would be pleased to hear from anyone who
could help to trace the copyright holder of this work.

Contents

List of tables

Acknowledgements

This book was undertaken on an impulse, engendered by my wish to share my experience of working with focus and commitment from the periphery of my clients' lives. I am grateful to Edwina Welham for responding so promptly to that first telephone call, and to all those others at Routledge who have encouraged this endeavour.

Particular people made it possible for me to embark on and complete this book. Phil Lapworth read each chapter as I wrote it and provided me with a generous, ever-available and scrupulous commentary. Tom Wilson accompanied my every agony, and each triumphant moment, with fortitude, patience, encouragement and wisdom. My daughters cheered me on and accepted, without protest, the scattered quality of my attention.

Several of my colleagues, especially Jennifer Mackewn, Phil Topham, Rosie Jeffries, Tracey Collins, Eira Makepeace and Josie Wells, have supported this endeavour. My experience of managing a counselling service at an ex-polytechnic in the West of England has been invaluable in developing my particular views about psychological therapy.

My memories of the patients and staff at Atkinson Morley's Hospital have been a valuable inspiration, and for this experience and for his sponsorship, I am still indebted to Professor Hubert Lacey. Finally, I am grateful for the lessons I have learnt from the four practitioners of psychological therapy who have accompanied me at different stages of my own personal life process.

Chapter 1

Why this book?

The 'talking/listening cure' is considered by the public and many health professionals as an imprecise, expensive, self-indulgent and slow route to psychological health and welfare. Counsellors and psychotherapists are divided about the morality and the efficacy of short-term psychotherapy and counselling. The critics of psychotherapy and counselling increase as the issues of abuse of power, crude and subtle, are debated: 'Therapists have put us on the couch for long enough; it's time we put them in the dock' (Madeleine Bunting in the *Guardian*, 24 Feb. 1994).

This book offers a way through the controversy by giving the central position back to the consumers of psychotherapy. Although still a minority, some of the most vivid and popular descriptions of the psychotherapeutic experience are the first-hand accounts written by clients. These accounts are valuable and enlightening, whether written in grateful praise (Cardinale 1984) or in more critical scrutiny (Dinnage 1989), and go some way towards redirecting attention away from the therapy hour and towards the client's life. Nevertheless, as Peter Lomas (France 1988: back cover) has commented in his recommendation of Anne France's description of her experience as a consumer of psychotherapy, the preponderance of accounts are given from the point of view of the practitioner. Almost without exception, approaches to psychotherapy or counselling place the practitioner in the principal role. Therapeutic models are offered to the expert professional with the implicit message that it is their responsibility to provide the client with a life-changing experience. Even person-centred models fall into this error by placing the onus of change on the practitioner's ability to provide 'core conditions' for growth of 'unconditional positive regard', 'congruence' and 'empathic understanding' (Mearns and Thorne 1988: 14–15).

Instead, this book views individual practitioners as secondary to the life pattern of an individual client's psychological development. To achieve psychological transformation, one client may use the services of a variety of professional helpers, as well as drawing upon the support of external resources and facing the common existential challenge of needing to 'cope constructively with the business of being human' (Gilmore 1973). Many practitioners will agree with this view, yet all are prey to the subtle and seductive notion of being the unique healer, wounded or not, whose singular knowledge, hard-won training and experience is enabling their clients to achieve the changes they seek.

The recommended approach is clear and yet rigorous, based on flexible adjustment to the client's development through a series of therapeutic relationships, each of which can be negotiated and accommodated by offering a stage-related professional service. At each stage, the client is invited into a clearly stated two-way commitment with an established focus related to the type of relationship operating between client and therapist. Length of time and breadth of focus are related and the process is likely to involve a series of therapeutic encounters with different counsellors and psychotherapists.

This is a book for practitioners of all the psychological therapies, whether they call themselves psychotherapists, counsellors, clinical or counselling psychologists. All these professional roles involve the use of some form of psychological knowledge to inform the practitioner's interactions with people who are experiencing mental and emotional discomfort which blocks their developmental progress. The approach offered is not linked to any one psychotherapeutic orientation. To an extent, it may be described as a collection of concepts concerning the four overarching professional issues of assessment, contractual commitment, personal development and the therapeutic relationship.

In addition, clients experiencing or contemplating psychological therapy may find some of these ideas interesting. The fictional case scenarios used throughout the book focus on the way in which clients experience and respond to practitioners. Their stories, and their psychological journeys, are the vivid reasons for providing psychological therapy. All the theoretical and technical preoccupations so much prized by practitioners are always peripheral to these central concerns.

THE CRITICS OF PSYCHOTHERAPY

I have already mentioned some of the criticisms which are levelled at the practice of psychological therapy. In Britain, a pragmatic and empiricist scientific establishment continues to influence general attitudes to any form of assisted psychological metamorphosis. This has been compounded and confused by a linked tendency towards an over-determined, if slightly mocking, respect for psychoanalysis as the expensive limousine in which the client with money to spend may, possibly, be carried through the mysteries of psychological transformation. Otherwise, psychological treatments are often considered to be the last resort for unfortunate individuals unable to cope with life's vicissitudes, and suffering from mental breakdown.

One result of these avoidant and hostile attitudes is that British practitioners have tended to polarise in their loyalties. There are those who seek the elite designation of *psychotherapist*, with its emphasis on protracted training and self-development in order to conduct an equally prolonged therapeutic engagement. In contrast the professional *counsellor* has tended to offer a friendly alliance between equals, in which one party offers a more skills-based and practical approach to psychological therapy.

> Counselling may be concerned with developmental issues, addressing and resolving specific problems, making decisions, coping with crisis, developing personal insight and knowledge, working through feelings of inner conflict or improving relationships with others. The counsellor's role is to facilitate the client's work in ways which respect the client's values, personal resources and capacity for self-determination.
>
> (British Association for Counselling 1992: 3.1)

The popularity of counselling in Britain may well be in the implicit message that this could resemble good old professional advice, similar to that provided by lawyers, accountants and plumbers, and therefore need not be linked with the stigma of mental disorder. The psychological therapies offered by the 'free at the point of delivery' (Beveridge 1942) National Health Service (NHS) are in much demand, although seen by most clients as a final admission of their failure to cope, somewhat dignified by diagnosis of mental ill-health. This increased pressure on mental health clinics has encouraged a broader and more pragmatic role for the (NHS) *psychotherapy* practitioner, who is now likely to employ a wide variety of techniques and to experiment with brief and more focused psychotherapy. A centre of influence has been the careful work of a team of practitioner-researchers based at Sheffield University (Barkham and Shapiro 1989, Culverwell *et al.* 1994). Nevertheless, a belief in the superiority and desirability of a psychoanalytic training remains entrenched in many medical settings.

In the United States, and in Europe, the use of the psychological therapies seems to be generally more accepted, and less stigmatised. It is argued by Vidaver, Archer and Peake (1988: 182) that one of the reasons for the American public's willing embrace of psychotherapy in its more accessible forms since the 1950s, is that: 'an emancipation of American thinking, in the form of literature from William Faulkner, Eugene O'Neill and Tennessee Williams, generated an intellectual ferment that placed high value on self-discovery, personal growth and understanding of behavior' (Peake, Borduin and Archer 1988: 182). It is probable that this intellectual interest in psychotherapy was itself imported by emigrants from mainland Europe. Somehow, the British social and medical institutions missed out on this earlier 'explosion on the scene' (Vidaver, Archer and Peake 1988) of the psychological therapies as a treatment of choice for a population in search of self-improvement.

Perhaps it needed the dogma of individualistic self-empowerment, endorsed by the Thatcherite 1980s, to encourage the rapid growth of counselling as a recognised British profession. I have already suggested some reasons for the increased acceptability of psychological intervention when this is offered in the form of facilitative counselling skills intended to increase an individual's mastery of problematic life events. This has led to the rapid development and expansion of the British Association for Counselling (BAC) as an umbrella organisation which offers membership and a code of ethics to a wide variety of people who have some interest in practising as a counsellor. Only a minority have sought BAC professional accreditation. Similarly, there has been a rapid growth, within the British Psychological Society, of psychologists with a special interest in counselling psychology, leading to a professional qualification. Again this is at present held only by a relatively small group of chartered counselling psychologists.

Interestingly, British models of counselling have rapidly adopted the role of junior partners within the major psychotherapeutic orientations, rather than following the American example of establishing a specialised and separate profession with expertise within the more instructional domains of education, health and other areas linked to benevolent social control. This specialisation has been validated by the creation, in the United States, of highly professional training courses in counselling, with mandatory and extensive practice placements. These stringent training standards are shaped and validated by the licence to practice required in every state.

To some extent, the alliances established between models of counselling and psychotherapeutic schools in the United Kingdom have confused the British public's perception of counselling as a new profession, and encouraged a homespun lay-person approach which sits uneasily with the complex theories of meaning developed by the major psychotherapeutic schools.

The recent development of the United Kingdom Council for Psychotherapy (UKCP) has gone some way towards formalising *psychotherapy* as a profession. However, the pressure to include a broad range of training institutions, each with their own variety of qualifications, usually linked to theoretical orientation, may not be helpful to the average UK citizen seeking a standard model of psychotherapy which can be trusted. There is, in any case, no empirical support for any generic superiority in efficacy being attached to a theoretical orientation. The development of a British criterion for competence, knowledge and experience which transcends theoretical orientation has been addressed, to some extent, by the qualifications required for accreditation as a BAC counsellor or as a chartered counselling psychologist.

During the same period, there has been a general groundswell, on both sides of the Atlantic, of a renewed critical appraisal, verging on condemnation, of the manner in which the psychological therapies have been employed. The three major criticisms levelled at the profession are that it has abused its power, ignored social injustice and exploited human distress for financial gain. Jeffrey Masson (1985) has spearheaded this onslaught, with particular emphasis on the self-protective theorising which enabled generations of Freud's descendants to ignore the painful issues of childhood sexual abuse, and to marginalise issues of gender. This indictment has been superseded since the 1970s (Dahlberg 1970, Pope, Sonne and Holroyd 1993) by the evidence of even greater betrayals in the form of sexual usage of clients, usually female, by therapists, usually male. Such unethical betrayals of trust have crudely demonstrated the dangerous asymmetric nature of power (Rutter 1990) within the therapeutic engagement. This imbalance, and its cavalier exploitation within a profession which was traditionally male-dominated, has been explored more extensively by feminist critics and is now an area for open discussion between therapists. The view promoted by this book is that, while practitioners cannot avoid the responsibility of power within the therapeutic engagement, they can refrain from the subtle grandiosities which such power can induce. One method would be to adopt the more straightforward and explicit role of a tradesperson, engaged to offer a service, and to work with and for their clients. This pragmatic attitude has been recommended since the seminal work of Alexander and French (1946) but is still rarely voiced in training programmes or in mainstream psychotherapy literature.

Alice Miller (1985, 1987) has argued that there has been a more general disempowerment of many psychotherapy clients. Their childhood experiences are liable to be discounted within the 'poisonous pedagogy' of repressive parenthood imposed through mainstream psychoanalysis and within society at large. David Pilgrim (1992) has consistently and coolly provided a professional psychologist's critique of the abandonment of collective responsibility and potential risk of victim blaming within the rapidly increasing field of private practice. His arguments dovetail with the more vivid denunciations of the novels of Fay Weldon (see, e.g., 1993), whose anti-therapy statements gain media publicity. The more gentle critiques of David Smail (1987) and Miller Mair (1989) underline the tendency of practitioners to conduct a one-sided dialogue rather than a meaningful discourse with their clients.

In all these critiques, the insidious professional narcissism induced by the intensity of the therapy session is to be discerned. The psychological therapist can be blinkered by an espoused and painfully acquired theoretical training, seduced by the expert role and confined by the setting within which he or she is reimbursed. Practitioners often work within what can seem to the client a closed system. Their reliance on their own theories, regarding the usefulness of transference insights, the prevalence of faulty cognitive schemas or the lack of enough unconditional positive regard tends to supersede the client's own experience in the external world. Above all, the picture is distorted by the prevalent belief of most practitioners that one particular therapeutic engagement is the *central* influence on a client's life.

As I have reiterated throughout this book, the psychotherapeutic situation is unique. Patients may look back upon it as the only time in their lives during which they feel themselves to have been understood and fully accepted by another human being.

(Storr 1979: 157)

This book aims to provide a creative response to critics by outlining an approach respectful of a client's ownership of their personal psychological development.

A fundamental and longstanding doubt about psychological therapy, particularly in its more psychoanalytic guise, is with regard to its efficacy. The doubts and disputes initiated by Eysenck in 1952 are still unresolved, especially in Britain, where the lengthy process of validation engaged in by American therapists during the 1970s (Meltzoff and Kornreich 1970; Luborsky, Singer and Luborsky 1975) is not generally known. Nor will this book attempt to engage with this thorny debate, except to acknowledge the impossibility of engaging in value-free outcome research, the futility of attempts to prove a superior theoretical orientation and the powerful influence of relationship and systemic issues within the therapeutic journey. The growing interest amongst practitioners in developing the evaluative approach of the 'practitioner-scientist' (Elton Wilson and Barkham 1994) to their professional activities is a hopeful development which may increase a more realistic understanding of process and outcome of the therapeutic engagement.

THE DEMAND FOR AN ACCESSIBLE AND EFFECTIVE APPROACH

Whatever the criticisms and divisions operating in the field of psychological therapy, there is a continuing demand for the 'talking cure' (Breuer and Freud 1955) and a growing acknowledgement of the need for more *effective* psychotherapy and counselling to be made available to more clients within a climate of limited resources in time and funding. The usual response to this issue is to presume that *short-term* or brief psychological therapy is indicated. This suggestion is seen by many practitioners as a meagre and cheese-paring solution which puts the cost-effective solution above considerations of quality. Even among those who extol the qualities of the brief psychotherapies there can be discerned an uneasy defensiveness, especially with regard to the appropriateness of short-term approaches for many client groups. The implication is that in the best of all possible worlds, longer-term psychotherapy would be the response of choice. Decades ago, Alexander and French (1946: v) described the prevalence, 'among psychoanalysts' of 'an almost superstitious belief that quick therapeutic results cannot be genuine'. The most recent handbook about psychotherapy demonstrates that little may have changed for psychoanalysis in the 1990s: 'Even where the contract appears not to have been made overtly, as in psychoanalysis, in reality the contract is for as long as it takes, even if that is many years' (Clarkson 1994: 5). While humanistic approaches to psychotherapy are critical of many aspects of psychoanalysis, the notion of the *length* of psychotherapeutic engagement as somehow indicative of its *depth* is not usually challenged. Indeed it is an aspect of psychoanalysis that is held in somewhat reluctant awe. This emphasis on *quantity* rather than *quality*, as the means to deliver conditions for true psychological change, has to be questioned and challenged by practitioners themselves if the profession is to withstand accusations of financial motivation and uncritical elitism.

The model offered in this book, of ongoing assessment, flexible commitment policies and areas of focus respectful of the client's life process, is not limited to brief psychotherapeutic engagements. It is offered to practitioners, especially those critical of short-term work, as an invitation to use a range of considered options, to *design*, in consultation with their clients, an appropriate and practical package of focused psychological change. This design would need to take into account and use the external realities of clients' lives, including considerations of available time and funding. The approach delineated in this book is intended to extend beyond the short-term versus long-term psychotherapy debate, through an emphasis on the client's own search for meaning within the materiality of their existence. All practitioners are invited to consider, *at point of entry*, a series of alternatives to any automatic offer of continuing long-term psychological therapy. The dialectic would then shift to questions of timing, motivation, and readiness for change, and would utilise the client's perceptions, participation and ability to choose. A flexible range of *commitments* replaces the more mechanistic therapy contract. Where there are concerns about limited resources, many mental health services have begun to modify their psychotherapy services towards a somewhat similar model. Nevertheless, this is often a reactive rather than a proactive development based on a need to justify the continuation of a psychotherapy service within a changing political climate:

However, in many areas, services in formal psychotherapies are often uncoordinated, unevenly distributed, and poorly integrated with other psychiatric and psychological services. Some are inadequately resourced to meet even minimal public demand. Further, they are often fragmented and subject to inter-professional tensions, themselves fed by anxieties about professional roles and by anxieties that conceptual differences between psychological therapies may contaminate rather than enrich a psychotherapy service. The current changes and uncertainties in the NHS are perhaps exacerbating these tensions, but they also provide some pressure to resolve them. The present situation is not conducive to

good patient care, is incomprehensible to most referrers and will undoubt-
edly become an anathema to purchasers.

(Kosviner 1994: 287–8)

The tradition of establishing some sort of 'contract' with clients has become
hallowed by usage and is rarely questioned. These are usually verbal
agreements, unlikely to be considered legally binding, and can appear to
favour the therapist's convenience with the emphasis on place, time and
payment. The tasks and goals of the therapeutic engagement may only be
specified in vague and open terms. A client in psychological pain is likely to
be disinterested in these parameters and willing to agree to almost anything
in the hope of some alleviation. The slowly increasing body of research into
the *client's experience* of counselling or psychotherapy includes some vivid
indications of the differences of perception, aspiration and valuation
between client and practitioner (McLeod 1990a and b, Howe 1993).

A shift of emphasis to the preoccupations and desires of clients need not
contradict the importance of a consistent 'frame' (Casement 1985: 61) as a
useful and necessary component in the work of a psychological therapist.
Any form of focused psychotherapy is likely to entail agreement as to time
and space, whatever the orientation of the therapist. The existential reality
of an agreed time limit is a powerful force for change, long recognised by
the major models of brief psychotherapy. This is a challenge to the traditional view, still held by many psychotherapists and counsellors, particularly
those working in the private sector, that long-term, open-ended therapeutic
engagement is always a superior form of psychological therapy.

THE LITERATURE OF BRIEF PSYCHOTHERAPY

The approach offered in this book is indebted to the literature describing
the wide range of innovative developments in the field of brief psychotherapy. These have taken place under the umbrella of two of the three
main theoretical orientations which inform the psychological therapies.
Cognitive behavioural forms of psychological intervention have always
been concerned to arrive at clearly specified outcomes in the briefest
amount of time and with the most economic expenditure of energy. Practitioners of psychodynamic psychotherapy have questioned the received
orthodoxy of psychoanalytic theory regarding the superiority of long-term
psychotherapy since Alexander and French (1946) developed the concept of
the 'corrective emotional experience' as the central curative factor in any
psychoanalytic therapy.

It is somewhat surprising to acknowledge that the challenging influence
of humanist and existential theorists has not extended to any widely
accepted and significant model of brief psychotherapy. Yet it is this orientation which has inspired and infiltrated all the major models of psychological

therapy, particularly through the work of Carl Rogers. He has contributed to our increased understanding of the interpersonal factors operating in the therapeutic relationship, and his emphasis on the necessary, if not sufficient, conditions for psychological change. But these very conditions, of unconditional positive regard from the therapist and of the natural growth processes inherent in clients in receipt of therapeutic benevolence, appear to militate against clearly stated limitations of time and direction.

Cognitive behavioural approaches to brief therapy are heavily influenced by theories arising from the schools of strategic and structural family therapy (Minuchin 1974, Haley 1976, Selvini-Palazzoli *et al.* 1980, Watzlawick 1983) which encourage the use of pragmatic problem-solving interventions into the immediate social environment or system within which clients are experiencing psychological distress and behaving dysfunctionally. Within the same broad theoretical orientation are the highly structured approaches of Ellis's Rational Emotive Therapy (1970), Beck's Cognitive Therapy (1976) and the hypnosis-based work of Erickson and Rossi (1979). Literature arising from this theoretical base describes the therapist as a skilled change artist, and does not, in any detail, explore the client's process of self-exploration as a lifetime search, with therapist as ally, as this book is intended to do. A useful summary of these approaches can be found in Cade and O'Hanlon's recent *Brief Guide to Brief Therapy* (1993).

In the psychodynamic field, the notion of short-term therapy, usually described as less than twenty-five sessions, is currently being explored by three main theorists: Davanloo (1980), Malan (1975) and Mann (1973). All these approaches emphasise the importance of careful, although not necessarily formal, selection for client suitability to brief psychotherapy. Interpretation of defences with swift and deliberate focus on transference issues characterises the work of both Davanloo and Malan. If anything, the centrality and the power of the therapist is increased in these briefer versions of psychoanalytic therapy, although Mann may be an interesting exception to this precept in that he emphasises the practitioner's empathic engagement with the existential reality of a time-limited contract as the major curative factor. It may be that Mann is a rare exponent of existential humanist theory as relevant to brief psychotherapy.

One of the most recent developments in short-term psychological therapy draws from a combination of theoretical orientations. This is the creative innovation of Anthony Ryle (1990), whose seminal text on Cognitive Analytic Therapy (CAT) draws on psychoanalytic, cognitive and behavioural theory to present a highly structured and clearly delineated approach. The client is included and involved throughout the clearly negotiated and time-limited process of therapeutic change. CAT therapists are encouraged to use and to share their thinking with their clients, and the use of clearly negotiated commitment on both sides of the therapeutic divide, combined with a flexible potential is explored, although only within the parameters of

12 to 16 therapy sessions. Ryle maintains that this approach can be beneficial to most clients, and argues that even the 'fragile borderline' personality may be reassured by a combination of optimism and freedom from long-term commitment. This model of therapy has contributed to the approach delineated in this book although it is considerably more manualised and uses specific and rigid terms and procedures. The theoretical understanding and skill of the CAT practitioner is still the central agent of change, rather than the developmental life process of the client.

The model of psychological therapy described in this book has been influenced and informed by the majority of these theorists in the field of brief psychotherapy. It reflects an integration of the major theoretical orientations and utilises *time-conscious* rather than purely time-limited procedures. I recommend the reader seeking more information about brief psychotherapies to the authors themselves, or to the excellent overview provided by Peake, Borduin and Archer (1988).

THE STRUCTURE OF THIS BOOK

I have attempted in this chapter to answer the question: 'Why this book?' by delineating its threefold purpose. It is a response to the need for more *effective* psychotherapy and counselling to be made available to more clients with limited resources of time and funding. It is not only a response to the critics of psychotherapy and counselling in general, but also a response to the critics of all time-conscious offers of psychological therapy. In the next two chapters, the two basic process models on which a time-conscious approach depends are outlined.

Chapter 2 consists of an introduction to *the process of structured commitment-making* in the form of a flexible 'flow-chart' progression of negotiated agreements regarding time and possible outcome, with the emphasis on initial assessment and continuous reviews. Chapter 3 proposes a stage model of *the enduring process of psychological change and personal development* applicable to a wide range of psychotherapy and counselling clients. Consideration of these stages can inform the practitioner's choice of relationship mode and focus, whatever the level of commitment agreed. Chapter 4 explores the use of *assessment* and *review*, as a shared process between client and practitioner, at the *intake interview* and at regular intervals or *choice points*. The use of focal themes appropriate to the stage indicated by the *life process* model within the structure of *contractual commitment* is illustrated in the next four chapters, each of which describes one of the four major types of commitment. Fictional case examples are used throughout the book to illustrate core issues of assessment, review and focus. Finally, the reader is invited to consider some of the implications and meta-considerations which span the terrain explored through this approach.

Chapter 2

A flow-chart for time-conscious and focused contractual commitment

DEFINING COMMITMENT

Central to a focused approach to psychological therapy is the importance of a commitment, agreed by practitioner and client, to the therapeutic engagement. Practitioners continually assess their client's level of commitment so as to match this with an appropriate offer of their own commitment. This is part of the process often described as making a *contract* with the client. In the previous chapter, I suggested some of the reasons that clients can be puzzled and repelled by this phraseology. A written legal agreement is implied, although this is non-existent, and the verb 'to contract' is unpleasantly linked to the notion of compression and shrinkage. I now prefer to express this in terms of a joint *commitment* with the client. This term has emotional associations which can be expressed in practical terms, as in the following questions, addressed to herself by an experienced practitioner: 'Am I willing to commit to the client? How much will this commitment take from me? How much is this client willing to commit to the process, at this time?' (Murphy 1994, personal communication).

There are always two levels to the psychotherapeutic commitment. The first level concerns the amount of time to be set aside by both participants in the therapeutic engagement. The second level of commitment involves an agreed area of focus linked with provisional anticipation of some achievement. Such a goal may be phrased in terms of an extended process: 'being listened to' or 'finding out about myself' or, in more clear expectation of some concrete achievement, 'having the courage to leave a violent partner' or 'conquering my depression'.

In this chapter I will take the reader through a series of choice points which assist in clarifying the factors which may influence the first level of commitment, time allocation. The model is useful if interpreted loosely and should never be used to *characterise* clients but as a guideline to the area of focus, expressed in general terms, and to the nature of therapeutic engagement likely to be useful to the client's personal development at a particular time. The *stages* of the client's life process, and their relevance to the area of focus and the goals likely to be achieved, will be described in the next chapter. The emphasis is on how the practitioner evaluates each situation, makes a clear and relevant offer at the outset of the therapeutic engagement, and remains flexible and alert to the client's process. To fulfil this aim, a balance is kept between covert professional judgement and overt agreement with the client.

Two major skills are necessary: to be able to make assessments and to conduct reviews. These are linked aspects of the therapeutic craft which differ between individual practitioners and are always in process of refinement. A broader and more detailed methodology is the subject matter of Chapter 4. In this chapter, the discussion of assessment and reviewing will be confined to time-related issues. The flow chart displayed in Table 1 outlines the major decision-making choices involved in the process of negotiating commitments.

COMMITMENT INDICATIONS AT THE INTAKE INTERVIEW – THE FIRST CHOICE POINT

The commitment explored by client and counsellor at the intake interview is the decision to initially engage in the therapeutic process. Both participants are involved in this decision, although clients may need to be reminded of their freedom and their power in this two-way procedure. The use of the life process model to inform the complexity of the assessment process is explored in Chapter 3. At the outset, the alternative *motives* underlying the client's arrival for the intake interview are under scrutiny. The practitioner aims to structure the interview with tact and clarity so as to discover and share with the client which of the three reasons given at the beginning of Table 1 are operating.

The choice of the holding arrangement

A client who is clearly *in crisis* is not usually available for an informed choice as to commitment. Sometimes the disorientation and desperation of the situation leads an individual in crisis to believe that they must arrange a therapeutic commitment so as to ensure some sort of stability. Clients who perceive an external problem or a recent traumatic event as a massive threat can nearly always be considered to be in crisis. A preoccupation with safety and survival is another valuable clue that this is not the time to discuss contractual practicalities. The distress manifested is extreme and the practitioner's function is to respond to the client's need to explore immediate issues of safety and survival with a combination of practical information and support for their established coping strategies. For all these clients, a *holding* arrangement is the most suitable offer. This can be the offer of a second intake interview as soon as any immediate risk is contained, or it

Table 1 Focused and contractual commitments

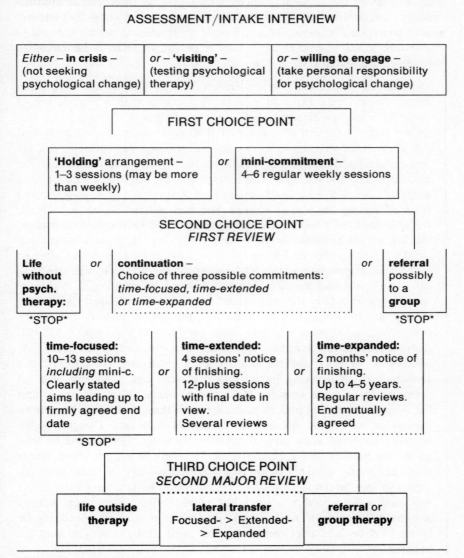

ASSESSMENT/INTAKE INTERVIEW

Either – **in crisis** – (not seeking psychological change)	*or* – **'visiting'** – (testing psychological therapy)	*or* – **willing to engage** – (take personal responsibility for psychological change)

FIRST CHOICE POINT

'Holding' arrangement – 1–3 sessions (may be more than weekly)	*or*	**mini-commitment** – 4–6 regular weekly sessions

SECOND CHOICE POINT
FIRST REVIEW

Life without psych. therapy:	*or*	**continuation** – Choice of three possible commitments: *time-focused, time-extended or time-expanded*	*or*	**referral** possibly to a **group**
STOP				*STOP*

time-focused: 10–13 sessions *including* mini-c. Clearly stated aims leading up to firmly agreed end date	*or*	**time-extended:** 4 sessions' notice of finishing. 12-plus sessions with final date in view. Several reviews	*or*	**time-expanded:** 2 months' notice of finishing. Up to 4–5 years. Regular reviews. End mutually agreed
STOP				

THIRD CHOICE POINT
SECOND MAJOR REVIEW

life outside therapy	**lateral transfer** Focused- > Extended- > Expanded	**referral** or **group therapy**

could be an agreement to meet two or three times, until a calmer discussion of the therapeutic option can be undertaken. These holding meetings should fit the need of the client in crisis and need not be regularly spaced out. Less experienced practitioners, and those maintaining an over-determined belief in the 'talking cure', are often troubled and disappointed by the sudden disappearance of clients who seemed enthusiastically committed at the first interview. Experience can show that willingness to postpone discussions of any formal contractual commitment and to respect the sense of emergency felt by a person in crisis is beneficial to both client and practitioner.

Duncan telephoned the psychotherapist, whose name he had been given by his doctor, very early on a Monday morning with a request for an immediate therapy session. Due to a cancellation, the practitioner was able to offer a session late in the afternoon. Duncan arrived early and paced up and down the hallway until the previous patient departed. He was dishevelled and sweating lightly as he sat, pale and resolute, in the chair opposite the therapist and blurted out his need to 'go into a long analysis'. His wife had finally asked him to leave home, saying she was tired of waiting for him to change. She had insisted on his leaving the house immediately and he had spent the weekend visiting several friends, staying up all Saturday night talking and weeping, unable to eat but drinking heavily. He had been asked to leave a friend's house after he had insulted a woman visitor and had spent the previous night walking off the alcohol and his pain. He was anxious to examine his marriage break-up and believed it was caused by his wife's unhappy childhood, saying that he would like to 'finish off' his mother-in-law. The practitioner responded with a gentle focus on Duncan's present emotional distress and physical needs. He asked Duncan about his immediate sources of support and his usual coping strategies. He checked out Duncan's usual drinking habits and discussed less damaging ways of releasing his present tension. He asked Duncan about his anger and his despair, accepting and empathising with these feelings, while monitoring the reality of suicidal or homicidal fantasies. Duncan began to relax his fixed stare and to breathe normally. He decided to telephone his brother and suggest a week's walking holiday to think things over. He would visit his bank and make temporary financial arrangements so that he could rent a flat. He agreed to write a long letter to his wife which he would not send but would bring to another therapy session in three days' time. It was decided that it would probably be better to delay any assessment interview until after his holiday with his brother.

A holding arrangement is also the best offer to be made to the clients whom de Schazer (1988) has well described as *'visiting'* the therapy room. These clients may make it clear that they view any problems they are experiencing as entirely owned by some external agency, often another person. This can indeed be a reasonably accurate description of the situation and may indicate the need for information about the availability of more pragmatic forms of professional assistance, such as legal, medical, social or financial advisors. Whatever the external situation, 'visitors' are not yet motivated to engage fully in personal psychological change. This lack of incentive can be difficult to discern and has been described by Norcross (Dryden 1991) as *'pre-contemplation'*. Quite often, a high degree of intellectual understanding of the therapeutic process confuses both client and practitioner into a contractual commitment which drags on inconclusively before disappearing into the dust of disappointed expectations. The phenomenon of 'visiting' can also be linked to a repeated misreading of the area of focus needed by this client at this stage of their life process. This more complex assessment issue is explored in Chapter 4. For the purpose of the intake interviewer's assessment of motive, it is enough to be alert to the signs of the client's being in pre-contemplation mode at this period of their life. A gentle probe as to the physical experience or behaviour likely to accompany the psychological changes being tentatively considered can provide clues which can then be discussed openly with the client. A relaxed acceptance of the client's need to explore the availability and the benefits of a therapeutic engagement, *without* commitment, for a session or three may be enough to enable subsequent motivated self-referral.

> Marion made several telephone calls to the therapy institute before arranging to see the senior practitioner for an assessment interview. She appeared calm and composed as she described a series of disastrous and violent relationships with men, culminating in the discovery that her 8-year-old son was being sexually abused by her latest partner, whom she had now left. It was this realisation that had brought her to seek help. She was anxious to check that there was complete confidentiality so as to protect her ex-partner and said that she had realised, from reading articles in magazines, that she was to blame and needed to change herself through therapy as soon as possible. The therapist explored the helpless despair underlying her composure and gently challenged her priorities. The discussion moved to her present needs to build a safer and more supported life for herself and her son. Information was given about local support groups for 'women against violence'. Marion was offered two follow-up sessions during the following weeks. She used these to strengthen her resolve to report her ex-partner to the police and returned for a final session a month later. At this last session she enquired about the cost and the likely duration of therapy, and decided that she was not ready at this stage for such a commitment. She was enjoying her new friendships with women and had a job in a community centre for physically abused women.

So, by a process of elimination, a client and a practitioner may find themselves in agreement that they are both *willing to engage* in the serious discussion of a exploratory period of therapeutic engagement. The client is clearly ready to contemplate the realistic possibility of psychological change and to explore their personal responsibility for the problematic aspects of their existence. Humanist schools of psychotherapy and counselling have been accused of an over-emphasis (Pilgrim 1992) on individual responsibility for the pain caused by social injustice and unavoidable trauma. In this model, there is an implicit acknowledgement of the limitations of individual change, in thought, affect and behaviour, in the face of cruel and hostile circumstances. The responsibility of the intake interviewer is to attempt an accurate assessment of the immediate needs of the client, and to be prepared to empower an oppressed client with appropriate information as to their rights and the availability of other professional specialisations and sources of self-help. The subtle dividing line between the need for external support and internal change is the crucial deciding factor which underlies an honest offer of psychotherapeutic engagement. Clients in need of mainly practical help are best responded to as being in crisis and held appropriately, although a few clients who seemed initially willing to engage may still need to use the *mini-commitment* to explore alternative sources of support.

The choice of the mini-commitment

Some motivation to look inwards and to acknowledge the existence of problematic patterns of thought, behaviour and emotion is the starting point for any engagement in psychological therapy. The choice of the mini-commitment as the outcome of the intake interview process entails an agreement to meet for between four and six regular weekly sessions. It is not advisable to shorten this initial commitment by arranging to meet more frequently than once a week. If bi-weekly sessions have been agreed, then the mini-commitment should be extended so that at least four weeks pass before the *review* session. Although flexibility and range is the signature of this approach, this period of four to six weeks seems essential in order to ensure sufficient time for a crucial period of exploration with each session important in itself, clear in content, focus and resolution. Client and practitioner need to work on building a *therapeutic alliance*, a process which seems to be tested best over a period of real time, with the space and proportion of the weekly cycle providing intervals for contemplation.

Returning to life after a mini-commitment

Indeed it is probable that the mini-commitment is the appropriate and, at this time, only suitable offer of commitment for clients in Norcross's contemplation stage (Dryden 1991). These are clients who are, at this time, only ready to explore the idea of psychological change but not to experiment with the consequences of change. As this underlying limitation of motive is uncovered in the process of the mini-commitment, it is important for the practitioner to acknowledge and respect the client's need to spend enough time in contemplation. In most cases, to continue into the time-focused commitment for another five or six sessions is likely to be beneficial. However, a few clients might need to continue contemplating the theoretical possibility of change by returning to their usual life patterns, for a period, with the added insight gained during the mini-commitment. To these clients, the practitioner can introduce the prospect of a future return to therapeutic engagement, or even suggest continuing their investigations through referral to a contrasting model of psychological therapy. Such an attitude displays straightforward acceptance of the exploratory phase of non-commitment which may be necessary and healthy for this client.

Using referral at the end of the mini-commitment

The choice of referral to another practitioner, at the end of the mini-commitment, is very often indicated when the practitioner comes to a firm conclusion that he or she does not possess appropriate or sufficient skills to work with this client. A practitioner, working in the highly concentrated manner recommended in this model, is likely swiftly to uncover problematic issues not displayed at the intake interview. If there is a well-researched and specialist therapeutic procedure available to the client, rapid referral is indicated and can be a positive outcome for both practitioner and client. Caution is needed here, however, and careful self-questioning regarding hidden motives and agendas. Sometimes a practitioner may be underestimating their own ability or avoiding an opportunity to widen their range of skills. Occasionally a potentially useful relationship issue is concealed in the interaction which has led to the practitioner deskilling themselves. This is particularly likely to occur in a situation where a relatively inexperienced practitioner is confronted with a knowledgeable client more experienced in the psychotherapy game.

Jane referred herself for therapy to a student counselling service in her first year at the university where she was a mature student. She described herself as 'permanently depressed' and disillusioned with all the previous counsellors she had encountered. She was anxious to ensure that she would be seeing the most experienced counsellor employed by the service and only had one free period to be available for counselling each week. At assessment, the intake interviewer reassured her of the general standard of counselling offered by the service and gained agreement that Jane would try out the short exploratory contract with the only counsellor available at the time. Jane responded to the warmth and interest shown by the trainee counsellor, and began to relax enough to share some of her disappointment with the chaotic and disorganised early parenting she had experienced. However, she continued to question the counsellor closely as to her ability to cope with herself as a client, describing the expertise of other counsellors she had worked with in the past. The counsellor took her own doubts about her ability to work with this client to her supervisor, who encouraged her to explore with Jane what it was like to know that she could be sure of remaining a client of this service while she was a student, provided she could maintain clear agreements as to time and space. This apparently simple question led to Jane bursting into tears of relief, and deciding, at review, to continue until the end of the academic year. When the trainee counsellor and Jane parted, Jane described their work together as 'everything she had hoped for'.

Alternatively it can be the client who, having used the mini-commitment to clarify and establish their need for continuing psychological therapy, decides that their needs may be met better by another practitioner. This decision can be a difficult one for client and practitioner but a well-conducted first review will usually bring to the surface any underlying issues and facilitate referral if appropriate. Conducting reviews at each choice point is central to the approach outlined in this book, and the recommended methodology is covered in detail in Chapter 4.

The use of supervision, or consultation, is a fundamental support when preparing for the first review and making accurate decisions regarding referral. Both practitioners and clients can have a blind spot in this area. Any discussion of referral can be perceived as a failure of the therapeutic engagement rather than the culmination of a particular piece of work. This approach holds an underlying belief in the value for the client of using a range of options during a lifetime of individual self-development. By including referral as continuing option in case discussion, supervisors encourage practitioners to adopt this attitude and to work on their all too human need for sole ownership and control. Another reason for referral, at the end of the mini-commitment, would be a purely realistic one due to some unexpected event in the life of client or practitioner. Such an event could occur at any stage of a therapeutic encounter and it is best to acknowledge the possibility at all points of continuation or re-engagement. Practitioners are advised to build up their own *resource directory* for referral purposes. Ideally, this should include a wide range of helpful professional agencies and individuals, as well as the names of other practitioners and specialists.

CONTINUATION OF THE CONTRACTUAL COMMITMENT

The mini-commitment is destined to culminate in a choice between three possible options for continuation in psychological therapy. This prospect is clarified during the intake process, and is held in view throughout each mini-commitment session so that client as well as practitioner can make an informed decision at the first review session. However, the practitioner has the primary responsibility for maintaining the professional alliance, summarising the main issues and ensuring that this *second choice point* is successful in leading to an appropriate choice of future commitment.

> Guy had been somewhat aggressive and mocking at the intake interview. He was a successful black accountant aged 35 with a thriving practice in his own community. He expressed scorn for the local 'white yuppies' but desperately wanted to feel accepted by his girlfriend's white middle-class parents. He relaxed as the counsellor explored the reality of racial prejudice and asked him how he felt about her own difference in experience, colour and gender. Guy agreed that it was an unfair society but said he wanted to change his way of responding to people in authority and particularly to women. He was offered four exploratory sessions which he used enthusiastically, unearthing links between his primary school experiences and his present patterns of reaction to his future mother-in-law. At the review session, he decided to continue with counselling for another six sessions, until his wedding in two months' time.

For the majority of clients, some form of *continuation* is the optimal choice. A well-conducted intake interview will have prepared clients to view the mini-commitment as a valuable exploration and initiation into some form of therapeutic engagement. Clients who were originally in crisis or 'visiting' will have been offered some version of the holding arrangement before committing themselves during the second intake interview. The highly focused exploratory work and relationship building undertaken with the client during the mini-commitment sessions culminates in the review session and a joint agreement as to which of the three main types of commitment is likely to fulfil the present needs of the client. This decision can arise from a clear recommendation from the practitioner, ideally prepared for in supervision or consultation. Alternatively, the choice may be agreed during a review which sets out the available and suitable options. In any case, the practitioner must prepare carefully to give a clear account of their understanding of their client's present thoughts, feeling and behaviour in interaction with their present situation and how this might be linked to previous strategies for survival. The presentation needs to be warm and positive and to include suggestions for future work within the therapeutic alliance. This is an extremely powerful moment for practitioner as well as client, and needs careful preparation and the use of good supervision, if available.

> Guy's counsellor worked in private practice, sharing a suite of offices with two colleagues. They met together for regular weekly co-supervision, and consulted a senior colleague once a month. Preparation for her first review with Guy was discussed with her peers before checking through

her offer of continuing commitment with the more experienced supervisor. She was aware of the cultural and age difference between herself and Guy. She had considered referral to an Asian male colleague so that Guy could explore, perhaps more openly, his difficulty with coming to terms with his anger and resentment regarding any situation dominated by older women. In supervision, she presented a thoughtful analysis of Guy's early experience of a matriarchal household, with a harassed, dominant and chaotic mother depending upon him to negotiate with white shopkeepers and landlords. He had remembered his crush on a white woman teacher at primary school as exciting, confusing but ultimately humiliating. He needed to differentiate these childhood experiences from his present achievements in a racially prejudiced society. The counsellor's colleagues encouraged her to postpone the possible referral, to affirm Guy's insights, and to suggest that they might use the counselling relationship to explore his fears and prejudices *in situ*. Guy listened carefully to these suggestions, and opted for a limited period of further counselling, after which he hoped to feel more prepared for his planned cross-cultural marriage. He might then consider going into therapy with the male therapist.

The choice of the time-focused commitment

The time-focused commitment is worth considering as an optimum option by most clients and practitioners. This would mean an agreement between client and practitioner to a time-limited commitment as a *continuation* of the mini-commitment, with a definite finishing date negotiated at the first review. This would normally mean an agreement to meet for another six to eight sessions, or a total of ten to thirteen sessions in all. Several research studies have reported that the major impact of therapy tends to occur within the initial ten to twenty sessions (Howard *et al.*, 1986, Kopta *et al.* 1992). Many clients are relieved and encouraged by the prospect of a circumscribed period of time linked to a clearly defined aim and measurable outcome. Others will be surprised by this prospect and practitioners need to be alert to the compliant client who is concealing a sense of rejection. In such case, it can be empowering to discuss the time-extended commitment as an alternative arrangement and, where appropriate, to offer the client the choice of options. The more confined the aims of the client, the more suitable is a time-focused commitment. The practitioner using this approach maintains a flexible and optimistic view of the client's personal journey and knows that it is possible that the client may re-engage in psychological therapy some time in the future. This type of contractual agreement is chosen when any further commitment appears unnecessary or unlikely to be maintained at this stage. Often there are practical considerations underlying the choice of a time-limited commitment: the client is moving from the neighbourhood, or has very restricted funds. All these pragmatic issues can be accommodated and respected in this model.

Having a clearly agreed last session makes *focusing* an essential and natural process. When arranging the exact number of sessions, it is useful to work towards the next 'natural break', often provided by a holiday period. Having established a firm *working alliance* during the mini-commitment, practitioners can discuss the benefits of working on the focal theme in order to achieve an agreed purpose by a specific closing date. The practitioner must, nevertheless, be prepared for a last-minute eruption of new issues or levels of concern as the fixed date of the last session approaches. At all times, the door needs to remain open to a future re-engagement in psychological therapy. This would probably be with the same practitioner, after a break during which new insights, emotional freedoms and behavioural changes can be tested outside the therapeutic relationship. Where this re-engagement is not requested, a follow-up session, after a few months, would normally be offered.

Within these flexible parameters, the time-focused commitment can even be offered to clients with a fragmented sense of self. This view conflicts with the strict selection criteria enforced within many of the brief psychotherapy approaches. I share with Ryle (1990) the view that these very clients, often diagnosed as fragile *borderline personalities*, are initially alarmed by the prospect of an apparently endless commitment to boundaries of time and space. The clarity of a time-focused commitment is less threatening but still offers adequate containment.

> Judy considered other suicide attempts during her time in the psychiatric ward. She attended a few group meetings and then retired to her cubicle, sobbing behind the curtains and swearing at anyone who approached her. She was referred for long-term psychotherapy but missed so many appointments that she was sent back to the ward, with a recommendation for informal befriending and counselling. The psychiatric social worker attached to the ward visited Judy. She was warm and practical, offering Judy six counselling sessions on the ward, to discuss the difficulty of agreeing to postpone all self-harm while seeing a counsellor. If Judy felt ready to commit herself to this agreement, then another eight sessions in an out-patient setting were on offer. Judy felt suspicious but also relieved. She was tired and scared by the risky isolation she was experiencing. This would at least be someone to talk to, and there was a clear way out of the relationship if it became painful.

The choice of the time-extended commitment

The difference between this choice and the much rarer decision to proceed with a commitment to *time-expanded* psychological therapy is signified by the type of motivation expressed by the client and by the presence of pragmatic resource constraints. The specific range of issues which clients wish to resolve will be clearly delineated and completion of the commitment will be linked to the achievement of these aims. Clients will have demonstrated trust in the therapeutic process, shown some insight into the repetitive nature of their reactive patterns and an ability to work within a therapeutic relationship. Choosing a time-extended commitment, instead of the time-focused agreement described in the previous section, depends upon one crucial issue. Can both client and practitioner fully agree that a minimum of four sessions' notice will be given, by either party, before terminating the continuing commitment to engage in psychological therapy? Both client and practitioner need to be free, in practical terms, to enter into this agreement, taking realistic account of employment, financial and holiday arrangements.

The specific task of the practitioner, at this choice point, is to make an assessment as to the motivation of this particular client as displayed nonverbally during the mini-commitment. Has the client demonstrated an ability to adhere to agreements regarding time and place? There is a strong belief that 'fragile' clients, with a chaotic lifestyle and a history of disruption and abuse, can benefit only from an offer of unlimited and long-term psychotherapy. However, as described above, the formal constraints of an extended commitment, with its emphasis on the healing aspects of regularity, dedication and clear boundaries, can also be perceived as oppressive and demanding. Supervision and consultation can assist a practitioner in this difficult and subtle judgement. Is this client now ready to benefit from a struggle with clear boundaries, or is an untidy and inconclusive failure to attend culminating in sudden departure more likely? When in doubt, the offer of a time-focused commitment with a clear option to return later can be made. A previous beneficial experience of psychological therapy is a highly motivating factor to return to make a time-extended commitment, having experienced a short natural break.

Practitioners in training are a particular sub-group of clients who are likely to seek out longer-term psychological therapy. For the majority of the training organisations with membership of the United Kingdom Council for Psychotherapy (UKCP), a lengthy period of personal therapy is mandatory, although this is not the case for many training courses in behaviour therapy, hypnosis or systems theory. Generally, it makes sense to ask trainees in any psychological therapy to experience, as consumers, the model of psychological therapy which they are studying and will be offering to their clients.

Assessment of these trainee clients can be tricky for practitioners using a time-conscious approach. A professional requirement to engage in protracted psychological therapy can diffuse the client's awareness of areas where self-development and psychological change are required. Painful and problematic issues can be masked or, conversely, maintained within the therapeutic milieu. Again the mini-commitment is essential as a forum for intensive focus and examination of motivation. Experiments in external changes in behaviour can be useful here, as well as careful monitoring of the trainee practitioner's ability to maintain a reasonable level of interpersonal skill and to form meaningful relationships. Above all, be prepared to challenge any tendency to hide within the therapeutic relationship and avoid external obligations.

No matter how little resistance clients have shown to boundaries of time and space, they can still benefit from careful consideration of the options available at first review. It is appropriate to discuss fully the reasons for giving four sessions' notice before completing the time-extended commitment and parting. The requirement is not for the participants 'to say goodbye', which could be construed as the emotional need of the practitioner, but jointly to honour and value the therapeutic work undertaken so far by the client and to signify future areas for self-development.

> At first, Jane felt tentative about her meetings with her counsellor at university. She realised that, with this calm and attentive woman, she was able to relax and talk openly about her fear of failure, her apparent inability to organise study time for herself and still look after Jack and the children. She was surprised to find that, unlike the psychotherapist she had seen at the hospital last year, this counsellor helped her to map out practical strategies for time management at home, while still understanding her need to be in sole control of the housework. She was suspicious and tense when the counsellor suggested that they use the sixth session to decide together about future counselling. Now she was managing better, would she have to prove her need for professional support? However, she had been assured in the third session that this was a service to which she was entitled, and she was determined to test this out. To her surprise, the counsellor agreed with her that she needed weekly sessions until the end of the academic year. The only condition made was that she, and the counsellor, give each other four sessions' notice before finishing. This seemed reasonable enough, and still gave her some sense of control. The counsellor was interested in her need to be different from her mother and she felt that she might now have time to think about the past.

In a time-extended commitment the focus is usually wider and deeper than that used in the time-focused commitment, although still steady and intense. The main themes have been mapped out in the first review and, if accurately predicted, are likely to surface in each session. The relationship between client and practitioner is likely to mirror the problematic interpersonal patterns which underlie most psychological distress. Existential reality and the therapeutic leverage of a time-conscious approach (Mann 1973) is

enhanced by relaxed recognition of the finite nature of professional assistance. At regular intervals, especially before a holiday or some other natural
break, the practitioner introduces a review session, taking care that the
client does not interpret this as criticism or potential rejection. John
McLeod (Mearns and Dryden 1990: 17) comments that the sparse research
into clients' attitudes to termination indicates 'emotional investment and
dependence on the counsellor, ambivalence about ending and an awareness
of impending loss of support'. Conversely, some clients are heartened by
the prospect of a clearly envisaged and successful conclusion to therapeutic
engagement. It can be the fear and avoidance felt by the practitioner which
shapes a client's aversion to endings.

The open-ended nature of the time-extended commitments encourages a
flexibility which can be extended up to the end of the commitment. Even if
the gains made seem minor and the unfinished business (Perls, Hefferline
and Goodman 1951: 140; Clarkson 1989: 42) seems vast, the four final
sessions can be used to affirm any enlargement of the client's survival
strategies and discuss potentials glimpsed. As areas for future change are
tentatively outlined, the client has time to decide whether to finish, to
continue or to plan how to achieve their goals outside the therapeutic
engagement.

> Jane was already dreading the end of her first year at university. She saw
> the long summer months stretching ahead without the orderliness of a
> weekly timetable. Most of all, she worried about her dependence on her
> weekly counselling sessions. These would end with the summer term and,
> although the date was highlighted in her diary, she was determined not
> to display her fears to her counsellor. However, the counsellor herself
> seemed to be thinking about the end. She had reminded Jane of their
> agreement to use the last four sessions to prepare for the future. Jane felt
> more positive as they celebrated her survival as a mature student, and
> began to list the little ways in which she was more relaxed at home, once
> even leaving the washing up to the family while she went for a long walk.
> She could see that there was a long way to go, and her fear of becoming
> like her mother was still very strong. She realised that her sharp feelings
> of sadness about saying goodbye to her counsellor were related to her
> unexpressed grief that her mother would probably never change. She felt
> relieved as she wept, and, at the last session, began to look forward to a
> break from intensity. She would postpone looking for another counsellor
> until she had finished her second-year exams.

The choice of the time-expanded commitment

In spite of the lack of research evidence that long-term therapy is more
effective than brief therapy (Smith, Glass and Miller 1980; Koss and

Butcher 1986) some practitioners with psychotherapy qualifications still limit their offers of commitment to their clients to the time-expanded commitment as outlined in Table 1. At least two months notice of termination is promised and required, and the expectation is of a time-span between two to five years, or even longer. The option of this form of long-term engagement is retained within a *time-conscious* approach because there seems to be a specific group of prospective clients for whom this can be an expectation and a considered choice. Once the habitual preferences of the practitioner have been questioned and contained, there is freedom to explore the reasons that a *client* might wish to commit themselves to an open-ended period of psychotherapy. This level of commitment is most likely to be the culmination of a preparatory series of personal self-development episodes, some of which may have taken place within a psychological therapy setting and others through tackling the risky business of living.

Even with this highly motivated client group, practitioners will need to make intensive use of the mini-commitment period up to the first review to uncover any indications that a more time-boundaried commitment would be equally beneficial. We need to take seriously the finding by Smith, Glass and Miller (1980) that 'the major impact of psychological treatment occurs in the first six to eight sessions' with 'a reduction in impact for the next ten sessions' (Peake, Borduin and Archer 1988: 32).

> Tim was a medical student with a particular interest in psychiatry which he claimed was purely intellectual. The day his girlfriend left him, he decided to go into analysis. He told his friends this was essential for his career and would enable him to display ego strength when faced with groups of angry and disturbed patients. He finally found a psychotherapist with an analytical training whose twice-a-week sessions he could just about afford. Within a couple of weeks, he had uncovered a painful pattern of unexpressed emotional need leading to continual avoidance of intimacy and subsequent relationship failures. He realised that the roots lay in his lonely childhood with elderly and hardworking professional parents. He continued to explore his resentment and his childhood experiences for the next two years while he qualified as a psychiatrist. His medical colleagues were impressed with his account of the insights gained in his analysis, and his masterly case descriptions. He continued to engage in a series of unsatisfactory emotional encounters.

At all times there is a danger of the therapeutic engagement being unnecessarily lengthened due to the therapist factors listed by Malan (1975: 8) as 'a tendency towards passivity', conveying to the client a 'sense of timelessness' and 'therapeutic perfectionism'. Until recently, lack of statistical evaluation has hidden the reality that even psychoanalysts only do longer-term work with a *minority* of their patients (Koss and Butcher 1986, Talmon 1990). However, the argument for the benefits of long-term psychotherapy should not be dismissed out of hand. When realised and contained, self-damaging behaviours are usually replaced by increased despair in thought and feeling. Clients clearly motivated to enter into a longer period of psychological therapy have usually prepared themselves to *work through* these profound levels of unease and disturbance. Some will have searched to find a spiritual path to fill this need, and others will have sought, and even achieved, a high level of personal and professional success. Some will themselves be practitioners of psychological therapy. Norcross, in his conversation with Dryden (1991) argues persuasively that personal therapy is one of the effective ways in which experienced practitioners can maintain their health as persons, in his view 'second only to the client's history . . . the critical determinant of psychotherapy outcome'. Another argument in favour of continuing psychological therapy for practitioners is the particular nature of their profession, although it is probably no more stressful than many other helping professions. The struggle against stress is itself part of the growth and development of self-awareness, a process which may be enhanced by occasional re-engagement in personal therapy.

The time-expanded commitment is the optimum choice for the client who, at the first review, has demonstrated an ability to maintain their coping strategies outside the therapeutic engagement and who is motivated by enough psychological pain to explore and transform hidden areas of their inner world. Reviews at regular intervals are recommended, as is the development of a clear 'criterion for ending' (Peake, Borduin and Archer 1988: 32), however distant this prospect may seem. In other words, there is still a need for some direction towards some outcome, however distant, to be clearly articulated even though this prospect displays subtle changes over time.

Ayesha had made a major decision for herself. She would go back into therapy again. This time it was her own free choice rather than the driven and guilty resolve which had underpinned her earlier encounters with counsellors and therapy groups. She had needed her first counsellor to support her as she left behind the drinking bouts and the violent outbursts which had punctuated her first marriage. The obvious distress of her children and her fear-filled dependency on her husband had impelled her to change herself for their sake. Then she had joined a therapy group, as recommended by the leader of the peer group for recovering alcoholics which she had joined. In the group, she had worked through her need to establish herself as a competent single mother, training and qualifying as a counsellor herself. Now she had, rather to her surprise, fallen in love with a woman and was once again struggling with the very same relationship issues which had destroyed her first marriage. They were less acute, and she could usually see and avoid an escalation of the old patterns. She was nervous as she outlined her aims to the small quiet woman sitting opposite her. Would she be seen as a neurotic woman, unsuitable to work as a counsellor? The therapist asked her to describe herself six years from now. What did she fear becoming, and what were her dreams? The pictures were clear and in vivid contrast. She had made the right decision.

THE THIRD CHOICE POINT – RETURNING TO LIFE WITHOUT THERAPY?

The notion of the client choosing *life without psychological therapy* as an option is emphasised throughout this chapter. As the practitioner is decentralised, so there is an added appreciation of the importance of the client's life experience, external to the contractual commitment. While important and influential throughout the therapeutic engagement, the concerns, decisions and relationships of the client in the course of their daily life are the forum in which psychological change has to be tested and developed. The time-focused commitment is, by nature, circumscribed and has a definite finishing date. The review process takes into account the main concerns discussed and achievements made as areas for continuing development. The break from psychological therapy is clearly envisaged as an extended opportunity to use the insight and emotional illumination of the therapy sessions in the process of self-development. The prospect of returning to take up a time-extended or, more rarely, a time-expanded commitment must be outlined with caution if the benefit of a time-limited focus is not to be diffused. Such a return would constitute one of the forms of *lateral transfer* indicated in Table 1. Another would be transfer from a time-extended into a time-expanded commitment. This can be a smoother relocation since the nature of the commitment may have undergone a gentle transformation as the area of focus has grown wider.

At all times, practitioners are urged to consider whether the therapeutic work might be better undertaken with another practitioner or in a group setting. As clients move to another stage in their *life process of psychological evolution* (see Table 2), so they may be best served by another therapeutic alliance. In particular, a psychotherapy group is very often the ideal setting for clients who have benefited from a short period of psychological therapy and need a sheltered environment to test out their new interpersonal skills.

SUMMARY

This chapter has defined the concept of psychotherapeutic commitment and expanded the issues underlying a practitioner's use of the flow chart displayed in Table 1. Choices available at the intake interview have been summarised and the issues arising from the assessment process will be further expanded in Chapter 4. Characteristic contractual issues arising from the four main types of commitment outlined in the flow chart have been discussed. A more detailed illustration of each commitment, linked with the area of focus arising from the use of the life process stages recommended in Table 2, forms the main body of the book.

Chapter 3

Stages to go through

Using the therapeutic relationship to discern the entry point within a life process of psychological evolution

In this chapter, a model for accompanying a client through six life-related stages of self-developmental change through the therapeutic relationship is presented. Table 2 sketches out the paradigm in diagram form. It is intended to assist the practitioner to find a focal theme for the chosen commitment entered into with a client. Early in the therapeutic engagement, usually at the first review, this hypothesis can be fruitfully shared with the client. The ideas expressed in the model arise from observations made during work with a wide range of clients, especially those bringing to the therapeutic engagement the painful experience of an abusive childhood. Using this model helps the practitioner to make a diagnosis, not of the client, but of the *area of psychological work* most appropriate to explore with this client at this time.

THE THERAPEUTIC RELATIONSHIP

The quality and nature of the relationship, which 'usually emerges silently and imperceptibly' (Gelso and Carter 1985: 159) between client and practitioner, has been widely accepted as the most important and effective influence on personal change through psychological therapy.

> Decades of empirical psychotherapy research have concluded that the therapists' interpersonal skills and capacity for forming meaningful therapeutic relationships account for more outcome variance than either theories or methods.
>
> (John Norcross in Dryden 1991: 35)

This intelligence, which is the main thrust of Rogerian theory (Rogers 1961), is now shared across all dominant theoretical orientations. Any approach to psychological therapy which does not acknowledge this principle runs the risk of being felt as dry, cold and task-oriented, ineffective for practitioner as well as client. The areas of focus delineated within Table 2 are linked inextricably to the use made of this crucial and yet subtle, ever-shifting interaction between client and practitioner.

In psychodynamic therapy, which includes the various psychoanalytic-based therapies (including, of course, self psychology), object-relations therapies, Gestalt therapies and various body-oriented therapies, awareness of the relationship is an indispensable tool. And even those who choose not to deal explicitly with the relationship, such as behaviour therapists, cognitive therapies and advice-giving counselors, will avoid a good many pitfalls if they are sophisticated about what might happen in the relationship between therapist and client.

(Kahn 1991: 3)

Of the many descriptions and discussions of the therapeutic relationship, Gelso and Carter's seminal article (1985) presents a threefold categorisation of this relationship in a manner which can assist in linking focal theme to appropriate use of relationship. Gelso and Carter (1985: 160) argue that there are three 'components' to this relationship: the *working alliance*, the *transference relationship* and the *real relationship*. While more categories of therapeutic relationship have been described (Clarkson 1990), these can usually be subsumed within the broader remit of these three relationship modes.

The *working alliance* is the essential relationship mode for the establishment of any contractual commitment as described in the previous chapter. It combines an emotional bond with an intellectual agreement. Practitioner and client are required to keep a hold on being 'reasonable' members of a working partnership, whatever the affective content of the therapeutic engagement. Such a relationship requires mutual trust in the professional integrity of the practitioner and in the agreed motivation of the client. Gelso and Carter quote research (Luborsky *et al.* 1983, Horvarth and Greenberg 1985) demonstrating that the working alliance can be established quickly, often in fewer than three sessions. It is the medium through which psychological problems are depicted, doubts and fears expressed and mutual aims discussed and agreed. Any ambivalence about the working alliance is a predictor of poor outcome.

The content of the working alliance includes the agreements made between client and practitioner concerning time, space, duration, goals and limitations of the therapeutic commitment. The integrity of the practitioner and the motivation of the client are the dynamic forces which create the working alliance. The establishment of this alliance is crucial to all focused and committed work with clients. If never established, or breached by a breakdown in trust, then the most skilful techniques or intense empathic perceptions on the part of the practitioner are likely to be wasted.

For several months after her father died, Joanna visited the psychotherapist, recommended by her best friend. He was said to be a skilful hypnotist although he had not mentioned this to her when they first met.

She was not sure how long she would have to go on seeing him and did not like to broach this subject herself. He was always encouraging her to 'relax and enjoy being the centre of attention'. They met for about an hour, usually on a weekly basis, for several months, making the next appointment at the end of each session.

The second category of relationship operating in any therapeutic engagement is inevitably the mode of interaction described by Gelso and Carter (1985) as the *real relationship*. Initially, this functions at a relatively impersonal level in that there are factual realities which affect any encounter between human beings. There are differences and similarities of age, gender, culture, and personal preferences which are apparent and influential from the first meeting, or even from the first telephone call. It is these *real* factors which can be the hooks for the *unreal* relationship, normally described as the *transference*. The practitioner's acknowledgement of the existence of valid issues of affinity and difference in the professional encounter is key to introducing a basic authenticity and honesty into the subsequent proceedings. Another type of reality to be encountered and acknowledged, where possible, is more crucially linked to the intimacy needed to facilitate a searching and vulnerable process of exploration. This is the subjective valuation of one human being by another, usually expressed as *like/dislike*. Again, these judgements may be fuelled by reactive, or transference, patterns based on past experience. Or they may be genuine indicators of personality and cultural preference. In any case, they can be subsumed by a working alliance based focus on *work/non-work* instead of *like/dislike*.

Joanna liked her therapist well enough but was not sure if the therapy was doing her any good. She presumed that he would know what was best for her and would be in charge of the process since he was an older and professionally educated man, like her father. He was much more friendly than her father and often told her about his own interests and plans.

The real relationship is implicated wherever a question arises in the mind of the practitioner regarding disclosure of subjective internal judgements or of factual information not immediately relevant to the therapeutic engagement. The practitioner of a time-conscious approach will be guided by consideration of how these real relationship disclosures are likely to be useful to the agreed focus of the therapeutic commitment. The real relationship influences, above all, the client's perception of a practitioner's authenticity and their validity as a guide and companion on a journey of personal development. Regardless of theoretical difference or superiority of qualification, a practitioner whose own character and lifestyle appears to be either chaotic or sterile, defensive or agitated, is unlikely to inspire trust in a therapeutic process of psychological change. Carl Rogers has defined ideal,

if somewhat stringent, criteria for those with ambitions to become practitioners in psychological therapy:

> we would endeavour to select individuals for such training who already
> possess, in their ordinary relationships with other people, a high degree
> of the qualities I have described. We would want people who were warm,
> spontaneous, real, understanding, and non-judgmental.
>
> (Rogers and Stevens 1967: 102)

In optimal practice, the real relationship is the medium through which
the concluding stages of a therapeutic engagement are conducted. At its
most transcendent, this person-to-person relationship can reach levels of
contact and silent empathy which can even be experienced as a *transpersonal*
relationship (Clarkson 1990). The real relationship is also fostered and
highlighted more overtly during an intake interview or any session which
turns out to be a *crisis containment*.

> Duncan looked intensely at the therapist. 'What would you do if your
> wife told you in the middle of the night that she had gone off you for
> good, and wanted you out of the house and out of her life?', he asked.
> The therapist paused. This period of crisis was not the time to explore
> Duncan's presumption that he had a wife. 'I would have felt desperately
> angry, frightened and sad', he said truthfully.

Gelso and Carter (1985: 161) argue that it is the theoretical orientation of
the practitioner which affects the 'salience and importance' given to any
one of the three relationship modes. For the psychoanalytic practitioner,
the transference relationship is the central agency for psychological change.
There is a virtual library of books describing and discussing the finer
categories of transference and counter-transference. For the purpose of the
practitioner working in the time-conscious approach, the transference
relationship is essentially an *illusory* interaction based on the existence or
absence of significant factors in a previous relationship which has been
formative in the past, for at least one of the two participants in the present
interaction. This distortion can occur early in the therapeutic encounter and
sometimes influences the basic working alliance before practitioner meets
client. It is important to remember that originally the interpersonal reactions
displayed in the transference were appropriate and adaptive strategies for
survival, protective of identity and self-esteem. Awareness of the swift
arousal of transference reactions is an essential factor in work with most
clients, especially those whose childhood has been experienced as damaging,
and whose concept of a consistent self is tenuous.

Often the transference relationship hardest to acknowledge and discern is
that which underlies an alliance which seems to be purely curative and
nurturing. This has been described as the *developmentally needed* relationship (Clarkson 1990) and arises from a *deficit* in parenting experienced in

the past. The warmth and attention offered within the best working alliance is linked, often out of awareness, to a childlike need which originally was not met, leading to an unreal level of significance being given to the overall therapeutic relationship.

> Joanna began to realise that her therapist was genuine in his warmth and interest in her. She wished that he had really been her father and dreamt of moving in with him so that he could really look after her all the time. She began to ask for earlier appointments so that she could see him more often.

Gelso and Carter (1985) suggest that a practitioner could choose to avoid transference, especially when working in brief or time-limited therapy, through adopting a strategy which challenges or disregards transference incidents and the conditions which tend to foster transference. For practitioners seeking to focus within an intense therapeutic commitment, this is probably an impossible and unhelpful task. The value of transference occurrence is that it discloses the stale patterns of interaction which are at the root of most psychological problems. Counter-transference reactions can uncover patterns owned by either practitioner or client, or even specifically related to the history of the therapeutic interaction. In any case the clue is in the inappropriateness of the reaction to the here-and-now situation. The main thrust of Gelso and Carter's (1985) description of the transference relationship is that all practitioners need to be familiar with concept of transference.

> Joanna's therapist became uncomfortable and irritated with the passivity of his client. He had tried out his best paradoxical injunctions and had provided a nurturing environment for her to explore her hidden disappointment and resentment with her cold and now permanently absent father. She persisted in her polite refusal of his accurate and empathic insights and began to weep silently at the very end of every session. He felt she was becoming over-dependent upon him and remembered the warnings given in his hypnotherapy training.

The competent practitioner is required to be aware that all three relationship modes *coexist* in every psychotherapeutic encounter. An image offered by an experienced psychotherapist (Leitman 1992, personal communication) illustrates the use that can be made of these three parallel relationship modes. It is as if the three relationships are tubes of mercury between practitioner and client. At any time the base of the tube can be held in the warm hand of a participant. The choice of which tube of mercury to expand, and whether to hold more than one (three is usually impossible!), can be made in or out of awareness. 'Therapeutic failures can be accounted for by under-attention to a given component in a particular case' (Gelso and Carter 1985: 192).

At the end of the next session, the therapist told Joanna that he would be away on holiday for the next few weeks and suggested a referral to a woman counsellor at the same health centre. Joanna took the note on which the counsellor's name was written with a sad but knowing smile. This was how her father, and all the men in her life, had always treated her. They passed her on. Outside the room, she tore up the piece of paper.

Up to this point, the main scenarios used to illustrate the text of this chapter have described a failed attempt to carry through a therapeutic relationship without a firm basis in the working alliance. In these circumstances, certain modes of therapeutic relationship can become particularly *risky*, as demonstrated below.

Risky relationship 1

The 'developmentally needed' relationship is a term which has been used to describe the 'intentional provision by the psychotherapist of a corrective/reparative or replenishing parental relationship (or action) where the original parenting was deficient, abusive or over-protective' (Clarkson 1990: 158). Entering into this relationship becomes *risky* when the practitioner fails to remember that it is also an unreal relationship and will not prove truly useful to the client until the transference elements, no matter how benevolent or positive, are unpacked. Only then can clients grieve for what they never had. Practitioners need to beware their own projective needs for a good enough parent.

Risky relationship 2

All therapeutic change is linked, at some level, to spiritual search. In the intensity of the therapeutic relationship, especially in the wake of a profound insight or a shared experience of deep feeling, a *moment* of the '*transpersonal*' relationship (Clarkson 1990) may be experienced. This is usually beyond words and is lost even as practitioners and clients, silently, acknowledge its existence. It is not a relationship mode to work in or to work towards. Psychological therapists can be grateful if this moment occurs, for it is a gift. However, they also need to be sceptical and be humble, and above all, to avoid the seduction of *counter-transference* reactions which contain a dangerous projection of self as guru!

Risky relationship 3

The 'real' or 'I–Thou' (Buber 1970) relationship can be a hindrance to setting up a working alliance, and much time spent in this mode may be an avoidance of acknowledgement of the painful transference patterns which brought the client into the counselling relationship. The real relationship is best fostered when there is a factual and externally based crisis and during well-negotiated closing sessions. Practitioners need always to check that their own needs for a real relationship is not being gratified through their therapeutic relationships.

A CLIENT'S LIFE PROCESS OF PSYCHOLOGICAL EVOLUTION

In Table 2 the stages of the life process model are linked to one of these three relationship components or modes. Indicated in the third column is the relationship mode (working alliance, transference or real relationship) likely to provide the optimal environment for the focal theme suggested. The first column is addressed to the practitioner and shows the point of entry and area of exploration which could be appropriate to offer a client at this particular point. At all times, practitioners are urged to pay attention to the client's life process of self-development rather than concentrating solely on the therapeutic process of psychological change. The table should not be used in a rigid manner but as a provisional and flexible guide. The relevance and accuracy of a practitioner's chosen point of entry can be checked and tested by a client's response to the suggested focal theme.

Although a client may work through more than one stage with the same practitioner, it is highly probable that the whole therapeutic journey will be facilitated by more than one practitioner and through other curative life experiences. This scheme argues that, for most people, the demonstrated progression from stage to stage runs through in the order shown. Clients may revert to therapeutic work at an earlier stage when a difficulty encountered in life reveals the need to deal with a different and problematic relationship pattern. This is particularly likely to be relevant to clients who have previously worked in a time-focused commitment with a sharper and more confined focal theme.

Using the Life Process stage model

Some cautionary notes

There is always a danger in proposing stages in a process of psychological evolution. The stages shown in Table 2 should not be understood as strictly vertical. They may overlap or be experienced in a cyclical fashion. Clients often go through several stages with regard to one issue before returning to go through the same stages with regard to another issue, or in response to some externally caused circumstance or trauma. There is usually some overlap regarding the *point of entry* and, in particular, the need to recycle the concerns listed at the early stages shown in Table 2. The mini-commitment described in the previous chapter is almost always necessary as an initial structural frame whatever the life process stage.

Table 2 Working with a client's life process of psychological evolution

STAGE *Possible point of* *entry/area of focus* *(after intake)*	FOCAL TASK *Issues relevant to this stage* *tied into a focal theme based* *on earlier experiences*	FOCAL RELATIONSHIP *Working Alliance (WA)* *Real Relationship (RR) or* *Transference Relationship* *(TA)*
PREPARATION *Build trust*	Work on present problems. Defences/symptoms understood as strategies. Re-education about power issues and child devt.	*WA* — main mode and essential focus. *RR* — explore factual/cultural components; and put aside. *TR* — note clues.
DISCLOSURE *Respect and listen as* *the 'story' is told* *objectively by the* *adult survivor*	Experiences named/labelled. Description of situations and sensations with associated self-image. Original strategies for survival described and validated.	*WA* — essential to cushion vulnerability of disclosure and insights. *TR* — noted but not made focal: counter-transference contained. *RR* — only needed if modelling required or for cultural enquiry.
CATHARSIS *Facilitate contact with* *client's early* *emotional reality*	Re-experiences as child did. Queries and, with practitioner as witness, ally and advocate, reframes experience. Natural needs expressed versus adapted needs/reactive patterns.	*TR* — likely to be central for both participants. *WA* — in background and used to maintain coping strategies outside sessions. *RR* — cautiously contain.
SELF-CARE *Share in the* *'corrective' emotional* *experience* *(Alexander and* *French 1946)*	Punitive and critical internal monitors replaced by insightful acceptance. Identity and related needs affirmed and restructured within cultural and social parameters.	*TR* — central; practitioner used to replace authority figures and previous models. *RR* — can be introduced to balance idealistic *transference*. *WA* — must be restated and used overtly.
RENUNCIATION *Encourage grieving,* *raging and letting go*	Sorrow and anger for lost ideals of childhood and parenthood. Acceptance of reality in past events. Allowing practitioner to step down from being the replacement ideal parent.	*RR* — can become more focal to replace idealisation. *WA* — maintained and wound down. *TR* — unpacked and worked with overtly, especially by client.
EMPOWERMENT *Observe the client* *getting on with* *existential issues of* *life*	Self-support and environmental support in place. Restructured relationships/partnerships. Confrontation/re-contracting with external social system. Use of groups/other networks/future therapy.	*WA* — available if required. Offer follow-ups/reviews. *TR* — likely to remain operational. Avoid intimate or financial connections. *RR* — contacts may be possible if abstinence maintained.

Preparation stage

At the beginning of psychological therapeutic work at any stage, the practitioner will need to build up trust and establish a strong working alliance. The primary importance of the working alliance is displayed in the table and it is this that forms the main *emotional bond* which facilitates psychological change. In the middle stages this alliance becomes less focal but remains an essential background to the therapeutic work being accomplished.

> Duncan contacted the therapist again two years later. He arrived looking embarrassed but resolute. In rather formal terms, he expressed his gratitude to the therapist for seeing him through a crisis. He looked back on that time as a turning point. He had realised then how much of an alcohol problem he had developed and had joined Alcoholics Anonymous. He was still a member of AA, and expected to be so for life. He enjoyed being able to help other alcoholics and took part in a variety of voluntary outreach work. His old firm had taken him back and he was earning enough to live comfortably and pay maintenance to his ex-wife. He felt he had changed himself a lot already. He had disclosed the depth of his degradation through alcohol and had learnt to be vulnerable and positive. He relaxed visibly as the therapist acknowledged the effectiveness and value of AA. However, Duncan felt something was missing and he knew there were early childhood issues into which he needed to go more deeply. His relationship with his father was still a painful memory. He had always avoided men socially and feared their judgement and competition. He paused, took a deep breath, and said he was ready to take the plunge now. Even though he was a man, the therapist had shown him kindness when he was desperate. Now Duncan was ready to trust him.

In this preparatory stage, it is usually important to explore the present problem areas and contributory influences as thoroughly as possible. Strengths and aims should have been established at the intake interview, which is the necessary precursor to every point of entry shown in Table 2. It is often a time for the practitioner to demonstrate acceptance of all the client's behaviours, no matter how dysfunctional, as strategies for survival. In the previous chapter, these reformulations were linked to the first review and the decisions about a choice regarding commitment. These survival strategies, which are still being used by a client and which Cognitive Analytic therapists describe as 'Target Problem Procedures' (Ryle 1990), can be used as focal themes throughout a therapeutic engagement. To understand this positive reframe of painful and shame-inducing problems, the client will usually require some information from the therapist about child development as well as the influence of social and cultural factors.

This re-education is particularly necessary if there has been a continuing history of power and authority misused, in the client's family of origin and in the surrounding culture.

> Duncan began to describe his father with a strange mixture of pride, fear and loathing. He had been the headmaster of the local prep school, and was a tall, handsome man, very popular with most of the boys. With these other boys, he was warm and jolly, ready to give the homesick ones special hugs, and to joke with the cheeky ones. Only with Duncan was he cold and withdrawn. Duncan had suffered doubly from being the headmaster's son. He was teased and ostracised by the other boys, and treated coolly by his parents so as to avoid any accusation of favouritism. Then he had been sent to the local secondary school where he was reviled as a child of the 'snob school' on the hill. He had attempted to gain popularity by importing first cigarettes and then alcohol, pilfered from his father's study. Soon he was himself dependent on these stolen goods and had a dubious reputation as the local bad boy, although still a loner. His father had found out, lectured him with cold distaste and threatened him with a beating. He learnt to drink in secret.

The transference and counter-transference issues likely to prove troublesome at this entry point reflect the participants' previous experience regarding trust and security. The practitioner may carry an over-determined wish to be helpful and a fear of being inadequate. This can be masked by the reality of the practitioner's professional need to increase their client load. The client has fears and expectations, based on past experience with powerful figures, about the competence, the confidentiality and the authority of the practitioner and the therapeutic setting. Increased awareness and open discussion of concerns relating to the working alliance are likely to increase trust without necessitating transference focus. Ann France (1988: 24) speaks on behalf of consumers of psychological therapies:

> Many are afraid that it will prove yet one more false avenue which leads nowhere and one, moreover, where the sense of failure might be particularly poignant, since it involves a personal relationship and the ability to communicate feelings which are often fundamental problems in themselves.

Disclosure stage

Here the focus is on listening to clients tell and re-tell the *history* of their painful psychological problems. Many clients do this in a relatively straightforward and unemotional way. Psychotherapists and counsellors, who have been trained to facilitate and value emotional expression above all, may feel uncomfortable with these objective accounts of painful and distressing experiences. There can be a danger in rushing clients into catharsis, by encouraging and inducing full demonstration of their deepest feelings. It is better to allow sufficient time for clients to gain full insight into the roots of the troublesome patterns which they are now experiencing. This will strengthen and inform them when they enter the next catharsis stage of vivid and emotion-laden recall of the original emotional experience.

> Judy described the night her father was arrested in a matter of fact way. She had been in bed and suddenly there was shouting downstairs. Her mother was screaming at somebody. Judy laughed briefly. Her mother never knew what was going on and then she got upset, and always took it out on Judy. She had been dragged out of bed and asked to tell the policemen what a good father she had. Her father had looked crumpled and old. He seemed to have lost his ability to smooth things over and make everybody laugh. She had wanted to protect him and hide him away and stop them picking on him. She looked earnestly at the social worker to see if she had understood.

For some clients, the disclosure stage may be experienced as powerful and satisfactory in itself. These clients are often are ready to leave this particular stage of involvement in psychological therapy before the practitioner considers closure to be appropriate. In the time-conscious approach, continuous alertness to a client's need to retire from therapeutic engagement is enjoined. Depending upon the exit agreements entailed in the type of commitment agreed (see Table 1), practitioners are recommended to trust the positive thrust of self-development. Neglect of this need for closure can lead to a stale repetitive process of intellectual insights being endlessly explored within the consulting room, while external life patterns remain the same.

> Tim began to relax more and to trust the analyst only after he had admitted his dislike of his parents. Even on their occasional visits to his boarding school, they had always seemed older than all the other parents. Then his father had retired early from the army, and now worked long hours as an insurance agent. Both his father and his GP mother were always tired and irritable. They insisted on a quiet house, and discouraged visitors. He longed to live in a noisy busy household like the one he had visited with his last girlfriend. Now he understood better his own pattern of social withdrawal, but there was very little to do about it. They went over and over the same story.

For another group of clients there may appear to be little difference between the disclosure and the next stage of catharsis. They have already disclosed their story, either in a previous therapeutic engagement or through their own insight, possibly gained from reading or discussion with friends. They are now ready to work through the emotional pain attached to these insights. In these cases, disclosure is made early, during the mini-commitment (see Table 1), and is accompanied by a clearly stated motivation to explore widely and deeply the issues arising. The commitment entered into is likely to be the time-extended or, perhaps, the time-expanded commitment. The entry point is more likely to be the stage of catharsis.

> Ayesha decided to take up the therapist's suggestion and lie down on the couch for the next session. She wanted to be alone with her feelings now, not to be distracted by anything, not even the quiet presence opposite her. She felt scared as she stared at the wall opposite with its two watercolours. This was it. She began to talk about her time in the children's home again, and this time she could smell the disinfectant in the corridors, and hear the echoes of her footsteps as she walked away from the front door. She felt her throat ache with the same painful tears and her stomach sicken with the same nausea. 'So you were learning how to cope with being on your own, again', said the quiet voice behind her. The tears pushed up into her nose, her eyes, burning and sore.

Counter-transference and transference reactions likely to characterise the disclosure stage are indicative of the defences being utilised to prevent premature emotional expression. Clients sometimes use self-mocking tones as they recount painful matters. Others show a need to justify and explain the behaviour of those whose past actions they have experienced as hurtful. Alice Miller describes a 'talented Czech author' who speaks glowingly of his 'gifted and many-sided father who encouraged his spiritual development and was a true friend' and yet who beat him regularly:

> This man spoke of these regular beatings as though they were the most normal things in the world (as for him, of course, they were), and then he said: 'It did me no harm, it prepared me for life, made me hard, taught me to grit my teeth. And that's why I could get on so well in my profession'.
>
> (Miller 1987: 93)

Practitioners, particularly those whose own stories are similar, may be tempted either to collude or to argue with these defences. They may wish to avoid any similarity to the original authority figure and be enticed into disclosing real relationship factors unnecessarily.

> Tim realised that his therapist came from a similar family to himself quite early in the analysis. One day he began to describe how his soldier father always shook his hand firmly, even before and after a beating. The therapist nodded sympathetically, and then they had discussed the different attitudes of parents from a military background. He could only have understood Tim so well if his own parents had been in the army.

Catharsis stage

In this stage the client once again experiences vividly the emotional reality underlying the psychological problems they have brought to the therapeutic arena. This stage could arise during any of the four contractual commitments outlined in Table 1, although, as described above, clients often need to spend enough time on the disclosure of their stories before entering fully into the emotions associated with these past events. Hence this cathartic experience is more beneficially worked through in full after the mini-commitment has highlighted the focal theme, and a firm alliance has been established. The working alliance is an essential background component at this stage and supports the client's need to maintain the coping strategies necessary for their daily life. The contractual commitment may be time-limited provided there are sufficient support structures outside the therapeutic setting, and a clear view of future options for re-engagement. As discussed in the previous chapter, even clients diagnosed as fragile borderline personalities who have a history of mistreatment can, after adequate attention to the disclosure stage, benefit by a well-contained and sensitive working through of buried traumatic memories. More usually, this work takes place during a time-extended or time-expanded commitment.

> By the end of the fifth session, Duncan realised that this therapy business was very different from the AA groups. The steady listening presence of the therapist, and the surprising links he made from time to time, often left him feeling tearful. He struggled to maintain his poise, emphasising the positive sense of self he had built up over the last few months. The deep gentle voice of the therapist was particularly disturbing. Sometimes Duncan imagined what it would have been like to have heard his father speak in these tender tones. Once he had agreed to continue in therapy, he began to joke about the similarities between the two men, both older than himself, both professional men. The therapist asked what had been his closest moment of contact with his father. Duncan looked aghast, and then began to sob as he remembered the strangely reassuring grip with which his father had held him across his knee during a beating.

A popular image which has crossed theoretical boundaries is the notion of catharsis as a process of healing for the inner child or 'the child within' (Whitfield 1987, Stettbacher 1991). The client begins to re-experience their life events, recent as well as in the past, in the manner a healthy child does. This means putting aside, for a time, what seem to be rational adult explanations for past events. As these defensive and adaptive screens fall away, the full impact of the earlier experience can be felt, queried and, with the alliance of the practitioner, tentatively reframed. In this process, the practitioner may be needed to be alongside the client as witness, ally and, occasionally, as advocate. However, these are roles to be undertaken with great caution. Here the client must lead the way and in particular, be in charge of any reframing of the experience. Otherwise there is an ever-present danger of distorting and disturbing the client's remembered reality. The practitioner needs to engage in a subtle process of timing and interpretation which avoids any personal bias or deliberate induction of memories which are later deemed to be false, and which are unauthentic for the client. Only if the reframe is accurate can the client go on to express and explore natural needs appropriate to the past event, and still relevant in the present.

> Marion decided to try therapy again when she was offered a job as manager of the centre. She could not understand what was holding her back from accepting. She should have been so pleased, and yet she was lying awake at night, sweating with fear. In the early hours of the morning, it was crystal clear. She was unworthy and would fail. It was connected with her shameful secret, her fundamental badness. She had betrayed her grandfather when she was eight. He would give her sweets and then fiddle about a bit in her knickers. She had not liked that bit much but she had gone back again and again, not only for the sweets but for the hugs and the attention. No-one else had made a fuss of her in those days, and then she had been stupid enough to tell her dad. He had beaten her and her mum, and she had never been allowed to visit her grandfather again. The other women at the centre kept saying that she had been 'abused' and that she was only a child. But she had not felt like a child then and now she could only be angry with herself for being so stupid.

To avoid entering into the transference relationship, or prematurely to challenge transference reactions during the purging process of catharsis would be to lose the advantage of working within the primary focal relationship. It is through being watchful for the main transference and counter-transference issues that a practitioner can most clearly discern and, when the time is ripe, uncover the adaptive patterns of interaction adopted by a client to defend against some original pain. The transference patterns are usually concerned with issues of *dependency* whether these are displayed as pseudo-competent avoidance of any dependency (counter-dependency) or as clinging, and sometimes angry, passivity. The progression of counter-transference responses often experienced are of over-involvement, swiftly followed by fear and resentment of these dependency patterns. The practitioner is hypnotically induced to play out the same historically based role as occurs in external relationships where intrusive dominance alternates with rejection and abandonment. Being alert and prepared for these reactions enables the practitioner to facilitate, with intense compassionate interest, emotional discharge of the client's real needs.

Marion was never late for a therapy session but she always came into the room slowly. She would sit down and start looking around the room, waiting for the therapist to begin. She said she needed to be asked questions although these seemed only rarely to evoke a response. She would sit still, watching the therapist hungrily but critically. Could this woman ask the right question this time, and put her out of her misery? The therapist fought with her defensive irritation. She longed to shake this client into activity. Surely it was clear enough. Marion needed to get angry with everybody who had contributed to her miserable childhood: her possessive and violent father; her weak and neglectful mother; and that dirty old man, her grandfather. Instead she sat there in dumb and stubborn self-hate, only active in her denial of these truths.

Self-care stage

As outlined in the preceding cautionary notes, the stages outlined in this model are likely to overlap. They are recommended as *ordinal* but not as *exclusive* and will usually recur on a cyclical basis. This is particularly true of the stage of self-care which follows immediately from any successful experience of emotional restructuring of established patterns. No matter how well clients seem to be coping in their daily lives, their choice to enter psychological therapy is indicative of some dissatisfaction with their internal experience and the patterns of social interaction. Self-care in this context does not indicate self-indulgence or an unrealistic abandonment of personal responsibility. Adopting such maladaptive strategies is likely to lead to increased discomfort in external relationships. To enter into the *corrective emotional experience*, first described by Alexander and French (1946) and generally accepted as central to the curative process of psychotherapy, means to challenge and replace the punitive and critical *internal monitors*. Theoretically, these are formed from childhood through a process of experiential and observational learning, and are particularly shaped by expectations and restrictions imposed by influential parental and other authority figures. It is continually surprising to note the human tendency to maintain the most persecutory and inhibiting factors of early conditioning to provide the 'drivers' (Kahler 1978) for their adult functioning. Alice Miller (1985) argues that manifestations of exaggerated harshness in the superego stem from a real childhood experience rather than an from over-determined drive to repress forbidden desires.

Since his marriage had broken down, Duncan had avoided all sexual relationships. At first this had been easy. He had needed all his energy to survive the painful experiences of detoxification. Alcohol had rendered him almost impotent for several years, and now he was used to being on his own. He succumbed occasionally to an urge to masturbate, but this was always followed by an overwhelming sense of guilt and self-disgust. He had developed a punishing routine for these occasions. He would volunteer for an extra night at the local night shelter, and spend the whole time cleaning down the walls of the kitchen, scrubbing the floors with disinfectant and making sure he did all the washing up, finding a grim pleasure in the greasy water and the raw red patches on his hands. Afterwards, he would think about his mother who had complained constantly of the bleak griminess of the school kitchens and cloakrooms.

Clients using psychological therapy will almost always be experiencing dissonance between their ideal self, or preferred identity, and the self-image they have constructed. The work of the self-care stage is to affirm and restructure their identity within realistic parameters. To do this means internalising a benevolent and nurturing internal parent to replace the critical monitor. The relationship with the practitioner is used as test-ground and model for this process. Transferences are imposed, both positive and negative, and the real relationship is investigated in the attempt to redefine a more authentic self in relationship to a more manageable social environment. The usual counter-transference reaction is to enjoy being idealised and flinch from the negative projections. Practitioners with a psychodynamic training may express a reverse, but equally distorting, response by refusing or discounting the positive transference and inviting only the negative relationship. Again, as with the catharsis stage, the transference relationship is central to the process of change, allowing the client to experience emotionally the contrast between betrayals and disappointments of previous relationships and the steady empathic attention of the practitioner.

At Christmas, Marion made a cake for the therapist. She was beginning to feel so much stronger. Her job was going well again, and she was sleeping better at night. It would be good to give the other woman something, to show appreciation, and one thing she could do well was to bake fancy cakes. The therapist, however, seemed embarrassed by the gift, putting it on a side table and wanting to find out what Marion was avoiding by 'trying to feed' her therapist. Marion was plunged into despair. Would she never be able to please the important people in her life?

Renunciation stage

Implicit in the process of remembering and restructuring the past are loss, grief and anger. For many clients the ideal of a golden childhood has had to be renounced. For others there is rage and piercing sadness that the past was as it was, and cannot now be reclaimed. Caution needs to be exercised regarding the interpretation of the past being used. The practitioner, perhaps more than the client at this stage, can hold on to the knowledge that all reality is subjective. Stern (1985: 260) describes the use of a 'pivotal metaphor' in all therapeutic reconstructions of the individual's developmental past. Most clients focus on one or two primary scenes which characterise the problematic issues with which they struggle. The more *time-limited* the commitment between client and practitioner, the more sharp should be this focus.

The expression of both rage and grief is usually necessary to enable clients to accept and renounce their lost ideals of childhood and parenthood. A full and aware discharge of these emotions can allow the actuality of the real relationship to be more focal, replacing the idealised and disappointing relationships of the past. This means unpacking the distortions of the transference relationship while maintaining what is needed of the professional clarity provided through the working alliance. To let go of the past is a type of bereavement, and is likely to restimulate memories of previous losses. Since this work might well coincide with discussions regarding the impending end of a contractual commitment, the practitioner might be prey to counter-transference reactions of guilt and over-compensation. Agreed termination dates might be postponed unnecessarily and non-therapeutically. Again there is a temptation for the practitioner to bask only in positive aspects, this time of the real relationship, the powerful position of real trust and a shared sense of affinity.

> Tim and his therapist had agreed to move to once a week sessions and then to finish in January. Christmas was particularly difficult that year. He went home for one day only and was on call at the hospital the rest of the time. He was the only psychiatrist on duty during the aftermath of the most painful season of the year. He remembered all the bleak Christmas days he had spent at the school when his parents were abroad. He could hardly wait for his next session with his therapist. He was obviously not ready to finish therapy yet. There was nobody else who knew about his past and who understood him.

Empowerment stage

This stage is often not included in models of progressive psychological change through psychotherapy or counselling. It is the stage when adequate self-support and environmental supports have been put into place. Restructured social relationships and intimate partnerships are being tested against a more authentic and realised personal identity. The effort of the client is directed towards making a new contract with their social environment. Creativity is redirected towards satisfying the healthy human need to love and to work. The reality of existence with all its dread and potential joy can be encountered face on. These clients may no longer be in regular contractual commitment with the practitioner. Or they may be still lingering in a therapy group although other support networks might be more appropriate. Occasional contact is maintained, perhaps by letter. The practitioner continues to keep available the working alliance in case a follow-up session or review is requested. Transference is still likely to operate and it is advisable to avoid intimate relationships. In particular, and often ignored, is the danger of any business connections with employment or financial aspects. Even more complicated is the temptation to engage in a social relationship based on friendship. The affinities established through the therapeutic real relationship can be seductive but are only rarely uncontaminated by transference aspects and can be disappointing outside the consultation room.

> At first, Tim enjoyed being in the training group. He had found out that he was the only member who had been in individual therapy with the group therapist. He was also the only other person with a medical training. He glowed when the therapist asked him about the latest research on lithium. Tim was glad to be of help and brought in books and papers which he handed over eagerly at the beginning of the next session. He realised how good it was to feel special.

SUMMARY

In this chapter a stage-related model of psychological evolution, delineated as a process of self-development embedded in the life of each individual client, has been presented (see Table 2). In addition, the importance and power of the relationship between practitioner and client has been described as the arena in which therapeutic change takes place. The general themes likely to emerge at each stage of therapeutic engagement have been discussed so as to enable the practitioner to assess a likely point of entry and area of focus. These considerations are likely to be structured by the type of contractual commitment entered into, as detailed in Chapter 2. Each stage of the process has been linked into conscious awareness and strategic use of three coexisting modalities of psychotherapeutic relationship, delineated by Gelso and Carter (1985) as the working alliance, the transference and the real relationship. Particular attention has been paid to the transference and counter-transference reactions likely to influence professional engagement at each stage of psychological self-development. The flexibility of the model has been emphasised and its relevance to all four types of contractual commitment. While some case scenarios have been used to illustrate points made in this chapter, more extended description of how to use this approach within each type of contractual commitment will be found in the specific chapters in the main body of the book. Above all, the spirit of this chapter has been to emphasise the centrality of the client's journey of self-development, and to remove the practitioner to the periphery. The psychological therapist becomes more like a tradesperson, whose skills in delineating specific areas of focus, and possible pitfalls, can be put at the service of the client, at any one time. The process, the outcome and the credit for its design, belong to the client and are likely to be elaborated in another setting.

Chapter 4

Assessment and review
A two-way process

The truth is that the assessment of a patient for psychotherapy is probably the most complex, subtle, and highly skilled procedure in the whole field. It is very important to say that it is not the same as a psychiatric history, nor a social history, nor a psychotherapeutic session – it contains elements of all three but is in fact more than all three put together.

(Malan 1979: 210)

It is a strange aspect of the counselling and psychotherapeutic profession that intake and review sessions are rarely discussed in any detail. Many trainees embark on their first experience of working with a client without any clear instructions as to what assessment has already been made by the referring agent, if there is one, or what to do about assessment themselves if the client has not been referred to them. Experienced psychotherapists and counsellors tend to avoid conducting assessments on behalf of other practitioners. Malan's high opinion of the art of assessment has not been shared to the extent that practitioners seek to become specialists in the discipline. In this book, the practice of assessment has been described as an ongoing process between client and practitioner which underlies the intake interviews and review sessions described in Chapter 2. A particular format (see Table 3a) for assessment is offered to practitioners, after more general considerations with regard to theoretical and diagnostic considerations have been discussed. Although designed for practitioners using the time-conscious approach, it could be adapted for use as a checklist by other practitioners.

THEORETICAL VIEWS OF ASSESSMENT

When exploring the subject of assessment, some writers lay particular emphasis on the need to use the first interview to select which clients are *not* suitable for psychotherapy or counselling. This is particularly true for psychoanalytically oriented and behavioural psychotherapies, although the reasons given for this careful selection are somewhat different. Clients are often considered unsuitable for any form of psychoanalytic psychotherapy if they display a high degree of distress which is acted out in disruptive or anti-social behaviour. Cognitive and behavioural therapists are more likely to select for satisfactory outcome, and may even appreciate a disruptive behaviour which can be clearly described and targeted for change. Both types of psychotherapy prefer to exclude clients showing a wide range of disturbance and distress, behavioural and emotional, as well as psychotic tendencies. Ryle (1990: 213) comments on the necessity to find a way of providing for 'the needs of the ordinary population of neurotic and personality-disturbed' individuals without resorting to a rigid set of selection criteria. His Cognitive Analytic Therapy has been used for a much wider range of patients in medical settings and is similar to the time-conscious approach in that it 'seeks the active collaboration of patients from the earliest sessions' (Ryle 1990: 212).

Humanistic and existential approaches to psychological therapy encourage a belief in the 'growth tendency' as described by Rogers (1961: 35) which is, 'in the last analysis, the tendency upon which all psychotherapy depends' and which, in theory, 'exists in every individual and awaits only the proper conditions to be released and expressed'. This welcoming attitude towards prospective clients is attractive but tends to under-emphasise the need to assess how motivated a client is, *at any one time*, 'to expand, extend, become autonomous, develop, mature' (Rogers 1961: 35). In other words, what psychological change in thought, feelings and behaviour is this client, at this time, able to visualise and aim at? If this question is not clearly put, to oneself and, sensitively, to the client at an early stage in the therapeutic engagement, it is probable that client and practitioner will enter a vague, inconclusive and possibly harmful process.

To integrate the optimism of the humanist into the realistic caution of the psychoanalyst and the outcome-oriented scrutiny of the cognitive-behaviourist is an ambitious task. Whether working in brief or long-term psychological therapy, assessment and review are core practitioner skills always in need of refinement. Interest in these skills is nourished by relaxed fascination with the variety of stories and situations brought by clients into the consulting room. The uniqueness of each individual client is balanced by the presence of common themes underlying human distress. These common themes underlie the diagnostic categories which are used by many practitioners. Clinical experience of a wide variety of clients does provide some commonalities, and at best, diagnosis can be informed by the observations of generations of observant practitioners. At worst, it can be used as a rigid template which restricts creativity and denies change in practitioner and client. Probably the most dangerous type of diagnostic categories are the informal assumptions made by the practitioner who claims to eschew all forms of assessment.

Peter felt tense and irritated by the end of his first session with a counsellor. She sat there, smiling, asking him to tell her how he felt. She was pretending not to see how strange he had become. All his mates knew. They had been avoiding him ever since the festival when he had freaked out. Now he was unable to stop the whirling pictures in his head. His feet and hands were itching and his skin crawled and shuddered. He felt someone was watching him, and the earnest gaze of the counsellor increased his sense of panic. The counsellor was asking him if he wanted to come back and see her again. She had not told him whether he was really ill or not, or what he should do. She had not even asked if he was on drugs. He got up abruptly and left the room. The counsellor sighed and made some quick notes in her book. She would tell her supervisor how difficult it had been to make a counselling contract. Peter was defensive and arrogant, and probably sexist. She thought how typical it was that he had tried to control the session, expecting her to give him advice, avoiding any real contact and then leaving before the fifty minutes was up.

MANAGING THE INTAKE INTERVIEW

The term 'intake' is used for this crucial first encounter since the assessment process for the psychological therapies is almost always used to decide whether *this* client is to be taken into the practice or agency and then offered a commitment to joint work. An initial assessment process needs to be welcoming and facilitative, while making clear that there are alternative possibilities and choices. This attitude of choice and plenty can be difficult to convey to clients, many of whom can feel disempowered by their need for some sort of psychological intervention. Others experience choice as confusing and indicative of possible rejection. Commence with a clear statement of the chance offered by this interview for a two-way assessment as to whether the services offered by the practitioner is likely to be useful to the client at this time. This can be coupled with an assurance that there are other possibilities to explore and that the intake interviewer will assist the client in using another professional service if necessary. Printed information clearly explaining the professional practices of the service offered can aid this process if given to the client to read before the interview. This can include information about the practitioner's qualifications, the use made of the intake process, likely induction procedures, the extent of confidentiality offered, financial considerations and other pragmatic concerns. If written sensitively, such preliminary literature can encourage the client to feel some control of the process even before entering the room.

However, not all prospective clients read information in advance, and a clear statement as to the purpose of this first meeting is usually helpful. The following points need to be covered before commencing the assessment process detailed in Table 3a.

1 Purpose of this assessment interview – to decide together whether psychological therapy is indicated at this time.
2 Length of time available for this interview.
3 What the practitioner has to offer in qualifications, specialisms and, where really relevant, theoretical orientation.
4 General description of options likely to be offered at the end of the interview.
5 Any remaining concerns or questions of the client before commencing intake.

Confidentiality and the practitioner's policy with regard to *maintaining safety* should be discussed as early as possible in the intake interview. Omission of this preliminary information is always hazardous, no matter how much in crisis the client appears to be, or, conversely, how apparently knowledgeable about psychotherapeutic procedures. It is professionally incompetent to allow a client to embark on any form of private consultation without making clear the *limits* of confidentiality available. Practitioners vary as to these limits, but it is usually prudent to make clear to clients that the obligation of all members of the helping profession is to maintain the safety of clients and all other individuals, especially children and other vulnerable people. Practitioners need themselves to be well-informed as to the legal limits of confidentiality between client and practitioner. This is a difficult area with very little certain protection for the practitioner required to disclose information by court order or in order to conform to changes in legal statutes.

Where there is, in the practitioner's judgement, real risk or danger to the client or any other person, then confidentiality might need to be breached. It is usually advisable to accompany this statement with an explanation that those consulted are likely to be professional persons with their own ethical codes. This can seem a ponderous and somewhat alarming warning to deliver, although the majority of prospective clients will accept the necessity for these limitations. Using a warm, firm but undramatic manner, while remaining in full contact with prospective clients, is helpful. Clients with self-damaging behaviours may challenge these standards but may also be reassured that there boundaries exist which might increase their own levels of safety. At worst, clients withdrawing at this point of the interview can be guided to services which do not need the same strictures and which can provide a listening ear for the distressed, no matter what risky behaviour is disclosed. Some suicidal or violent clients may be encouraged by an explanation of the difference between expressing violent thoughts and feelings and performing dangerous actions.

The first time Judy met the psychiatric social worker, she was very wary. She had agreed to talk to someone but she was not going to give in. The doctors who had pumped her stomach had tricked her out of her decision to die. She had to hang on to her one sure way out of all the pain. She had the pills hidden away in the shoes in her locker. The worst part of the group meetings on the ward was the silence at the beginning. She wanted to tell them about her longing to go to sleep forever but then they would start to search her belongings, and her way out would be gone. The social worker seemed to know a bit about her. She took it for granted that Judy was still thinking about killing herself, and also seemed to know that these thoughts were frightening. She suggested that Judy use the first few sessions talking about all these conflicting feelings, to the social worker and to the nurses on the ward. Later, when Judy left the hospital, she would have to agree to keep herself safe if she wanted to continue the counselling sessions. All that could be postponed. It sounded OK and, anyway, nobody could stop her if she really wanted to do it.

In addition, it is ethically sound for practitioners, no matter how experienced, to inform clients that they may, from time to time, be consulting professional colleagues and may, therefore, discuss the client with other practitioners holding to the same code of ethics. Offering new clients a copy of the code of ethics subscribed to by the practitioner is a useful practice.

DIAGNOSTIC ISSUES RELEVANT TO INTAKE INTERVIEWS

As already indicated, theoretical schools differ in their approaches to the use of diagnosis as part of the intake process. Malan (1979: 210) firmly recommends that the interviewer meeting a client for the first time must think simultaneously of a number of issues. I am grateful to a colleague (Evans 1987) for inspiring the following summary of Malan's advice:

> Think psychiatrically – diagnosis influences prognosis. Think psychodynamically – identify the intrapsychic and psychosocial conflict operating, now and in the past. Think psychotherapeutically – using professional experience to predict the themes and the process of therapy in this case. Think practically – what is actually possible, and available for this patient.

Malan (1979: 213) adds to this advice a particular emphasis on the danger of establishing too significant a relationship within the first interview. On one side, there is a need to establish sufficient initial *rapport* to gain an alliance with clients to enable both participants to establish a focal theme. On the other side of the equation is the need for flexibility and openness to referral elsewhere or withdrawal from contractual commitment. In the time-conscious approach, assessment practitioners are required to work for a high level of attentive awareness and presence at all times and especially in the intake interview. This can be offset by firmly distinguishing the intake interview from the usual session of psychological therapy. Different methods can be developed to indicate its distinctive quality. Taking notes can be a powerful communication, particularly if this is accompanied by an explanation that this is not likely to happen in a normal session. Also powerful is the message conveyed by sensitive postponement of full engagement with emotion-laden themes until the level of commitment has been resolved.

The psychiatric practice of taking formal histories and examining the mental state of clients can be a disempowering and alienating procedure. However, the typical format of what is usually called a 'clerking' interview as carried out by students of psychiatry is given below as a background checklist for information which can be relevant to assessments.

Presenting complaint – History of presenting complaint – Family history – Personal (developmental) history – School record – Work record – Sexual history – Past medical history – Social history – Personality traits – Mental state, judged on appearance, behaviour, talk, orientation, mood, thought content, memory, concentration, general intelligence, insight.

The psychiatric interview is usually a lengthy question-and-answer interview.

The medical student groaned inwardly as he entered the day-room. Judy had turned the television on loud and was apparently absorbed in a 1930s black and white movie. This was the third time he had tried to take Judy's formal history. Well, at least she was alone in the room. He tried again to explain that this was part of the treatment. Without a proper record, they would find it difficult to help Judy. She was watching him with a smile. He was about the same age as her, and not as tall. He felt nervous. She had a reputation for making angry threats. Suddenly, she relented and told him to go ahead. He got out his list of headings and embarked on the interview. It was easy enough getting the historical details. She seemed to enjoy telling him about her family, their ages and their interests. She particularly relished the story of the fight which had ended with her smashing up the living room. She was amused by his tentative questions about her 'relationships', and boasted of a 'brilliant' sex life. It was only at the end when he started on the routine mental state questions, about what day of the year it was and could she count back from thirty, that she became impatient and told him to f*** off, she'd had enough.

Many practitioners are wary of collecting items of information, preferring to explore the likelihood of a therapeutic alliance. This preference might lead to a practitioner overlooking important information, such as the following significant items:

1 Any medical condition, past or present.
2 Medications prescribed, particularly if mind-altering.
3 Excessive use of caffeine, alcohol or other recreational drugs, legal or illegal.
4 Unusual dietary or eating patterns.
5 Experiences of losing touch with consensual reality.
6 Previous hospitalisation for psychological distress.
7 Name of present medical consultant, usually general practitioner in UK.
8 Previous or current experiences of psychological therapy.

Obtaining permission to consult with other professional people who have been contacted by a prospective client is nearly always advisable. Neglecting to do so can lead to confusion and lack of support from colleagues when this becomes necessary. Again, there are a few clients who will threaten to withdraw rather than give this information. Exploration of the reasons for this mistrust are often enlightening in themselves, and offer an opportunity for negotiation and reassurance.

Diagnostic categories

There are three main categories of psychological distress where generally accepted diagnostic considerations are likely to be useful to practitioners. Care should be exercised in accepting clients for psychological therapy who display extreme signs and describe severe symptoms of *psychosis*, *anxiety* or *depression*. These symptoms might be evident in clients suffering from a psychosexual disorder, manic episodes, obsessive-compulsive behaviours or an eating disorder. Knowledge about these signs and symptoms does not necessarily lead to excluding clients from therapeutic engagement but ensures that appropriate and achievable therapeutic interventions are offered. Insufficient knowledge can lead either to damaging psychotherapeutic engagement or to stringent exclusion practices. Both of these consequences contradict the main purpose of assessment, at intake and at review, which is to ensure that clients gain eventual benefit and ease from psychological pain. Practitioners are recommended to familiarise themselves with at least one diagnostic manual and to take advantage of any opportunity to observe psychiatric procedures, suspending judgement while doing so.

Although the *ICD-10* is still used in some NHS settings, the *Diagnostic and Statistical Manual of Mental Disorders* (American Psychiatric Association, 1987) or *DSM* has grown in popularity in the UK and is regularly revised. The manual provides a multi-axial approach which can be usefully adopted by all intake interviewers. Five different aspects of prospective clients are examined separately. These are as follows: symptoms of psychological distress; personality factors; level of physiological health; psychosocial and environmental stressors; and evidence of recent healthy psychological functioning. Information about these five areas can be gained verbally and through impressions.

Possibly the most powerful and essential information is given by the accepted *signs* of anxiety, depression or psychosis. To assist practitioners, some of these are indicated below, together with indications for referral. This should not be considered an exhaustive list as it is based on the *practices of the author* and does not, in any way, attempt to summarise a diagnostic manual.

Signs of anxiety: agitated repetitive behaviours; increased pulse, hyperventilation; changes of body heat; skin conductance changes (sweat); fight or flight body movements; cognitive confusion displayed verbally and behaviourally, accompanied by a belief in personal ineffectiveness, vulnerability and helplessness. None of these symptoms are helpful in dealing with any real experiences of physical or social threat.

Referral of clients with symptoms of neurotic anxiety should be considered by practitioners when there are severe phobias, obsessive-compulsive behaviours or intense and generalised free-floating anxiety accompanied by suicidal ideation. However, suicidal ideation in itself does not exclude an offer of commitment with a clearly stated policy regarding safety and damage limitation. Some clients need to use medication for temporary containment of their most frightening feelings while using psychological therapy. The success of this combined treatment usually depends on the level of co-operation between medical and therapeutic practitioners.

Signs of depression: avoidance behaviours and postures; inappropriately flat affect; lack of self-care displayed as inadequate diet and personal grooming; sleep disturbance; early morning waking; uncontrolled weeping accompanied by a belief in personal failure and lack of self-worth. None of these symptoms are helpful in gaining social support and affiliation to repair real experiences of loss or bereavement.

Referral of clients with symptoms of neurotic depression should always be considered by practitioners when there is evidence of life-threatening behaviour affecting bodily functions (appetite, sleep or self-neglect) especially when these accompany delusional ideation which may include psychotic phenomena. Again, close co-operation with a medical general practitioner prescribing anti-depressants may be beneficial.

Signs of psychosis: reported disorders of perception, illusions and hallucinations, including auditory, visual, olfactory and somatic experiences; thought disorders including obsessions and delusions; loosening of associations; bizarre speech; incoherence and inappropriately flat affect; reported odd beliefs and unusual perceptual experiences; marked lack of initiative, interests and energy; social isolation, withdrawal; catatonic rigidity or excitement.

Referral should be considered if a combination of these signs and symptoms are present and in particular if the intake interviewer has become so wary, guarded or uneasy that any prospect of a trusting alliance is unlikely. Clients who have already been diagnosed as psychotic and are contained by medication can be rewarding clients to offer a clearly defined commitment. Work focused on reality testing and mutual problem-solving is indicated.

> Peter felt awkward and watchful. His earlier experience of this counselling business had been disappointing and frightening. He had been left alone to cope with increasingly threatening hallucinations. If only that uptight woman had taken control like the young doctor he vaguely remembered from the night he landed up in the casualty ward of the local hospital. Would this smiling Irishman ask the right questions? He began to describe some of his most bizarre experiences and beliefs. Before he had started the regular injections, he had certain knowledge that his every movement was monitored by two small demons. He wondered aloud about the existence of a parallel universe with windows into his soul. The counsellor seemed unalarmed and seriously interested as he asked Peter how often he now had these thoughts, and whether they still seemed as real to him now. He went on to ask Peter about his friendship circle, and how he spent his leisure time. Peter described the day centre he attended, where he had a few mates, but went on to talk about the loneliness of being a mature student at the local college. Talking through some strategies to improve his college social life, Peter began to feel accepted and normal again.

Of the five pivotal aspects of psychological functioning described by the *DSM-III-R* (American Psychiatric Association 1987), psychotherapists and counsellors are likely to be more familiar with the notion of 'Axis II' *developmental and personality disorders*. While personality traits are 'enduring patterns of perceiving, relating to, and thinking about the environment and oneself, exhibited in a wide range of important social and personal contexts' (American Psychiatric Association 1987: 305), they become problematic when they are linked with social functioning or personal distress. Perhaps the line between supportive problem-solving counselling and more intensive psychotherapeutic intervention is marked by the amount of focus on personality structure in the therapeutic interaction.

When personality traits are perceived as severely maladaptive and inflexible, they are often described as personality disorders. These disorders are usually first manifested in childhood or adolescence and could continue throughout adult life, perhaps fading in their more florid manifestations in mid-life, only to erupt again if senility occurs in old age. The *DSM* (American Psychiatric Association 1987) places personality disorders on a separate axis of mental distress from symptoms of psychiatric disorder. This enables a practitioner to differentiate between the presenting problems and more deep-seated developmental problems. In psychiatric diagnosis the prognosis is usually more gloomy if a personality disorder is diagnosed. In counselling and psychotherapy, any focus on personality difficulties normally indicates an interest in a fundamental level of psychological change. However, when personality problems are accompanied by severe impairment of social and personal functioning, it is important to be alert to the possibility of further disintegration (including psychotic symptoms), if intensive therapeutic work is engaged. Be prepared to refer the client, possibly to a containing therapeutic environment or community. Alternatively, limit the engagement to a supportive problem-solving approach.

> At the team meeting, the social worker described her first meeting with Judy. She related how Judy's initial truculence had faded as she had begun to describe her special relationship with her father and her fear of being weak and ordinary like her mother. The nurses on the team had observed Judy's intense mood swings on the ward. She could be joking and good-humoured at one moment and then suddenly withdraw into scowling silence. Judy had increased the superficial cuts on her arms during the last week. The social worker decided to go slowly, working to build up Judy's confidence in therapy, and to resolve the present problem of where she was going to live.

The *DSM-III-R* (American Psychiatric Association 1987) describes on Axis II three groups of personality disorders, which fall into the following groups or clusters:

1 odd or eccentric behaviours: paranoid, schizoid and schizotypal.
2 dramatic, emotional behaviours: histrionic, narcissistic, anti-social and borderline.
3 anxious, fearful behaviours: avoidant, dependent, compulsive and passive-aggressive.

It is important to note that the grouping emphasises behaviours. Typically, personality problems involve observable behaviours which disrupt social interaction but which may or may not be regarded by the individuals themselves as undesirable or unusual.

CONDUCTING REVIEW SESSIONS

As with intake interviews, practitioners take the main responsibility for the process of review. It is their professional judgement which will steer the session towards agreement about future commitment. There are two main themes for any review session. The first theme is focused on the immediate past. What has been achieved, what remains incomplete and what major concerns have been uncovered? Linked to this theme is evaluation, which can be two-way, of this experience of psychological therapy. The second theme concerns the possibility of continuation at this time. This theme is focused on the future. What would be the value of extending the therapeutic engagement at this time, for the client? In what way have the aims and goals of the client altered? The answers to all these questions need to be sensitively negotiated, with careful attention to here-and-now influences arising from the review process itself. Clients may construe review sessions as a kind of test in which they have to prove their distress and their value as clients. For clients whose self-esteem has been eroded and damaged in the past, it is imperative to ensure their full understanding that continuation is a likely outcome of the review session, and that the final decision will be negotiable. Practitioners can recommend and may hold strong views but the client is the customer and needs to be reminded of this. Review sessions share with assessment a need to balance professional judgement with the danger of ignoring issues of power and covert influence.

> Peter had enjoyed his first few sessions with the counsellor. They had proved to be the high point of each week and he was beginning to feel less shy with the young male students in his class at college. The women still alarmed him, especially the chatty outgoing ones who touched him lightly as they talked, and then flitted off laughing. Were they laughing at him? He wanted to talk about this fear to his counsellor, but realised that this might mean talking about those weird sexual fantasies he had experienced at the festival. When the counsellor suggested they discuss whether to continue the sessions, he felt alarmed. Perhaps after all, the man could read his mind, in spite of his denials. He wanted to get rid of Peter and his disgusting and repellent ideas. Peter looked down at his feet, and mumbled something about being busy on Tuesdays next term. 'Would another day be better?', asked the counsellor, 'because I would like us to go on meeting'. Peter looked up sharply, trying to match the warm tone of voice to the judgement he expected to find on the man's face. Maybe he would be allowed to continue seeing a counsellor.

USING A CHECKLIST APPROACH TO ASSESSMENT AND REVIEW

The focused approach offered in this book is underpinned by a constant process of assessment and review. These are procedures for which the practitioner takes main responsibility but which is shared as fully as possible with clients. As already discussed, the very concept of 'assessment' seems to be an uncomfortable issue for some practitioners, particularly the large number influenced by a humanist wish to avoid all judgemental thinking. More diagnostically minded practitioners accept the task of evalua-

Table 3a Ongoing assessment and review

Client's name/no.	Intake/review/last session notes

....

GP info. .... Drugs/diet, etc. ....

Previous psych. therapy: ....

(1)	Description of client and of process/personal and interpersonal (present focus)
(2)	Problems/concerns/themes/issues (present focus)
(3)	History: family/social/losses/gains/survivals (past focus)
(4)	Aims and goals/obstacles visualised (future focus)
(5)	Unfinished business (present and future focus)
(6)	Therapeutic alliance concerns/themes (past and present focus)
(7)	Transference issues to be considered (past and present focus)
(8)	Life process stage (use Table 2). (Any diagnostic considerations?)
(9)	Commitment agreed: Continuation?/Referral?/Close? (use Table 1)

© 1996 by J. Elton Wilson

tion and prediction as necessary, especially where client selection for suitability is concerned. Researchers design and use tools such as the 'Prognostic Index' developed by Luborsky and his colleagues (1988), which can then form the basis of the traditional psychiatric interview. Between these highly structured protocols and the tentative explorations offered by a client-centred counsellor during a first session, there is a wide range of methodologies for assessment purposes. Most experienced practitioners establish an initial checklist of some kind, which can be used with most of their clients, and which can be referred to from time to time. Trainees are usually grateful for guidance in conducting initial sessions and will tend to use the methodology of their trainers and supervisors.

In Table 3a a detailed form of assessment, suitable for use both during the intake process and while conducting reviews, is offered to the reader.

The format displayed in Table 3a culminates in the practitioner's decision as to which type of contractual commitment (see Table 1) to discuss with this client at this time. This decision in turn is informed by a tentative judgement regarding the stage reached by this particular client in their life process (see Table 2).

Each section of the suggested format for assessment and review has a particular time-related focus. This is to counteract the tendency for psychological therapists to focus exclusively on past events. The proponents of 'solution-focused' therapy as originated by de Shazer (1985, 1988) have proposed a therapeutic approach which is almost entirely future-oriented. This specific strategy is, at this time, particularly popular with cognitive therapists who use it to build on the well-established methodologies of behaviour therapy. Instead of attending primarily to the history of problematic issues, these practitioners ask about the conditions, or *contingencies*, in which clients are either able to overcome their difficulties or are able to achieve some element of the positive outcome which they seek from therapeutic engagement. This approach could be viewed disparagingly by psychoanalytic and humanist practitioners as an avoidance of the expression of the painful emotions which underlie maladaptive patterns of thought and behaviour. In the format presented in Table 3a, a balance between past-, present- and future-oriented foci of interest is recommended to the practitioner in the belief that theoretical understandings can be stretched beneficially by including elements from novel and effective methodologies.

Unpacking Table 3a – a checklist for assessment and review sessions

Describing the client and the process

For every assessment or review session, this is an essential function for the practitioner. The subtle skill of *paying attention* to the person of the client, in the present moment, is often overlooked. It is an ability which needs continual renewal and of which true mastery is only occasionally achieved. The practitioner needs to possess the presence to take in the client on a person-to-person level as fully as possible while remaining aware of their own internal responses as well as observing the interpersonal process between themselves and the client. This endeavour is far more complex than the brief notes of *age, gender, relationships held* and *occupations followed*, which will also be allocated to this part of an assessment format. Vivid keywords can be useful in prompting recall of the impressions received when reading through these notes at a later date. If genuinely attempted, this level of attention can be used to inform the outcome of an intake interview or a review session. It is imperative that previous descriptions of the client are temporarily put aside whether they have been contributed by others or are held in the practitioner's own memory. Ideally, an element of person-to-person immediacy would pervade every therapy session. For review purposes, practitioners can aspire to renew some of the freshness of their first encounters with their clients so as to assess the level of change which has taken place.

Focusing on the problematic issues

This requirement might seem a direct contradiction to the recommendations of the previous section. However, for the client sincerely seeking alleviation of psychological distress through psychotherapy or counselling, problematic concerns are an integral part of their moment-to-moment existence. To ignore this might be to fall into the error noted by Koss and Shiang (1994: 664) and forget that clients 'typically come to psychological treatment seeking specific and focal problem resolution, not for personality "overhauls" as assumed in the past'. Discovering and clearly articulating the *predominant problematic concerns* preoccupying the client at this present time is an essential part of the decision-making process required by the end of the session. Often these problematic issues are expressed as themes rather than discrete concerns and this can be linked to a focal theme which can then be used to indicate the life process stage likely to be useful as a point of entry into work with this client.

> Judy sat huddled in the corner of the shiny leatherette sofa in the hospital day-room. She waited for the alert and lively woman opposite to begin the dreary questioning about her childhood and her family which had preoccupied the two psychotherapists she had seen in the hospital. She was surprised when she was asked whether she was comfortable where she sat, and then, when she had moved to a more upright and supportive chair, what was frightening and sad in her life on this particular day.
>
> Judy began to describe what it was like having to hide away her thoughts and feelings so that she would not be diagnosed as mad and locked away for ever. What would help? She wanted to understand what had happened at home and how she had found herself suddenly smashing the television set and attacking her mother and her sister in a blind rage. She paused, wearily awaiting the questions about her early childhood, about which she remembered so little. The woman opposite was leaning forward, interested only in how she usually got on with her family – was she close to her mother, her sister, other family members? She did not seem shocked when Judy blurted out that she felt nothing for anybody except her father. He was the only one she had liked, and now he had gone away to look after some other woman's kids. He had disapproved of her for the last few years, and now he was gone. Was this part of the reason why she had taken the overdose? Yes, because she felt so guilty and bad but no-one would listen to her at home, or at the hospital.

The social worker offered to do just that, listen to her story and leave her to decide by the sixth session if she wanted to continue. Judy knew already that to continue she would have to agree to stop cutting her arms. However, that was not being asked of her now, and it would be a relief to tell someone about what had happened between her father and her boyfriend.

Visualising the future – hopes and expectations

Sensitive exploration of the client's hopes and expectations is likely in itself to increase the likelihood of a beneficial conclusion to a therapeutic engagement. A 'solution-focused' (de Shazer 1985) and realistic discussion of aims and goals as visualised by the client at this stage of the therapeutic engagement can be empowering in itself. Clients are encouraged to explore their present strengths and strategies for survival, and to visualise realistically how these might be expanded in the future. To a large extent, this can be a process of re-education as the client realises that personal growth and expansion can be envisaged, without loss of their present sense of identity. Problematic issues already discussed can often be reframed as evidence of the survival capacity of the client. It is encouraging to both client and practitioner if the goals of psychological therapy are depicted in realistic and tangible terms. The more abstract the discussion, the less easy will it be to check the outcome at the next assessment or review.

At the review session, Judy told the social worker about her father's cleverness and physical strength. She was proud that he also had a 'sort of' social work job. She predicted that everybody at the hospital would be charmed by her father, and would agree with him that she, Judy, had very little reason to complain. Surely her father had been right to send her boyfriend to prison and to arrange for the abortion. The social worker commented on her loyalty to her father, and asked her if this was very precious to her. Judy glowed as she related how her father had treated her as eldest son rather than eldest daughter, at least until her young brother was born a few years ago. How did she live up to this expectation? She had always been tough and bold, not a weak girl. Here she drooped in her chair, she remembered how weak and helpless she had felt in the abortion clinic, and how soft and fat her body had felt ever since.

The social worker commented on her change of mood. She said she had noticed how Judy had squared her shoulders at the beginning of the session as if prepared for a fight. She wondered if Judy had used some of her old courage in agreeing to attend these sessions, and asked her what she hoped for now. Judy said, without much hope, that she would like to feel strong again, and get back her father's respect. What about her own self-respect? Yes, but that was the same thing for Judy. What would be one way in which she would act differently if she liked and respected herself a bit more? Judy found this difficult to answer. She was surprised to find herself thinking how good it would be to stop living at home. She could imagine herself in a flat somewhere, with friends visiting.

What's likely to be unfinished, now and in the future?

This question can increase the realistic optimism which is a crucial attitude to engender in assessment and review. Whatever the achievements of the client, there will be areas which are still unexplored. Clients are never completely cured or fixed, and the skill of the practitioner is in sensitive acceptance of the continuous nature of personal development. However, the emphasis is on caution in this subject area, particularly when conducting reviews. Clients need to celebrate their progress, however small, and the aim is not to discourage but to make their ongoing life's journey central to the therapeutic process. The unfinished business of one stage of this journey can point the way towards the next stage.

Judy moved into the hostel a week later. At first it was fine but, after her father's visit, she got very drunk. She had wanted him to see her as separate and grown up, but his reproachful reminders of how much the younger children missed her made her feel guilty again. She watched him uneasily as he set about charming the other girls, making them laugh. Would she ever be free of him? Perhaps it was time to tell the social worker about her father's secret.

Evaluating the alliance – how might we work together?

Peake, Borduin and Archer (1988: 20) describe this discussion as an essential part of a new client's 'role induction' which in itself 'facilitates progress in psychotherapy, both by providing an advance plan on how this curious process works, and by generating hopefulness to combat the sense of demoralisation'. The working alliance has already been described in Chapter 3 as an emotional bond combined with an intellectual agreement. These two are both necessary in order to agree pragmatic parameters of the alliance, including the length and frequency of sessions, financial considerations and the extent of confidentiality offered. Too often these pragmatic elements are left undiscussed, relegated to the position of ground rules which must never be challenged or discussed. Encouragement of such discussion can strengthen the value of *time and space boundaries* as the container inside which trust can be built.

Clients' *expectations* of therapeutic engagement need to be explored fully and respectfully. McLeod (1990a: 7) describes the research findings which show that clients enter into an *evaluation* of the competence of the practitioner who is often expected to provide 'expert diagnosis, advice, recommendations and action to resolve the problem'. While such requirements are likely to dismay many practitioners, prepared only to facilitate the client's own potential competencies, they may well indicate the amount of demoralisation (Frank 1985) experienced by clients seeking psychological therapy. This mismatch in expectations between client and practitioner is so commonly demonstrated that it deserves acknowledgement and open debate where possible. Only then can clients experience a sufficient level of the *'emotional connection'* described by McLeod (1990a: 9) as an essential component for successfully entering the therapeutic engagement.

At review sessions, all the concerns discussed above can be deepened and widened to include considerations of client motivation and therapeutic integrity. Has sufficient trust been established to continue? How does the client rate the practitioner's contribution to the therapeutic engagement so far? Are the ground rules experienced as consistent or oppressive? Has the practitioner adequately maintained the container of the commitment? How indicative of fluctuations in motivation are the missed or forgotten appointments? Conversely, does the client's unbroken record of punctuality indicate enthusiasm for the session or a learnt pattern of obedient conformity?

> Judy was careful to be late for most of her first six sessions. She would arrive about ten minutes after the agreed time, never later, and glance challengingly at the clock. The social worker did not comment on this until the sixth session which was to be a review. To Judy's surprise, she was asked if she found the sessions too long and would prefer a shorter session. This suggestion so disarmed her that she was able to admit to testing out the social worker's patience. The thought of having shorter sessions was alarming. She wondered if the social worker was sending her up, although she seemed sincere enough. Anyway, she would make sure she was on time for the next few sessions.

What is the pattern which gets between us?

At an initial assessment session, key patterns of interaction may be observed. With caution, these observations can be shared with the client. This can be a useful test of the client's understanding of the power of these transference reactions to distort relationships. Such insights need to be used sparingly and in a straightforward and empathic manner. Review sessions provide an important opportunity to reflect on patterns which have already become apparent. In the time-conscious approach, practitioners are encouraged to use review sessions to give a clear account of their understanding of their clients up to this time. Interactional patterns are connected to learnt strategies for survival while leaving space for major links to significant figures or events from the past to be made by clients themselves.

> Judy's wrists were conspicuously bandaged on the third session. She asked drearily if the sessions would stop now. She was reminded gently that the agreement had been that she would need to decide whether she was ready to stop cutting herself if she wanted more than six sessions. Judy had been surprised that the social worker never discussed her with the other hospital patients. She had not taken all that stuff about confidentiality very seriously. She had expected them all to laugh about her behind her back. It seemed that she was used to people letting her down, and had constantly prepared herself for rejection by any therapist. The social worker paused in her recollections. Judy looked at her suspiciously. What was coming now? So far this woman had stuck to her word. But she was sure to get tired of her and find another favourite. That was what her mother had always done with every new baby. Suddenly, the memories flooded back and she began to talk about her painful jealousy as each sister and brother arrived. Yes, she had expected to be replaced, even here.

Deciding on the focal theme – what stage is this client likely to work through this time?

At the initial assessment, this decision should be made with caution. The whole of the assessment process described culminates in a practitioner's tentative hypothesis as to the point of entry into each client's life process of psychological evolution. Clues are to be found in the *attitude* of the client to the problematic issues and concerns expressed. Extreme caution verging on distrust can indicate that the preparation stage may be the main arena of work for this client.

> The social worker said she thought Judy had experienced her father's withdrawal from their very special relationship as a major abandonment. Her brother had taken her place and her mother had always seemed to disapprove of her. She had decided to throw herself into a relationship with the toughest person she could find, a squaddy from the nearby army camp. Her father's interest in her was revived, if only because he was so angry, searching for her in the woods and threatening to kill the soldier. Now she sought out confrontation and crisis. Only then did she feel alive and the centre of attention.

Clients who report traumatic events and a high level of social distress and dysfunction may need to be contained by a short period of preparation for work in the disclosure stage. Others arrive at the assessment session with a reasonably clear picture of the emotional charge which is being repressed, and the concerns which are tied up with these feelings. For these clients only enough of a trusting working alliance has to be put in place before accompanying them into the stage of catharsis. Clients who have already experienced difficult emotions and the accompanying insights, either through previous psychological therapy or other modes of personal development, may need accompanying through the changes accomplished during the self-care stage.

The next two stages, of renunciation and empowerment, are more likely to be considered as points of entry by practitioners conducting review sessions. However, there are clients returning to psychological therapy, either with the same practitioner or in a new professional context, who are still hanging on to stale feelings of anger, disappointment and grief. Practitioners conducting therapy groups or facilitating self-help groups are likely to find themselves considering whether some individuals are mainly in need of a supportive fellowship as they continue with the process of self-empowerment.

Deciding which commitment to enter

As already stressed, each new client is likely to need some time in the preparation stage, whatever the practitioner's assessment of the likely area of focus. Making standard the offer of a mini-commitment, as a preliminary two-way experiment in contractual commitment, provides the necessary forum for this work. Some clients, at the very beginning of their journey of self-discovery and psychological expansion, may be more appropriately offered a holding arrangement while they work through a current crisis or spend some time visiting, in pre-contemplation (Dryden 1991) of the experience of psychological therapy. Another group of clients may, even after the most careful assessment and offer of commitment, decide that the period of contemplation offered by a fully extended mini-commitment was all that they needed at this time.

Wherever the practitioner has achieved some clarity about the area of focus, then continuation into a time-focused, time-extended or time-expanded commitment is indicated. These options are described in detail in Chapter 2 of this book. The first review session provides the major point of choice. At all times, practitioners are encouraged to explore sensitively whether a client is really clear about continuing. Just as clients need to build up a trusting therapeutic relationship and confidence in the benefits of psychological therapy, so many practitioners need to develop trust in the self-healing potential of a client's return to the continuing 'business of being human' (Gilmore 1973). At intake interviews, uncertainty can usually be allayed by offering a second or even a third intake to provide the opportunity to prolong and refine the assessment process. The three overarching

Table 3b Ongoing assessment and review form as completed up to Judy's first review

	Client's name/no. *Judy xxx* *female, unemployed.*	Intake sessions *(Psychiatric in-patient, on* *mild medication).*	First review After six sessions, no drugs now. Out-patient.
1	Description of client and of process/ personal and interpersonal (present focus)	*Looks younger than 20* *yrs. Baggy overalls* *hiding her ?underweight* *body. Angry and scared;* *shows courage and* *ability to respond.*	*Makes good contact;* *open with feelings; rapid* *mood changes; healthier* *appearance; painted* *nails! No bandages.*
2	Problems/concerns/ themes/issues (present focus)	*Unable to contain rage;* *intense guilt-ridden* *relationship with father,* *self-damage; suicidal* *intentions.*	*Feelings about father* *confused; self-esteem* *and separation; hints of* *more 'secrets'.*
3	History: family/social/ losses/gains/ survivals (past focus)	*Closest to father until 15* *years then some violence* *linked to a sexual liaison.* *Overdosed when father* *left.*	*Brother's birth felt as loss* *of identity as father's* *favourite. Mother lost* *to each new sibling.*
4	Aims and goals/ obstacles visualised (future focus)	*To decide whether to con-* *tain suicidal intentions/* *continue counselling.* *Family loyalty vs. need to* *talk re father.*	*To decide about moving* *away from home; to* *explore mother's role; to* *use full time of session!*
5	Unfinished business (present and future focus)	*Separation/individuation* *from father. Possible dis-* *closure of painful secret.* *Continuing self-damage.*	*Some painful disclosure* *pending. Restore contact* *with mother. Father's* *influence still strong.*
6	Therapeutic alliance concerns/themes (past and present focus)	*Clarify commitment,* *confidentiality and self-* *damage issue. Trust low.* *Responds to honesty.*	*Continuing counselling* *is conditional on client* *ceasing to self-damage;* *confirm confidentiality.*
7	Transference issues to be considered (past and present focus)	*Mother and sisters* *disliked; recent psycho-* *therapy faiiure; beware* *temptation to force dis-* *closure re family.*	*Father is some sort of* *social worker! Mother* *experienced as rejecting* *and preferring siblings.*
8	Life process stage (use Table 2). Any diagnostic considerations?	*Preparation stage: needs* *a safe enough relation-* *ship and more self* *esteem (diagnosed as* *'borderline personality').*	*Disclosure stage: will* *need time for this as* *loyalty to family high.*
9	Commitment agreed: Continuation?/ Referral?/Close? (use Table 1)	*Mini-commitment to con-* *tinue if self-damage con-* *tained by agreement.*	*Only time-focused* *commitment possible* *now. May return to Psycho-* *therapy Dept.*

questions for practitioners to ask themselves, and to be ready to answer by the end of all intake interviews and review sessions, are as follows:

1 Is this the right time for *any* contractual commitment?
2 Am I clear enough about the *area of focus* now required?
3 What *stage* of psychological development is this client traversing?

The answers to these questions depend on the practitioner's professional judgement. Table 3a should be used as an aid to making this judgement. Practitioners unused to such a structured approach, and those in training, may prefer to work through the nine sections of the table after the assessment or review session. Clients can be asked to re-contact the practitioner after the session for a final offer. As practitioners become more experienced in the time-conscious approach, this should become less necessary. Equally, as clients themselves become experienced in making choices about the duration and form of their psychological therapy, the process of continuous assessment and review will become a shared task.

Table 3b shows how the table might be used for Judy, the fictional client described throughout this chapter. If rigid diagnostic exclusions were applied, clients with this degree of psychological distress would not normally be offered any form of psychotherapeutic commitment. In this example, a flexible and carefully calibrated approach is illustrated. Assessment is used as an aid to increase choice in contractual commitment and to ensure that the client works in the area appropriate to her probable stage of personal development.

SUMMARY

In this chapter the use of a structured procedure for assessment and review purposes has been recommended. Table 3a provides a detailed template for practitioners to use in order to facilitate decisions regarding which of the four commitments (see Table 1) the practitioner should offer and which life process stage (see Table 2) is influencing the client at this time. In addition specific issues involved in the management of the intake interview and the review session are discussed, with particular attention being paid to the use of diagnostic categories. Theoretical perspectives are discussed briefly and a pragmatic argument made for assessment and review to be rigorous without being inflexible.

Chapter 5

The mini-commitment
Contact, commitment and clarification

The purpose of the mini-commitment has been described briefly in Chapter 2 as a 'crucial period of exploration with each session important in itself, clear in content, focus and resolution'. Ideally, this contractual commitment will have developed out of a careful process of assessment at the intake interview. It is different from the holding arrangement (see Table 1), recommended for in-crisis or 'visiting' clients who are likely to benefit more from an uncommitted, flexible and less formal offer of between one and three sessions over an appropriate period of time.

In this approach, the mini-commitment is a focused period of exploration which will usually be expected to continue into the time-focused, time-extended or time-expanded commitment. However, it is always useful to keep in mind the prospect of clients terminating at the end of the agreed period of four to six weeks. If this becomes likely, then the review session can be advanced so as to ensure that at least one session is used purely for closing down the present work. Some form of exploratory period appears to be used by the majority of practitioners from all theoretical orientations. However, the particular demands made on the practitioner during this investigatory period are rarely discussed in any detail. Nor has the influence of this 'period of four to six weeks' on the outcome of psychological therapy been much researched, although its significance as a test of motivation and therapeutic engagement is likely to be recognised by most practitioners.

These first few sessions can be predictive of the process and outcome of any therapeutic engagement. A growing body of evidence (Hartley and Strupp 1982, Luborsky *et al.* 1983) is quoted by Gelso and Carter (1985: 164–5) to support the concept that 'early measures of the working alliance predicted treatment outcome'. It is in these initial sessions that a client's need and readiness for psychological therapy is fully tested. Each session needs to be concentrated on building an adequate working alliance (see Chapter 3) and also to be complete in itself. Working in this way, a clearer picture will emerge, at the end of each session, of the focal theme appropriate to the client's present stage in their life process of psychological evolution (see Table 2).

The mini-commitment requires a complex combination of skills. There is a natural tension between establishing a human relationship of trust and empathy, maintaining clear boundaries and achieving consensus as to aims and aspirations. To facilitate trust, practitioners need to be relaxed and attentive. To establish professional clarity and avoid misunderstandings, ground rules need to be agreed. To ensure sufficient mutuality of purpose, some focus on the goals of the therapeutic encounter is needed.

SIX STEPS FOR EACH COMMITMENT

In this chapter, these tasks are worked through in six steps, each generating specific questions to be explored and, if possible, resolved. At each step, the experiences of fictional clients will be used to illustrate the variety of skills needed to ensure a productive resolution of the mini-commitment, as well as the potential pitfalls which can occur. As with the previous case examples, practitioners are shown as realistically as possible, struggling with their own preconceptions and making mistakes, as well as occasionally hitting the right note. Each of the other three commitments, whether time-focused, time-extended or time-expanded, will also be described as traversing the same six steps, although none with the same need for intensity and economy of focus. The six steps are summarised in Table 4.

Step 1: Making contact – the working alliance is an emotional bond

Who are you and where am I?

The quality of psychological contact experienced between the two partici-pants in any therapeutic relationship is fundamental to the working alliance. Argyle (Argyle and Trower 1980) and other social psychologists interested in interpersonal communication have brilliantly illustrated the speed with which human beings establish a non-verbal discourse which then informs and influences the course of their relationships. Psychotherapists and coun-sellors are trained to listen with more than their ears and to be aware of subconscious communications transmitted by clients and of their own reactions. They will be observing their mini-commitment clients closely and the question 'Who are you?' will be being asked and answered non-verbally as well as verbally.

There is, however, a danger in this technical ability, if it overlooks the mutuality of this interpersonal scrutiny. Clients will be equally alert and attentive in their observation of practitioners. More is at stake for a client, and the quality of the practitioner's presence can be the vital factor which decides the issue of a establishing a reasonable level of trust. Asking ourselves the question '. . . and where am I?' can be a constant reminder of

Table 4 Six steps for every commitment

Step 1: Making contact — the working alliance is an emotional bond
Who are you and where am I?
Do we like each other, and does it matter?
Do we trust each other enough?

Step 2: Testing the commitment — the working alliance is contractual
What do you require of me, professionally?
What do I ask of you, as a client?

Step 3: Expectations and pitfalls
What do you hope to gain?
What was your previous experience of psychological change?
What do you fear?
How will you stop yourself getting what you want?

Step 4: Telling 'the story' — entering the client's life process
What brought you here, now?
Where have you been?
How was it for you, then?

Step 5: Working with the focal theme for this stage
What keeps happening again and again?
If this is the pattern, how was it learnt?
What do you need to re-learn?
So, what work is needed now?

Step 6: Reviewing the commitment — past and future
Shall we continue?
What are the alternatives?
How shall we work together now?
Have the goalposts changed?

© 1996 by J. Elton Wilson

the dialogic nature of self and other awareness. The present generation of Gestalt practitioners are developing a refinement of traditional Gestalt practice (Yontef 1980) which comes nearest to describing this aspect of establishing meaningful contact. 'She must practice inclusion, show her presence, be committed to the dialogue, be non-exploitative, live the relationship and be an experimental phenomenological experiential guide' (Clarkson and Mackewn 1993: 168).

To be centred, alert and alive, practitioners need to be reasonably unguarded and open as well as possessing some genuine social skills. Non-defensiveness is probably the most influential and inaccessible contribution to any successful human encounter.

beginning with our parents, we encounter people throughout our lives who have so much to defend that we learn, at worst, to keep our feelings to ourselves, or, at best, to expect the expression of those feelings to be met with little more than a defensive riposte.

(Kahn 1991: 15)

In these early therapeutic meetings clients are likely to feel highly defensive and disempowered. Practitioners can respect and accept this level of self-protectiveness while deliberately relaxing their own defensive reactions. In addition, the normal courtesies of consideration and genuine civility are not to be despised for their contribution to this crucial first contact. Keeping in mind one of the main themes of the time-conscious approach can be helpful here. The client is now the customer, and can expect a reasonable level of respect and attention to accompany demonstrations of professional competence. Included in these 'ordinary' social skills is the manner in which practitioners greet their new clients, introduce themselves and ensure reasonable levels of physical comfort. One answer to the question 'Where am I?' could be 'At your service!'.

Marion had made it clear to the therapy institute that she would wait until she could be referred to a woman therapist. She remembered too well how embarrassed and angry she had felt with the male social worker to whom she had been allocated when she was fourteen. In the last two years, she had learnt to trust and like most of the women she worked with now. She imagined that her therapist would be equally warm and friendly, although wiser. But the woman sitting in the chair opposite her now was very different from the women at the refuge. She was dressed in expensive but dull clothes, and she had a posh accent to go with them. Worst of all, she seemed to hold back from any form of greeting. She asked Marion for her name, pointed out a chair to sit on, and then sat in silence. She did not ask any questions or refer to the assessment interview. When Marion began to talk about the room – why was it so like an office, and why did it not have lamps and comfortable chairs? – she responded strangely. Was it so important for Marion to be comfortable, she asked. Marion felt judged and criticised. Still, she had made her mind up to see a woman therapist, and now she had got one, without too long a wait. She had better make the most of it.

Do we like each other, and does it matter?

Once the working alliance has been initiated by paying sufficient attention to presence, the next unspoken concern of practitioner and client is likely to be whether they find each other compatible. In everyday human encounters, this judgement is likely to be based on physical appearance, similarity of views and a shared background (Argyle and Trower 1980). These factors are equally influential in the therapeutic encounter. Again there is a tendency for practitioners to downgrade the importance of these normal social reactions. By paying attention to their own reactions to clients, however arbitrary and reactionary these may seem, practitioners can gain important information about the ways in which the working alliance may be used. Suppressing or ignoring these reactions can be dangerous. They could provide clues as to any transference or counter-transference reactions which may have influenced the therapeutic encounter from the earliest contact between practitioner and client.

> Guy telephoned the number he had been given by the doctor. A cut-glass female voice apologised that there was no-one able to talk to him right now but that she looked forward to returning the call as soon as possible, and would be grateful for a contact telephone number, and the time of his call. He felt like slamming down the receiver. She sounded old and posh, a bit warmer than his future mother-in-law, but they could have been at the same school. He felt again the helpless rage of a frustrated and powerless 7-year-old. The telephone was beeping at him. He might as well leave his number. At least he could check the old biddy out and, irrationally, he imagined she would somehow know if he just rang off.

Differentiating between unrealistic judgements arising from transference reactions and the commonplace attributions observed by social psychologists is one of the skills needed by practitioners in order to develop a working alliance. If a feeling of like or dislike seems to be exaggerated or intense, inapplicable to any current reality, it is likely to be a transference reaction. For the working alliance to operate, a reasonable level of interpersonal acceptance is necessary. Clients who feel a strong dislike of the practitioner to whom they have been referred are unlikely to engage enough in a therapeutic relationship to unpack the significance behind this pattern of dislike. Practitioners, on the other hand, can make a deliberate choice to put aside their initial feelings of antipathy towards a client for long enough to develop enough dispassionate interest to use their reactions in the client's service.

> The therapist felt embarrassed as she started to describe Marion to the supervision group. She reported the bare facts first. Marion was thirty-five, working in a women's refuge as an unqualified social worker. Slim and dressed in rainbow colours, she had peered intensely at the counsellor through her spectacles, the large frames and thick lenses making her eyes appear enormous, demanding and fault-finding. She had been critical of the setting, and then kept asking about the therapist's qualifications. When Marion had started to talk, her voice had a whining, complaining quality. It had been difficult to take a family history. The therapist hesitated, and then blurted out that, for the first time, she really felt

dislike for a client. Should she continue seeing Marion? Surely she would never be able to feel a close therapeutic relationship. The supervision group was sympathetic. At least two of the group recounted similar experiences. The supervisor suggested that the therapist use her dislike as information, and increase her interest in Marion as a person. Perhaps other people had the same reaction to Marion, or, if not, what was going on between Marion and herself? Was Marion angry, frightened or just hostile?

Do we trust each other enough?

Does trust depend on liking someone? This is a crucial question which has rarely been fully explored and on which there are some theoretical divergences of opinion. Almost all approaches to psychological therapy agree that warm and positive feelings between client and practitioner facilitate the formation of a working alliance. For many psychoanalytically trained practitioners this affiliation is traditionally labelled as a useful but essentially unreal element of the positive transference. This scepticism extends to affectionate feelings experienced on either side of the therapeutic encounter, and any expression of genuinely caring feelings has until recently been considered inadvisable. These views have been creatively criticised by Kahn (1991) and others, as requiring psychotherapists 'to behave in ways which are formal, rehearsed and distancing' (Lomas 1987: 63). For cognitive-behavioural practitioners positive feelings provide a necessary, but not sufficient, foundation for introducing interventions designed to bring about psychological change. For many humanists this basic connection is itself the change agent, and arises from the real relationship between client and practitioner.

It is probably rare that a trustful working alliance can coexist with feelings of extreme dislike or repulsion on either side of the professional divide. Nevertheless, it is possible to build sufficient trust on a basis of mutual respect and positive expectations of progress. Clients seem to prize above all the experience of being heard and understood in a professional setting where confidentiality is respected. These early sessions are likely to be influenced by factual or cultural issues, which need to be respectfully acknowledged and briefly explored in order to put them aside.

In building trust, practitioners should be cautious of placing too much verbal emphasis on the need for a therapeutic relationship. Susan Oldfield warns that

> although safety, reliability and confidentiality may form the foundations for trust, the offer of an intimate, on-going relationship may be daunting as well as comforting ... it is in the area of making and sustaining relationships that many clients find difficulty.
>
> (Oldfield 1983: 17)

The current popular belief among practitioners that the counselling relationship is the major fulcrum for personal transformation through psychological therapy has tended to influence some practitioners to concentrate prematurely and verbally on the therapeutic relationship. During the mini-commitment, and perhaps throughout their time in psychological therapy, clients are concerned, in the main, with problematic issues in their external life relationships. Constant reference to the need to build a close relationship with the practitioner can seem confusing, irritating and somewhat narcissistic.

> At the second session, Marion's therapist sat back in her chair and watched Marion as she ducked into the room, head lowered at first and then defiantly raised to stare challengingly at the other woman. The therapist was reminded of a nervous and highly strung dog, a red setter perhaps. Too thin, and ready to snap at strangers. As the therapist reminded herself to stay interested, Marion began to relax. Perhaps this woman was not so bad. Her eyes seemed softer today, and she seemed readier to ask questions which Marion could answer, instead of expecting her to remember about being a baby. This time the questions were more to do with Marion's present life. Marion was eager to explain about her job offer, and how she felt trapped and confused by the responsibilities she was being asked to take on.

Step 2: Testing the commitment – the working alliance is contractual

What do you require of me, professionally?

Although the first glimmers of trustful rapport may originate from the quality of non-verbal communication established between client and practitioner, the working alliance is vitally dependent upon clearly enunciated contractual agreements. In asking this question, practitioners give their clients permission to make crucial enquiries, especially with regard to confidentiality, the nature of psychological therapy and professional qualifications. In their responses to these questions, practitioners will have an opportunity to establish their own minimal but necessary ground rules. These will already have been explored in any well-conducted intake process, but will almost always need to be explored further. For instance, some clients may need a more lengthy debate clarifying the circumstances in which complete confidentiality could be restricted in order to maintain safety. For these clients, the mini-commitment may be entirely focused on a decision whether to accept the practitioner's ground rules and all six sessions could be occupied with the background to their objections. In this investigation the underlying problematic issues are likely to surface and become central.

> Marion was reminded by the therapist, at the end of the second session, that she had not filled in her GP's name on her index card. The therapy institute was very strict about having this information. Marion looked furtive, and hurried out, saying she would like to talk about it next time. She rang in to cancel the next appointment. Two weeks later, the therapist experienced Marion to be as hostile as she had appeared at her first session. She glared at the therapist, and began immediately to describe how terrible the last two weeks had been. She filled the session with her complaints about her work place, her neighbours and the teachers at her son's school. At last the therapist was able to ask about her absence. This led to an evasive description of difficulties with work shifts and buses. The therapist held her ground. Was the request for her GP's name anything to do with it? Marion looked startled and then defensive. She wanted to know why this was so important. She never went to see her GP anyway. She didn't believe in using drugs. She could look after herself, and her son, with homeopathy and herbs. The therapist asked gently if she had some reason to fear medical doctors. Marion looked startled, and then ducked her head. Looking down, she began to talk about the hospital doctors, and their endless conversations with her mother. They had not asked her about anything. And then there had been a thick file which followed her about.

During these early sessions, clients are likely to be evaluating their experience in terms of the practitioner's ability to relieve their psychological pain. Clear statements regarding the practitioner's belief system and competences may help to build a shared understanding of how client and practitioner might work together. Especially with clients new to psychotherapy and counselling this can seem to be an educational process. Sharing a theory of change explicitly with a client can help to defuse areas where there are marked differences in expectations. Research reported by McLeod (1990a: 7) demonstrates that many clients tend to look for, and value, 'expert diagnosis, advice, recommendations and action to resolve a problem'. These findings need to be taken seriously. Psychotherapists and counsellors who try to ignore or interpret this requirement are likely to provoke resistance to an alliance, and to delay the therapeutic process. This does not mean giving advice or playing the expert but it may entail an honest description of the practitioner's view of their role and how they hope to be helpful to the client. It is helpful to phrase this in clear everyday language and, at this stage, not to include more esoteric theoretical beliefs regarding the 'healing magic' (Orlinsky and Howard 1977: 492) of the therapeutic relationship.

What most clients want to know is how the practitioner may be useful, what they will try to do and what they are not likely to do. While this explanation will vary according to theoretical orientation and training, practitioners who take seriously the stated needs of the client may find that they can stretch their area of expertise. The move into integrative or eclectic psychotherapy is usually client-led as practitioners realise that they are being asked for levels of knowledge and skills not covered in their previous professional training. Working to establish a shared direction, client and practitioner not only test out the working alliance but begin to fulfil the general purpose of the mini-commitment which is to investigate what work is to be achieved at this time.

> Marion wondered when she would start to feel better. So far, the therapist had begun to seem more caring, but Marion was still lying awake at night, weeping and worrying. She had once been told by a woman chaplain, who had found her crying in the side chapel of the church, that talking to a therapist about her childhood would make it possible for her to forgive her mother. She wanted that so desperately. But she didn't feel better about the past. A sort of angry confusion had been added to her ever-present sense of guilt, and she still had not talked about everything that had happened. Would the therapist be able to make her talk about her mother?

What do I ask of you, as a client?

At this stage, clients are required to conform only to seemingly pragmatic arrangements, already made at intake, as to time, place, arrangements for cancellation, and the agreements as to fees and duration. These may need to be restated, underlined and even re-negotiated during the mini-commitment sessions. This does not mean an obsessive focus by the practitioner on contractual arrangements, but a readiness to discuss and explain the usefulness of a therapeutic 'frame' (Casement 1985: 61). Clients may have agreed to arrangements which they are finding irksome and which seem to be designed only for the convenience of the practitioner. The extent to which this is true can be accepted, realistic adjustments made, if necessary, while exploring any emotional issues underlying both current resentments and initial compliance. As these interpersonal interactions begin to be clarified, so the alliance can be openly described as a container within which experiments in relationship patterns can begin.

> Guy always arrived at the door on time, but would then hurry into the lavatory. Five minutes later, he would enter the consulting room, neat and tidy, smelling of aftershave. Not for another five minutes would he be able to relax his guarded posture, unfolding his arms to gesture and grimace as he mimicked the voices of past enemies who had put him

down as a no-good Jamaican. At the third session, the counsellor asked if their meeting time was working out as convenient for Guy's work schedule. Guy looked surprised, and then relieved. He hated arriving sweaty and untidy at the last minute. His immaculate grooming was symbolic of his escape from the shame of poverty and a defence against racist prejudice. He could not sit down in his counsellor's white middle-class home until he had restored his sense of dignity by combing, washing and scenting his body. It had not occurred to him that he could rearrange the time of his session to accommodate this need.

Step 3: Expectations and pitfalls

What do you hope to gain?

By the end of the mini-commitment, client and practitioner will evaluate the purpose of the therapeutic engagement, revise and restate the client's aims and goals, and decide whether and how to continue. This question initiates the search for clarity, and will be returned to at the first review session. At intake, these aspirations are likely to have been stated briefly, or vaguely. For approximately six sessions there is time to look deeply into a client's longings for peace, or for growth, or for change. From session to session this may change and, if practitioners can open up to their clients' dreams with understanding, then permission is given to explore and expand aspirations. If, at intake, clients had difficulty with making their aims and goals explicit and concrete, then these early sessions can provide the encouragement to do so. Practitioners can enable this process by asking clients to visualise themselves as they would be if they achieved their aims. How would they look? What would they think, do or feel differently? These questions need to be used sensitively and care taken not to produce a rigid or unrealistic goal which becomes another source of distress. Writers advising how to make Transactional Analysis (TA) 'contracts' caution against collusion with aims which implicitly discount or damage the client's essential self:

> Most of all avoid contracts which involve 'getting rid of' some part of the self. For example, 'I'll stop being vulnerable' or 'I'll cut out my angry feelings'. These contain a belief that there is something wrong with the client as they are and invite the counsellor to collude with this belief.
>
> (Lapworth, Sills and Fish 1993: 18)

The subtle difference between the mini-commitment and some short-term TA 'contracts' is that it is focused on finding the place in this client's life process at which to engage at this time, rather than concentrating on specific areas of change. Clients demonstrating the self-destructive wishes quoted above are providing valuable clues as to the extent to which they may need to work in the preparation stage described in Table 2.

> At the fourth session, Marion's eyes filled with tears. 'You look as if you want something so much', said the therapist as she reminded her that, at the assessment interview, she had said she only wanted to be understood. Now the therapist was asking if she wanted anything more. Yes, she wanted to stop crying every night, to stop being so frightened all the time, and most of all, to stop caring about everything so much. 'What would you be like then?', asked the therapist. Marion muttered that she would need a head transplant or something. The therapist asked if her head was filled with painful thoughts and memories and suggested, gently, that she might need to share these before she could let them go. Marion took a deep breath. This was it.

What was your previous experience of psychological change?

It is vital to gain information about previous therapeutic engagements. These are likely to have shaped the client's attitude to a working alliance, and will continue to be an influence, for good or for ill. It is advisable to conceptualise all previous practitioners as potential colleagues in the present process. There is an all too human temptation to be critical, competitive or defensive towards previous practitioners. Even where there seems to be evidence of inadequate practice and the use of techniques foreign to one's own practice, it is wise to withhold judgement, while hearing and accepting the client's experience. How will the client describe you to the next practitioner? For many clients it may be necessary to 'chew over and spew out' (Perls, Hefferline and Goodman 1951: 202) what was previously perceived as nourishing. Important information is contained here. What does the client need now, and what still needs to be worked through?

> Guy was mockingly critical of all 'do-gooders'. He described with sneering vividness the youth club leaders, the teachers and the university lecturers who had made him their 'token black genius'. The counsellor felt momentarily estranged by his lack of appreciation for all these well-meaning mentors who had perceived his intelligence and encouraged his meteor-like career. She noted how angry he sounded. 'They didn't want to know anything about me – never saw me as a person', he said fiercely, 'only what I could do to make them feel good.' The first of his sponsors had been the nursery school teacher. 'She was a bit like you', he said, watching the counsellor carefully.

Where genuine abuse of power appears to have taken place, however, practitioners cannot maintain such a neutral and professional interest in their client's complaints regarding a previous practitioner. This difficult ethical situation demands careful and genuinely empathic acceptance of the client's experience and will need to be taken to supervision or some other form of professional consultation as soon as possible.

Included in this area of investigation is any previous deliberate attempt to achieve psychological change or growth. Accounts of groups attended, books read or studies undertaken are all invaluable information about a client's motivation and preferred ways of learning. Do clients enjoy reading about psychotherapy and counselling, or have they been inspired by physically and emotionally active exercises suggested by a workshop leader? Practitioners save time by starting work where there is an 'open door' (Ware 1983: 11) rather than imposing their own views of what is needed for personal change.

What do you fear?

This question arises naturally out of the previous enquiry. All clients are likely to have some ambiguity about engaging or re-engaging in psychological therapy. Even if previous therapeutic experiences have been useful, they are likely to have been disturbing and only painful emotions may now be remembered. Other clients are likely to be all too aware of the bad press which psychological therapy has received, especially in the UK. Will they be forced to hate their parents, regress into dependency or lose their ability to cope with their day-to-day lives? Accepting these negative expectations in a straightforward way allows the practitioner to introduce the notion of the working alliance as a safe enterprise, within which the client can retreat and re-negotiate the pace and the depth of the therapeutic process.

How will you stop yourself getting what you want?

Again, this question is linked with the previous question. Knowing what is fearful about therapeutic engagement, clients are likely to know how they react when the going gets tough. Of all items of information gleaned during the mini-commitment this one is likely to prove the most valuable and long-lasting. People can be extraordinarily insightful about their escape routes and the ways they can trip themselves up. Once revealed, ways of frustrating these obstacles and avoidances can be debated. Again, this is an introduction to the oversight available through using the working alliance.

Guy had been very clear at the intake interview about what he expected to gain from seeing a counsellor. He wanted to sort out his feelings about women, especially older white women, before his marriage to a white girl. He had read about psychotherapy and expected to delve into his past and to talk about his childhood. He saw himself as a fast worker, with sufficient insight to sort out his mixed-up feelings and get back on track with his successful lifestyle. He had not expected to feel so exposed and tearful by the end of every session. He began to fear that this vulnerability would affect his work and be visible to all his colleagues. He began to make jokes in the sessions, especially when he had described a painful episode from the past. The counsellor asked him if this was how he usually dealt with sad or angry feelings. 'I can't afford to have them, not in my job', Guy snapped. He felt trapped. He did not want to stop at this stage but there seemed no alternative. He was disbelieving when the counsellor suggested that he could symbolically leave his more acute feelings in the room. Towards the end of the session, he wrote down what he was feeling on a large bit of paper, which was then folded and put into a cupboard. To his surprise, this seemingly childish manoeuvre seemed to work. At the next session, he reported a reasonably stable working week, although he had been a bit tearful in bed with his fiancée.

Step 4: Telling 'the story' – entering the client's life process

What brought you here, now?

Although this question belongs chiefly to the intake process, it can be retained as a continuing area for exploration and interest for every session. What has brought this client to the consulting room on this day? If a client's main concern remains the same, then the root problematic issue is clear, and the practitioner's focus is on the original strategy for survival which underlies the painful repetition. Perhaps the time has come to move into experiments with alternative responses to pressure or threat. If a client presents a series of different problematic issues, then the strategy for survival may lie in any link between the issues. If a client is no longer clear about what is troubling them, or why they are turning up for each session, then it is advisable to check motivation, and even to consider whether the client's need for psychological therapy might be satisfactorily contained within these preliminary sessions.

In asking this question, caution may be need to be exercised. It can remain a silent question held only in the mind and heart of the practitioner. Some clients may feel criticised if too heavy an emphasis is laid on their reason for attending sessions. All that is required is to find out how the presenting problem presented at intake relates to the client's life.

Where have you been?

Telling one's life story has become an underestimated aspect of the healing possible through engagement in psychological therapy. So much priority can be given to the process of dialogic relationship (Yontef 1980) between client and practitioner, that the content of the dialogue can be overlooked, and even scorned for lacking a 'here-and-now' quality. Erving Polster (1987) holds that 'every person's life is worth a novel' and encourages his Gestalt clients to recount their story:

> It revives the mind's attention to prior experiences, presenting them anew, almost as though they were happening again. The better these reproductions, the more vividly the listener feels the new life a story may give to a previous event.
>
> (Polster 1987: 26)

Stories require a listener, and will be told all the more vividly if the listener is sincerely fascinated, accepting the truth of the experience narrated and yet listening for patterns and themes. In this way the fundamental story, the archetypal myth by which a person lives emerges from the narrative and is used to unpack and clarify the present dilemma.

How was it for you, then?

This simple question is loaded. Many clients in the mini-commitment will not yet be ready to share, in any depth, the feelings attached to their stories. It is the question which will indicate at which stage of their life process (see Table 2) this client is likely to be working. Clients at the preparation stage will prefer to return to the present issues rather than make too vivid in the present their key experiences from the past. There is likely always to be an element of preparation in these early sessions, but clients for whom disclosure is the entry point will be ready to deepen their stories with a detailed 'description of situations and sensations with associated self-image' (see Table 2). Clients genuinely ready for catharsis will have worked through their story before, either with another practitioner or through their own self-development.

> Marion found it quite easy in the end to tell the therapist about the problem with her grandfather. It was almost as if she had gone over and over it so often in her head that the whole story was waiting to pop out. It did not seem to belong to her, but to be about another confused eight-year-old girl. She had not felt abused by him, only embarrassed and sad, but the therapist began pointing out that her grandfather's behaviour had been an abuse of his adult power. She wanted to switch off the other woman's calm voice, just like she did all the television programmes on this subject. It was the younger men like her father who were abusers, who hurt and bullied women so that they lost all their confidence and huddled in refuges, ashamed to go out on the street. The therapist listened as Marion's voice rose, shrill, accusing all men of being oppressors. 'Your grandfather was different from other men?', she asked gently. Marion paused, remembering how he had looked at her that last

time, ashamed and accusing all at once. Suddenly she realised that he had used her need for attention to get his own dirty little pleasures. He was not so young in those days either, he was in his fifties. She began to weep inconsolably.

And so it goes on. Each stage in the life process of psychological evolution may begin to become apparent through asking this apparently simple question. Clients who need to change their fundamental self-care strategies will have moved on from expression of past pain and be ready to challenge the past with its punishing and repetitive patterns of interaction. While clients whose present work is to renounce the past and move towards a greater freedom and self-empowerment will give more retrospective responses, and be more able to link their past story with their present desire for change.

Ayesha was tired of it all. Every time she went into any form of therapeutic situation, the same story had to be told – being abandoned by her parents and going to the children's home. She still felt tears in her throat but she wanted to finish the business this time. She wanted to move on.

Step 5: Working with the focal theme for this stage

What keeps happening again and again?

Although the answer to this question may have already begun to emerge from the client's story, the extent of repetition is not always clear to the story-teller. This question, held in the practitioner's mind as they listen, is crucial. Repetitive patterns underlie all areas of psychological pain which are available to personal change. Unexpected traumatic events and experiences of social injustice are external to individuals. Psychological therapy offers an opportunity to change habitual responses to these assaults. This does not mean teaching clients to adapt to insult and injustice in their external world. Psychological therapists need to question their tendency to:

continue down the middle of the road, bringing people into line so that they can function within the system and cope. We continue to locate all symptoms universally within the patient rather than also in the soul of the world. Maybe the system has to be brought into line with the symptoms so that the system no longer functions as a repression of soul, forcing the soul to rebel in order to be noticed.

Hillman and Ventura (1993: 154)

This question is particularly central to the life process stages described in Table 2 as preparation and disclosure.

If this is the pattern, how was it learnt?

Realising the patterns in our responses is the first step to understanding the system within which these patterns were formed. For clients, this realisation can be liberating. Most people experience being helplessly drawn into a habitual response which then leads to yet another distressing situation and increasingly painful feelings. There seems to be no choice and no escape. Realising that this all originally involved a learning process leads to hope that it can be replaced with new learning. It is this question which can hoist a strategy for survival out of the unconscious and into awareness. No longer need these reactions be viewed only as maladaptive, inevitable, mysterious and shamefully out of our control.

> Marion began to realise why she had continually ended up with men who hurt her. Her father had been known as a 'hard man' for as long as she could remember. Her mother had tried to excuse him by recounting the unlikely story of Marion's birth, and how he had cried and held her in his arms on that first day. So, perhaps, that was it. She had tried to make that happen again, with other 'hard' men.

The need to focus on this question is typical of the life process stages of disclosure, catharsis and self-care.

What do you need to re-learn?

For the purpose of the mini-commitment, finding an answer to this question is in preparation for the first review. It is phrased here in cognitive terms although any effective psychological evolution has to include emotional and physiological re-education. Again the focal themes listed in Table 2 can be used as a guide since they all describe some transformation of attitude or understanding. A subsidiary question to be asked, inwardly and silently, by every practitioner is: 'Can I teach you anything?' It can be a humbling experience to realise that a client is reaching out towards a personal metamorphosis which is still incomplete in the practitioner.

> Marion described herself as a selfish coward, and she always had been, leaving her mother's house when she was fourteen and never returning. Her mother had been left to cope with all the kids, and her father had gone on drinking. When he had died, she could have gone back to visit her mother. He would not be there to beat her up. But now she shrank from her mother's whining voice and helpless need. She had got her life together, pushed out all the male bastards from her life and she dreaded being sucked down into the past again. Her sharp self-critical voice rose as she attacked her own need for safety and discounted her struggle for survival. The therapist realised how much energy there was in this attack

and asked if she was really angry with her mother for being 'sucked down' and not getting her life together. Marion drew in her breath sharply as her rage and grief over her betrayed childhood spilled over. Later, her therapist compared the raw expression of Marion's rage with her own constrained attempts to discharge her current frustrations.

So what work is needed now?

Once aware of their survival strategies, clients can begin to consider changing them, or, at the very least, having alternative ways of keeping themselves feeling safe. This question revives the specific aims and goals which have been discussed in general terms during the intake process. During the mini-commitment, practitioners prepare to offer their speculations, not only regarding the client's problematic strategy for survival, but also as to alternative and less problematic strategies. For many clients, this question may be premature and complex. To find the focal theme in the survival strategy and then to engender a positive belief that this was not only learnt but could be re-learnt is sufficient. Through careful observation, sensitive interaction and the use of Table 2, practitioners attempt to discern the life process stage reached in their clients' personal journeys. This decision will enable practitioner and client to focus more clearly. Clients will demonstrate the accuracy of the chosen focus by their responses. The process is led by the client with practitioner as escort and, sometimes, as guide.

Guy's counsellor realised that he was moving rapidly towards an explosion of remembered pain. His insight into the way his childhood had shaped his present behaviours was sharp and acute. He had described his childhood in vivid terms, and was beginning to question the way his mother had used him as her 'little husband' to protect her and deal with the world outside. His longing for someone to look after him had been met by white schoolteachers, interested in him as a curiosity, a clever West Indian. He had felt like a stranger everywhere. There was only a short time left before the agreed number of sessions drew to a close. The counsellor asked Guy if he would be willing to visualise himself as a little boy, and to speak for this boy. She explained that this might bring out even more strong feelings than before, but that he seemed ready for these now. Guy's eyes filled with tears as he restored to consciousness the needs of the courageous small boy he had been. How would he be able to meet these in his present relationships?

Step 6: Reviewing the commitment – past and future

This section links with, and should be informed by, the issues addressed in

Chapter 4. Practitioners are advised to use the headings from Table 3a to inform the review process. The questions addressed below will provide additional information. Skill and subtlety is needed throughout this enquiry to discern the future area of focus. The flexible series of templates provided in Table 1 will provide a guide regarding continuation of commitment, whether this is time-focused or time-extended. Candidates for a time-expanded commitment have already been described in Chapter 2 as being a 'highly motivated client group' with an 'ability to maintain their coping strategies outside the therapeutic engagement' in order to commit themselves 'to explore and transform the hidden areas of their inner world'. Yet without some visualisation of a therapeutic destination, even these clients could be trapped unnecessarily in a redundant and inconclusive process.

Shall we continue?

This question is the culmination of the mini-commitment. Clients need to know that they have some choice in the matter, and yet not feel rationed. In settings where commitment is severely limited to six sessions, the question may not even be asked. In this approach, an argument is made for some sort of continuation to be available, even if this is confined to the time-focused commitment. If brief therapy is demanded by the setting or is the practitioner's preference, then a package of ten (plus or minus) sessions with a carefully conducted review at the sixth session is recommended. This recommendation is phrased somewhat reluctantly as any form of rigid prescription opposes the spirit of this approach. A glance at Table 1 will remind the reader of the advantage of remaining flexible and adaptable to clients' needs.

There will always be some clients who express a wish to terminate their commitment immediately. Where this is the case, it is advisable to make an agreement to use the sixth session for review purposes and then to have a final session to close down the therapeutic engagement.

What are the alternatives?

Referral options, as well as other forms of self-development outside of psychological therapy, are prepared by the practitioner with this specific client in mind. Even if clients seem fully engaged and wish to continue, awareness of other therapeutic options can be liberating to clients and relieving to practitioners, especially those with an exaggerated sense of responsibility. Particular caution is needed when discussing alternative options with clients who have experienced a series of rejections and whose encounter with the therapeutic profession has already featured several referrals.

It was several years before Joanna decided to try psychotherapy again. She tried out a woman therapist this time, whose name she found in a directory. She had plenty of letters after her name, and seemed knowledgeable enough at the first interview. Joanna had read enough and thought enough to realise that her loneliness and occasional acute experiences of depression were linked with her father. The first few sessions were revealing, and she began to feel hopeful that she could sort herself out. Then her therapist asked if she might need to work through her feelings with a male therapist in due course. Joanna agreed coldly that, in theory, this could work. However, in her experience, male therapists were all just like her father, and likely to be on his side. Belatedly, the therapist remembered Joanna's description of being 'passed on like an unwanted package' after her father's second divorce. She took a deep breath and apologised for her clumsy lack of understanding. Joanna was surprised, embarrassed and delighted. She was not used to apologies.

How shall we work together now?

This question will need to be reformulated as a tentative recommendation by the review session. Keeping the question format will remind practitioners to keep the dialogue open, where possible. While many clients appreciate the offer of a shared endeavour, for others this question may seem intrusive or too matter of fact. Too frequent and too explicit an exploration of the therapeutic process can be counter-productive, like pulling up a plant to examine its roots. For practitioners, however, silent exploration of this question is a necessary part of their own 'internal supervision' (Casement 1985: 57–71).

Have the goalposts changed?

Practitioners using Table 3a for ongoing assessment and review will be addressing this question as they discuss goals. It is included here as a reminder that, during any period of commitment, the desired outcome may have changed completely or become blurred. By the end of the mini-commitment, a clarification of the purpose of therapeutic engagement is almost always necessary.

At the beginning of the sixth session, Marion's therapist announced that they would need to hold some sort of review. Marion immediately felt suspicious. At the last session, she had cried and stormed over her mother's weak stupidity. Was she being asked to justify her need for therapy? Had she gone too far and alarmed this reserved and quiet woman? She listened suspiciously as the therapist summarised the sessions so far, sympathetically recounting how Marion had managed to survive and then abandon the repeated patterns of physical, emotional and sexual abuse she had experienced since childhood. She was surprised to be offered an option of continuing therapy in an open-ended way, on condition that she agree to give four sessions' notice of ending. The last bit of this offer sounded a bit like a trap. She liked to be able to move on quickly when things didn't work out. No discussion and no emotional traps for her now. She hesitated, and then decided. Maybe this would be different. It sounded professional enough and, although she still did not really like her, the therapist had been useful so far.

SUMMARY

In this chapter, the use of the mini-commitment, in the form of approximately six initial weekly sessions of psychological therapy, has been discussed in depth. An introduction has been made to the proposition that all contractual commitments outlined in this book can be conceptualised as progressing through six phases or steps. These steps should not be confined by being mapped on to particular sessions, although there may be a temptation to use them in this way for these initial sessions. The order indicated is to guide the practitioner's focus as it develops. The issues addressed are likely to persist throughout the time of the commitment. For instance, the story will be told, expectations rehearsed and the working alliance tested at every session.

Chapter 6

The time-focused commitment
Using time as a tool

> It should also be known that time limited psychotherapy is not for the beginning therapist. It is difficult, intense and moves very rapidly. Previous experience with long-term psychotherapy is an important pre-requisite as is personal therapy, preferably psychoanalysis.
>
> (Mann 1981: 42)

This cautionary and somewhat inflexible pronouncement could be used by less confident practitioners as a justification for not using a time-conscious approach in their work. It is probably correct that some experience of long-term psychological therapy, whether as client or practitioner, can contribute to a practitioner's ability to discern focal themes and decide upon the possible stage of personal development reached by a client. Nevertheless, many less experienced practitioners work in settings where time for psychological therapy is necessarily limited by a variety of factors. In this chapter, encouragement is given to all practitioners and their clients to enter optimistically into a therapeutic engagement where advantage is taken of this very limitation.

The time-focused commitment is described, in Chapter 2, as the *optimum* option for many clients. This blunt opinion is not shared by the majority of psychotherapists and counsellors at this time, in spite of continuing evidence as to the powerful effect of the first ten to twenty sessions of psychological therapy. The power of this 'dose effect' (Howard *et al.* 1986; Kopta *et al.* 1992) is most likely to influence the practice of cognitive-behavioural therapists, respectful of the growing body of research underpinning short-term approaches to psychological therapy. Nevertheless, the most rigorous theoretical argument for a twelve-session therapeutic engagement is made by Mann, a psychoanalytical practitioner, who has also been described as a 'decided existentialist' (Peake, Borduin and Archer 1988: 43). He argues that consciousness of time is a major influence upon all forms of psychological distress and provides the pivotal issue upon which effective psychotherapeutic engagement is dependent. His work, and the less specific application of time limits explored by Alexander and French (1946), has informed the manner in which the time-focused commitment is outlined below.

DEFINING THE TIME-FOCUSED COMMITMENT

In this book, the time-focused commitment describes a continuation of approximately six further sessions after the mini-commitment, so that the duration of the entire therapeutic engagement between practitioner and client, at this stage of the client's life, is likely to have an upper limit of fifteen sessions (see Table 1). The exact number of sessions is not, however, the defining characteristic of this type of therapeutic engagement. The time-focused commitment is distinguished from other forms of contractual commitment in the following ways:

1 Time is focused because there is a specific closing date, agreed between practitioner and client.
2 The extent and nature of psychological work undertaken is focused within the stage of psychological change reached by clients in their life process.
3 Therapeutic concerns are focused on to a particular *focal theme*, already conceptualised by practitioners and recognised by clients.
4 Aims and ambitions are focused because there is an agreed purpose for this particular commitment.

In this book, each therapeutic commitment is depicted as progressing through six steps (see Table 4). In this chapter, each of the six steps traversed in the time-focused commitment will be considered in the light of these four distinguishing characteristics.

Step 1: Making contact – the working alliance is an emotional bond

Who are you and where am I?

There is an urgency and a poignancy in attending to this question when there is a specific closing date. It is sometimes argued that any form of time limit is likely to confine the relationship between client and practitioner to a business-like association and to exclude any possibility of deep and meaningful connection. This view confuses quantity with quality. Working in a variety of time-limited settings, practitioners report that an intensity of contact is necessary if this type of psychological therapy is to be effective. In Malan's (1975) extended study of brief psychoanalytic therapy, he summarises this 'single unifying factor of extraordinary simplicity', as follows:

the prognosis is best when there is a willingness on the part of both patient and therapist to become *deeply involved*, and (in Balint's words) to bear the tension that inevitably ensues.

(Malan 1975: 274)

From a recent cognitive behavioural viewpoint, Cade and O'Hanlon describe themselves as 'continually pointing out' to all their brief therapy trainees,

the importance not only of listening to what the client is communicating, including the feelings that are being expressed, but of finding ways of demonstrating to the client that this has been done. Just listening is not enough. If nothing is fed back, the client cannot know whether he or she has been heard.

(Cade and O'Hanlon 1993: 43)

For person-centred practitioners, there may be more difficulty in linking the concept of intense person-to-person contact with any therapeutic engagement which includes an agreed limitation of time. The implication of most of Carl Rogers's (1961: 131) seminal papers is that all the necessary therapeutic conditions, including the 'optimal and maximum condition' of the client being 'psychologically *received*', take time to develop. Nevertheless, films made of Rogers working with Gloria (Shostrom 1965) demonstrate an immediacy of connection unhampered by the time limitation of a single session therapeutic encounter.

The degree of connection between client and practitioner as they enter into a time-focused commitment is built out of contact established during the earlier mini-commitment sessions. There is a danger that too concrete a focus on the purposes agreed and themes established at the first review may lead to a loss of this all-important sense of mutual awareness at this stage. Silently repeating the self-directed question of 'Who are you and where am I?' can remind practitioners of the essential mystery of every human encounter and reinstate the liveliness of a shared therapeutic endeavour.

Judy felt very different as she entered the out-patient wing of the hospital. She had moved out to the hostel only last week, and now she would be having her remaining counselling sessions in this busy, brightly painted building. She glanced apprehensively into the big group room, hoping she would recognise some of the patients on her ward, but then she remembered that this was not the day for in-patient art therapy. She found the social worker's office and knocked on the door. She felt shy and strange as she entered the room. It was warm and light, with a desk, two comfortable chairs and plenty of plants, very different from the shabby hospital day-room where they had met till then. Somehow Judy's counsellor looked different too, almost a stranger, although her bright, searching gaze was familiar. Judy felt weary suddenly. Now they would have to start discussing whether she should leave home permanently, just as she was beginning to feel close to her mother for the first time ever. That was the 'work' for which they had agreed to use this eight-week 'contract'. She had felt so grown up and motivated last week, but now these words seemed off-putting, technical jargon. She wanted to run away, to get drunk or to drive as fast and as dangerously as she could. The counsellor was standing still, watching her. 'Which chairs shall we occupy for our sessions here?' she asked gently. She seemed almost tentative, ready to start again with getting to know Judy. Suddenly the new situation seemed more hopeful. Judy sat down by the window and began to talk.

Do we like each other, and does it matter?

The potency of full attention is not always experienced as benevolent if the reactions displayed by clients under Davanloo's (1980) revealing scrutiny are to be taken as evidence. Issues of like and dislike will continue to be of interest when a time-focused commitment has been agreed, but can now be differentiated from the working alliance which has been established during the mini-commitment. The alliance must survive all these fluctuations between positive and negative feelings and provide a space for practitioner and client to use these emotions as information regarding the accuracy of the focal theme. Consciousness of a clearly fixed ending date is likely to accelerate the arousal of strong emotions emanating from previous relationship patterns. These transference reactions are invaluable indications of the strategies for survival employed by clients. When time is limited, practitioners aim for early confrontation of the unreal nature of these reactions. These challenges have to be gentle enough to be acceptable and yet clear enough to face the client with the focal theme or 'central issue' described by Mann (1973: 18) as revealing, in a non-threatening and highly empathic way, a part of the self which has hitherto been painfully hidden. If their life stage of psychological change (see Table 2) has been accurately assessed, then clients are more likely to accept challenges, and to be aware of the painful issues which need to be explored.

Do we trust each other enough?

It is the dissonance between the mutual trust established through the working alliance and the precarious and unrealistic feelings aroused in transference which is the curative experience sought. Where there is an agreed purpose, a reasonable level of mutual trust is even more necessary where the focal theme is a fundamental attitude of mistrust based on earlier experiences. Both client and practitioner rely on each other as working partners. Any failures of trust due to real blunders or misunderstandings on the part of practitioner *or* client have to be acknowledged and talked through swiftly.

> Judy was shaking with anger as she entered the social worker's office. How dare this woman refuse to see her father, except with Judy there, and even suggest that he should find his own therapist if he was feeling distressed at present. Surely she realised that he was sad, hurt by Judy's criticisms. He needed help, and here was the only person that Judy had ever trusted refusing him that help. She was just like Judy's mother after all, hard and cold. She started to sob loudly as soon as her counsellor spoke. She did not want to listen to explanations about 'boundaries' and confidentiality. She did not want to be seduced by the comfort of this woman's presence. The social worker stopped talking. She waited until Judy looked up, face blotched and furious. She said she understood how angry and hurt Judy was feeling. She realised now how much Judy longed to heal her father as well as herself. Maybe this was what she had always tried to do, since she was little. She wondered whether Judy would like to have a list of people who would be able to offer her father some advice and help at this time. Judy thought this over, and then began to laugh. Yup, she had done it again. Little Miss Fixit for the family. She felt embarrassed, and grateful to be relieved of that familiar role.

Step 2: Testing the commitment – the working alliance is contractual

Issues of trust in a professional commitment are worked through verbally and non-verbally. Professional issues discussed during the mini-commitment sessions are likely to be tested behaviourally during any continuation of commitment.

What do you require of me, professionally?

Where there is a specific closing date, agreements made as to confidentiality, duration, cancellations and fees need to be kept extremely clear. In particular cancellations will need careful handling since these will attenuate and possibly weaken the intensity of the process. Because the time-focused commitment is particularly vulnerable to cancellation, no matter how justified, practitioners are advised to make each session valuable and complete in itself. This means keeping in mind the agreed purpose and focal theme at all times and, where possible, sharing this consciousness with the client.

> After four sessions, Guy decided to tell his girlfriend that he was seeing a counsellor. He was enthusiastic about the whole adventure, especially

now that there were to be only six more sessions. He felt amazed by the discoveries he had made about himself, and the ways in which he now saw the world. He wondered about other people he knew. Were they really as absorbed with sport, clothes and motors as they appeared to be? He took Amanda out to dinner, and began to ask her about her feelings, and to describe some of the ways he now understood their relationship. She was amused at first, and then disturbed and angry. She wanted to know how much he talked about her to this other woman. She was not soothed by his protestations that the counsellor was old, as old as her mother. She asked angrily when his next session was to be, and then asked him to show how much he put his love for her first, by cancelling this and coming shopping with her for wedding presents instead. At first Guy refused to do this, but gave in later on that night when he found her weeping in bed. He felt embarrassed and angry when he next met the counsellor. He had left an answer-phone message explaining his absence, and was willing, even eager, to pay for the missed session. His counsellor accepted the fee, while reminding him that their agreement had been for a number of sessions, rather than for time alone. He exploded with anger. She was trying to control him and take advantage of his good nature. Suddenly, Guy realised that it was Amanda with whom he was really angry, and not just with her, but with all the women that he had tried to please by giving up things he really cared about.

What do I ask of you, as a client?

Again this question is likely to have been explored fully at the first review, and during the earlier sessions of the mini-commitment. The working alliance needs to be enough in place so that the increased pressure of time and focus can be borne. To benefit from this time-limited agreement, clients need to bring their willingness to explore themselves as well as their problem areas. In Chapter 2, an argument was made for offering a contractual commitment with clearly defined time boundaries to clients with a fragmented sense of self, often diagnosed as fragile 'borderline' personalities. Ryle (1990: 122–4) argues cogently for the use of a time-limited period of insight-based Cognitive Analytic Therapy as a 'safety net for both patient and therapist, guarding against the emergence of malignant destructive transference–countertransference relationships so easy to set up by inexperienced therapists with these powerful patients' (Ryle 1990: 123). For many of these clients there can be a truly 'corrective emotional experience' (Alexander and French 1946) in fulfilling their side of an agreed, contained and temporary commitment. Only then might they feel ready to consider returning, after a break, to the demands of a time-extended psychotherapeutic engagement.

As Judy's final session with the social worker approached, she began to feel a mixture of relief and dread. She longed for a break from the painful memories and the mixture of grief and anger which threatened to erupt at every session. She thought that she might 'lose it' at any moment. She imagined herself crawling on the floor, hanging around the counsellor's knees and begging to be put to sleep for ever. Yet this new quiet thoughtful part of herself would miss those releasing moments of clarity, when the same jigsaw piece fitted into yet another puzzling situation. Her counsellor called it the 'aha' moment and Judy always enjoyed a moment of mastery, very different from the shaky sense of control to which she usually clung. She began, silently, to consider the counsellor's suggestion that she might try out the psychotherapy unit again, not immediately, but perhaps in a few months' time.

Step 3: Expectations and pitfalls

What do you hope to gain?

Where there is a clearly agreed length of time, this question needs to be brought to the surface regularly. As expectations fluctuate and shift, valuable clues are given as to what might be the 'smallest, simplest step towards change' described by Talmon (1990: 120) as sufficient to initiate decisive alterations in perception, feelings or behaviour.

> Reviewing the first ten years of my psychotherapy practice, I found out that most of my therapeutic failures resulted from working too hard and saying too much. In my present therapeutic sessions, I look for the smallest simplest step toward change. My expectation is that when my client leaves the session remembering one new point (or tries out one new behaviour), it is plenty. Nevertheless, my thinking and clinical formulations are often still very complex. On the basis of my training, I might entertain multiple formulations of the present problem, ranging from dynamic to behavioural, cognitive to systemic.
>
> (Talmon 1990: 120)

While Talmon (1990) is intent upon making a powerful case for 'single-session therapy', his views are an encouragement to all practitioners and clients to use every session, particularly those working towards a specific closing date, as contributory towards an ever clearer agreed purpose.

What was your previous experience of psychological change?

Where there is a specific closing date all previous experiences of personal development need to be brought to the surface, acknowledged and valued. These may include some form of psychological therapy but are more likely to be linked to previous experiences of psychological distress. The problematic issues now being brought to each session are likely to resemble, in pattern, troubles worked through in the past. There are several ways in which this exploration can be useful. Previous strategies can be remembered and re-mobilised provided they do not sabotage the present aim of the client. If, however, these previous experiences reveal outdated strategies for survival, reactions to confusing or threatening childhood experiences, these become available to examination. Linked in to the focal theme, these adaptations can be unpacked, tracked back to their origins and gently challenged.

> Guy wondered if he had been right to ask for brief counselling. He smiled engagingly at the counsellor as he told her that she was probably his only real friend. He hoped she would be flattered and pleased by this confession, perhaps spontaneously offering him some more sessions. The counsellor did not do this but began to ask him about his other friends, and reflect on the companionship he seemed to enjoy with Amanda. Guy realised that he had felt isolated many times in the past. Each time he had taken up a new interest, usually an active sport, and buried himself in this until he had achieved enough success. Most of his friends were people with whom he played squash or golf. He enjoyed the brief intimacies of physical competition, so different from having to 'watch his back' every day at the office. This seemed to be a useful coping strategy, his counsellor commented thoughtfully, and it would be very different to talk about his occasional feelings of loneliness to anybody else, even Amanda. Guy realised that he had imagined Amanda would be unable to bear even the slightest hint of weakness on his part. Perhaps this was not true.

Where a client has had some previous psychological therapy, this is likely to be contrasted, favourably or unfavourably, with the present agreed commitment. Most of these comparisons will have been worked through in the preliminary weeks of the mini-commitment. However, clients may still retain some previously gained notion that a time-limited commitment is likely always to be inferior to an open-ended arrangement. Such a grudging acceptance of the present therapeutic engagement is likely to undermine the working alliance unless it is acknowledged and defused at an early stage. Conceptual criticisms of the time limitation are likely to surface again as the closing date becomes imminent, but these are likely to be intellectualisations reflecting at 'the deepest level the wish to return to past time, to make past time now and thereby to restore infantile omnipotence and, with it, timelessness' (Mann 1973: 9).

> Joanna found her preliminary sessions with the psychotherapist startlingly enlightening about her relationship with her father. More disturbingly, she began to realise how much she had missed not having a

mother. She had always joked about her easy teenage years, free from all the mother–daughter hassles experienced by her friends. She felt unprepared for the yawning gap between sessions and she had decided to accept what the psychotherapist called brief focused therapy. She had not wanted to become too dependent on this woman's caring interest. Now she was surprised to find herself feeling angry and critical. For all his faults, her previous therapist had surely been more relaxed. With this therapist, every session seemed to hold a reminder that time was passing. She did not want to be reminded of the closing date, nor of her mother's absence, and her father's death. Surely these could not be the only reasons for her depression. It was all too simplistic. Perhaps this woman was not really as experienced as Joanna had believed her to be. At the next session, the therapist wondered aloud if Joanna's silence might be hiding some feelings of disappointment or anger. As she voiced her criticisms, Joanna's shrill complaints collapsed into tears. Nobody had ever been there only for her, she realised, and now nobody would ever take her mother's place. She was too old to be loved. The therapist quietly accepted Joanna's despair and acknowledged the pain of her discovery. At the end of this session, Joanna felt exhausted, drained but strangely calm, almost exhilarated.

What do you fear?

In a time-focused commitment, this 'horror of time' (Mann 1973) is often a crucial fulcrum for the resolution of a client's 'central issue' as described in the focal theme. Practitioners need, however, to be sensitive and subtle in the way they draw attention to this factor. Even when clients do not demonstrate any conscious awareness of the closing date, the 'basic tendency of the organism to complete any situation or transaction which for it is unfinished' (Perls, Hefferline and Goodman 1951) is likely to operate beneficially. It could be counter-productive to this quiet, yet urgent, process if anxieties about ending are artificially inflated and inappropriate links made to previous losses or bereavements. Once again, practitioners are urged to avoid any assumptions about the importance of *this* therapeutic relationship until its significance is affirmed by the client. This entails maintaining a delicate balance between avoidance of painful previous experiences of loss, in practitioner as well as client, and too premature a focus on the existential truths of termination.

Other fears, even if already faced during the mini-commitment, are likely to resurface strongly in any time-limited therapeutic engagement. Will clients be able to cope with the strong emotions surrounding their focal theme? Will their external relationships with friends and partners be damaged forever? Will they be able to cope with their responsibilities at work and at home? All these are valid questions which can lead to creative experiments within the safe enough environment of the consulting room. Remembering the power of a small but significant change of belief and/or behaviour is essential in the time-focused setting: 'I try not to do too much. If I can find just one issue, just one idea, just a teaspoonful, that is useful to the client, the intervention can be a successful one' (Bloom 1981).

How will you stop yourself getting what you want?

To some extent this question can be transformed, in this context, to a time-related query. How will clients stop themselves from using the limited time available and sabotage their optimistic acceptance of a specific closing date with a clearly articulated focal theme. Mann has expounded eloquently upon the all-pervading human desire for permanence which stems from 'the sense of timelessness residing in the unconscious of all humans' (Mann 1973: 7). To agree, in principle, to work together with an agreed purpose, focusing on a 'central issue' (Mann 1973: 17–20) and to be satisfied with completion and termination would be, in his view, to achieve maturity and to triumph over universal existential angst. Clients who have chosen the time-focused commitment can be encouraged, within the working alliance, to consider ways in which they might try to 'restore infantile omnipotence and, with it, timelessness' (Mann 1973: 9) so as to avoid losing the 'fantasised all-giving, all-loving early important person' (Mann 1973: 56). Once clients have drawn up into awareness the particular way in which they might already be avoiding change, this can be used to sharpen the focal theme.

> Guy decided he would make it clear to Amanda that he would not be missing any more counselling sessions. To his surprise, she did not argue about this and seemed, if anything, to respect his decision. Now Guy began to question his counsellor closely. Did she feel he really needed the remaining time? Did she feel pleased that he would be fulfilling his commitment to her? It seemed to him that she responded to these questions without enthusiasm. He became suspicious that she was only interested in the money he was paying her. He asked if he could pay by cheque instead of cash, and then forgot his chequebook for two sessions. He was torn between guilt and triumph when his counsellor accepted his explanations and apologies without comment. He asked her if she was secretly 'pissed off' with him and complained that she was not telling him what he would need to do to be a good husband to Amanda. The counsellor commented on the power and authority he seemed to be ascribing to her. She reminded him of his recent discovery that he had conducted most of his life believing that, in order to survive, he must please a powerful woman. Certainly, this had been true for the little baby boy, she added gently, as she held his gaze. Guy felt sad, angry, embarrassed and amused, all at one time. He had to face it. This woman

was not going to play the part of his needy, bossy mother. It was time to let go of the dream, the struggle to get his mother to love him and look after him.

Step 4: Telling 'the story' – entering the client's life process

Most clients will have sketched out their stories during the preliminary sessions of the mini-commitment. Once practitioner and client have an agreed number of sessions, and a specified closing date, there can be a shared, but mistaken, assumption that there is not enough time to go over an important episode from the past, or to expand on the background to problematic issues in the present. If the practitioner accepts responsibility for holding the client's focal theme clearly in mind, then what appears to be repetition can help to clarify a central discomfort, the unfinished and unsatisfactory issue which is likely to resurface rapidly in the sharpened focus of a time-limited encounter.

What brought you here, now?

It has already been suggested, in Chapter 5, that it is advisable for the practitioner to ask this question, silently, at every session, whatever the agreed commitment. As the surface issues bringing clients to each session seem to shift and change, so the power of the underlying theme can be clarified. Clients will recognise their own patterns and can begin to explore alternatives.

Where have you been?

Linking the client's account of their lives, past and present, to the agreed purpose of the time-focused therapeutic encounter, practitioners can encourage a sense of the persisting search for meaningful existence which has informed even the most chaotic personal history. The past is reformulated as a journey, during which, usually out of awareness, survival strategies were designed, tested out and then repeated until they became problems in themselves. Cognitive restructuring may be all that a client needs to achieve during the agreed time limit. This is likely to be particularly true of clients whose sense of self has been severely damaged by their early formative experiences, or by a more recent severe trauma. The entire work of the time-focused commitment may satisfactorily be contained within the disclosure stage described in Table 3a. These clients are likely to return to some form of therapeutic commitment in due course, when they feel safe enough to re-experience the emotions which drove their earlier strategies and compulsions. Practitioners may experience disappointment with what seems like a purely intellectual outcome, even though this is likely to have been signposted by the client in the manner in which they have described their aims.

> Judy had stopped cutting herself, but her mood swings were as alarming as ever. She only felt calm on the days of her counselling sessions with the social worker. She found herself thinking deeply before and after the sessions, writing pages in her diary and not feeling the same need for sedatives. As the agreed number of sessions drew to a close, the social worker reminded Judy that she had said from the beginning that what she wanted most was to understand what had happened to herself and to her family. Judy felt immediately relieved. She had achieved something, after all, and she was not being asked to confront her father and mother, even though she could see clearly now where they had failed her.

How was it for you, then?

Whatever the life process stage (see Table 3a) reached by clients, they are likely to use their history to support the necessary work of this intensively focused commitment. Clients ready for catharsis will rage and grieve over the past, while clients working on self-care or renunciation will interweave their narratives with insights already gained. Clients seeking support in their accomplishment of issues of self-empowerment, are likely to muse upon the past, looking for comparisons with their present patterns of behaviour and emotional stability.

> Tim decided to take advantage of the personnel department's offer of 'self-development' interviews. He arranged a couple of interviews with the organisational consultant brought in for this purpose. He was surprised and impressed with the accuracy of her observations. She commented on his self-sufficiency and ability to work long hours without the support of a colleague. He began to tell her what he had discovered about his childhood in analysis. He became thoughtful and quiet as he talked. Realising that his time with this receptive listener was short, he began to wonder aloud how he might engage in more of a social life. It was a strange and disturbing question. Why was this an issue now? He thought he had worked through his regressive needs and had reached a reasonable acceptance of his occasional depressions.

Step 5: Working with the focal theme for this stage

This step is reached swiftly and decisively in a time-focused commitment. As already indicated, the essence of any time-limited approach to psychological therapy is the need to uncover and work on a central issue, agreed between client and counsellor.

What keeps happening again and again?

The essence of a focal theme is its repetitive quality. As the underlying similarity of painful and troublesome events begins to emerge, both client and practitioner may feel daunted by the power of the pattern. Having agreed to limit the time of the therapeutic encounter, it is advisable to limit expectations regarding the extent to which these patterns may change in the short term. Clients working on one of the earlier stages of psychological change can be reminded that identification and observation of a disastrous pattern usually takes place long before changing behaviours and avoiding emotionally toxic situations. Even at the final empowerment stage, it is likely that there is a dreadful familiarity about the central issue bringing a client back into personal development work. A useful image is provided by the last three verses of Portia Nelson's 'Autobiography in five short chapters':

III

I walk down the same street.
There is a deep hole in the sidewalk.
I see it is there
I still fall in . . . it's a habit
I know where I am.
It is my fault.
I get out immediately.

IV

I walk down the same street
There is a hole in the sidewalk.
I walk round it.

V

I walk down another street.

(Nelson 1985)

Clients reading this poem are likely to identify which verse they have reached, and may be heartened by the optimism of the final verse.

If this is the pattern, how was it learnt?

The most repetitive events of a client's life story, related earlier, can now be connected to the inevitable learning which has taken place in the past. There is often immediate relief in the realisation that what seems to be illogical, or even crazy, repetition of painful experience is based on earlier experience during which certain responses were learnt as a survival strategy and has become, out of awareness, a typical reaction to a wide range of situations. Another source of information, where time is limited, is the attitude of the client towards the specific closing date already agreed. Clients will reveal the limited ways in which they were able to negotiate for their own needs, the lack of clear boundaries in the past, or the rigid rules within which they learnt to operate.

What do you need to re-learn?

Practitioners working within a time-focused commitment need to press home the notion that what has been learnt can be replaced with new learning. This re-education is likely to begin immediately, within the therapeutic relationship, even though it will need reinforcement through external life experiences.

> Judy told the social worker that her old boyfriend had been looking for her. It was a dramatic story that she told. He had returned from Germany to the local army camp and had stormed straight round to her mother's house. He had threatened to beat up her father for making Judy have an abortion all those years ago. He had shouted and wept, saying that he was prepared to marry Judy in order to 'get his baby back'. Judy stopped, wide-eyed and breathless. She looked expectantly at her counsellor. Surely she would react with horror, warning Judy not to get involved with this man again. The social worker did not seem very concerned. She asked Judy whether she was still at all interested in this man. He had not featured much in their discussions, except as a part of her painful attempts to regain her father's full attention. She commented on Judy's obvious excitement. Judy felt deflated and asked, sullenly, whether her counsellor cared about her at all. The soldier was a violent bastard, especially when drunk, not that she was frightened of him, of course. The social worker explored Judy's obvious disappointment before checking on the level of risk involved. Once again, she reiterated that Judy did not have to be in a crisis situation to be the centre of her counsellor's attention.

So, what work is needed now?

The more defined and circumscribed the therapeutic engagement, the more crucial is the need for these learnt patterns to be openly experienced between practitioner and client. Only in this immediate therapeutic encounter can safe enough experiments be attempted which oppose and disprove the beliefs concealed within the focal theme. These experiments may not be behavioural, or even prepared and carried through in full awareness by the client. Their experimental nature will be revealed by the client's experience that something new is taking place, here and now, in the psychotherapeutic space. When time is focused, attention to change is more acute. The practitioner's task is to ensure that the smallest movement towards change is honoured and affirmed.

Step 6: Reviewing the commitment – past and future

When there is a specific closing date, and approximately six sessions following the mini-commitment, it is advisable for the practitioner to encourage relaxed informal re-evaluation throughout the therapeutic encounter. This does not mean changing the focal theme or lightly discarding the objectives already agreed between client and practitioner at the first review. If client and practitioner are clear that this particular period of intense personal development is likely to be followed by others, then consideration of future psychological change can be part of the present process.

Shall we continue?

This question in its obvious form is not likely to be asked by the practitioner. The time-focused commitment differs from all the other commitments described in this book in that client and practitioner consciously agree to use a temporary inflexibility for an agreed purpose. However, there is a sense in which practitioners may benefit by continuously monitoring the intensity of this type of work. At any time, but more usually after two sessions of optimistic and rapid progress, clients may display an apparent failure of motivation, even complete amnesia about the purpose of this particular therapeutic engagement.

> The participation of the therapist throughout the beginning phase is relatively easy. The total dynamic set of the patient favors the therapist in his work. The smoothly functioning gears begin to grind in the middle phase. Improvement in the patient tends to reach a plateau, and the first glimmers of disappointment become known either in the stated failure to improve further, a return of complaints or, more often, a sense of withdrawal, of moving away from the therapist. The patient may have less to say or may feel that all that needed to be said has already been said. Often the patient conveys an attitude that asks, 'Where do we go from here?' Clearly the patient's enthusiasm has begun to wane.
>
> (Mann 1973: 55–6)

It is this silent question that needs to be picked up and explored by the practitioner. Most often this can be done overtly by encouraging clients to explore their doubts and disappointments. Often it is only at this point that a client, who has previously cheerfully chosen to work in a time-limited way, will admit to fears of abandonment, betrayal and failure. The realistic basis for these emotions needs to be acknowledged and accepted by the practitioner in a non-defensive manner. However beneficial the therapeutic engagement has been, there are likely to be disappointments and dissatisfaction. The freedom to voice these feelings may in itself be a reparative emotional experience. A truly open exploration can bring into clear consciousness the levels at which these ambivalent feelings are not related to the present situation, the professional commitment freely entered into by client and practitioner. If the focal theme selected is reasonably accurate, then these emotions belong within the work which is being done, and which now can become more conscious.

> With only one session to go, Guy became quiet and almost morose. He claimed that he had not realised that next week would be the last session. He said he was sick of being hemmed in by other people's arrangements for the marriage, and even for the honeymoon. His life was no longer his own. And now, his counsellor commented, perhaps he was feeling hemmed in by the arrangements they had made together, two months ago. Guy grinned ruefully. He knew it was illogical to complain of a contract which he had specified so clearly. He took a deep breath. The truth was that he felt scared of facing this wedding alone. Impossible though it was, he wished that she could be there alongside Amanda and himself, a sort of 'best woman'. Perhaps that was what he would have liked his mother to have been, the counsellor said gently: the best mother in the street. But his mother had been far from that, Guy admitted miserably, and, even if she was still alive, she would have been a terrible embarrassment at his wedding. As he wept openly for the first time, he realised again how difficult it was going to be, letting go of that old dream.

What are the alternatives – to us working together?

This question may arise whenever the specified closing date is discussed. Both participants remain aware that there is work to be done outside the consulting room, and after this time-focused commitment has been completed. In Table 1, it is made clear that there will then be a stop as far as the practitioner's work with this client, at this time, is concerned. However, this does not preclude the use of the third choice point to offer a follow-up session in a few months' time. At this time, future psychotherapeutic options might be considered. These could include a possible return to the same practitioner for a time-extended or time-expanded commitment, referral to another practitioner, referral to a psychotherapy group, or the use of a peer support group to enhance psychological growth. Of these options, group psychotherapy is a particularly beneficial and appropriate experience at this stage. There is a hot-house quality to this intensive time-limited period of psychological growth which can be sheltered, tested out and developed in a group setting. Hans Cohn (1986) routinely agrees with his individual clients, from the outset of their work with him, that they will progress to participation in group therapy led by him. Although Cohn's model is based on a more traditional form of long-term existential psychotherapy, it seems ripe for adaptation to the approach outlined in this book.

Joanna's agreed period of brief focused psychotherapy had come to an end. At the last session she thanked the woman therapist for helping her understand how much she had been hurt by her mother, as well as her father. The therapist asked if Joanna would like, in due course, to take part in a psychotherapy group. She herself facilitated several groups and might be able to offer Joanna a place. Joanna hesitated. She was interested, but did not feel ready to expose her newly discovered sensitivities to strangers as yet. The therapist affirmed Joanna's stated need to 'lick her wounds' and left the offer open for her to consider at some future time. She asked Joanna whether she had enough supportive people in her life at present. Throughout the brief therapeutic encounter, Joanna had been talking through her discoveries about herself with two of her closest female friends. They met each weekend at the health club and shared their hopes, fears and vulnerabilities. Joanna felt confident that these two women would be there for her if she began to feel wobbly again.

Another choice to be considered, as the time-focused commitment draws to a close, is that of eventual lateral transfer (see Table 1). While it is essential not to fudge the clarity of the specific closing date, the general affirmative optimism of this approach supports open discussion that a client may, in due course, re-engage with the same practitioner, probably within a time-extended or time-expanded commitment. Implicit in this discussion is acceptance of a stage-related life process of psychological evolution, with psychological therapy as a resource used by clients in the course of their personal journeys.

Judy realised that she was in danger of becoming sloppy and sentimental about her counsellor. She wanted to buy her a really amazing present so that she would never be forgotten. She spent a lot of time looking in classy gift shops. How could she find out what the social worker really liked? There were so few clues: just the bright coloured scarves she always wore. There was only one session left and she still had not worked it out. She looked desperately round the room at the plants and the pictures in her counsellor's office. She was not really listening to what was being said: something about the journey Judy was on, and what ways she would 'support herself' during the coming weeks. She would be fine, she responded curtly, as she always had been. She was good at surviving, wasn't that what they had been looking at: her strategies for survival? The social worker remained quiet, watching her.

Judy realised that her words had sounded shrill and unconvincing. She said, more steadily, that she had her friends at the hostel, and at the day centre and there was her appointment with the consultant next month. She admitted that she was beginning to think that it might, one day, be worth trying out that psychotherapy place again. Did the social worker think they would offer Judy another chance?

How shall we work together now?

Having unpacked any reluctant or ambivalent feelings, and reaffirmed the existence of alternative options for psychological work in the future, the intensity of the present task is likely to be reclaimed with energy. Clients are likely to question practitioners closely about their progress and their fears that the distress which brought them to psychological therapy may return. These questions can be misread by practitioners who are themselves doubtful about leaving the past behind. It is important for practitioners to remain aware of their own residual yearnings for the magical restoration of the security and dependency which belongs to a reasonably happy infancy, and which, for many of us, has not been satisfactorily consolidated. Unless this universal desire for blissful unity has been acknowledged, worked through and challenged in a practitioner's own psychological therapy, it will be difficult for them to work in a time-focused commitment. What is needed is relaxed, warm and skilful facilitation of a client's growing aware-ness of their compulsive efforts to restore and repair the past instead of engaging with the challenges of their present life.

At the very last session, Guy's counsellor said that she realised how difficult he had found the last few sessions. He had moved from an intellectual understanding of the roots of his problems with women to actually re-experiencing this complex mixture of rage, suspicion and longing. Now he had the tools to separate the distress of his boyhood from his present relationships. Guy enjoyed the notion of skilful self-management, but wondered aloud if he would be able to do all this without the counsellor's help. She smiled warmly at him. Just realising he might sometimes need another person was already a sign that he had moved away from the compulsive self-reliance which had been his major way of avoiding close relationships. Guy admitted that he had begun to trust Amanda with his feelings, and was really enjoying her new openness with him. He had even begun to see some of the ways in which Amanda's warmth had been learnt from her mother. She wasn't such a bad old biddy after all. And perhaps, the counsellor commented, he could say goodbye to her with the same words. He started to protest, and then as they laughed together, he felt again the healing tears run down his face.

Have the goalposts changed?

If the agreed purpose of this time-focused period of intense psychological change has, to a large extent, been fulfilled, then there will be an inevitable change of aim. There is a danger that client and practitioner will move too quickly into planning the next stage of the client's psychological work. No matter how time-limited the therapeutic engagement, time is needed to celebrate what has been achieved. No matter how small may seem the shift in understanding, in emotional response or in behaviour, it is crucial evidence that psychological change is taking place. Only when the satisfaction phase of each developmental cycle of change has been fulfilled can the next cycle be visualised. Part of this celebration may be an acknowledgement of remaining resentments and disappointments, especially where these attach to the practitioner. As these are fully aired, so they can be released leaving clients free to take away a realistic and 'good enough' experience of their relationship with the practitioner and of their own ability to change and grow. Most clients will benefit from a discussion of the 'unfinished business' (Perls, Hefferline and Goodman 1951: 140; Clarkson 1989: 42), and this can lay the foundations for future work in the arena of self-development. In any case, it is vital that the door is left open in some way, either through the offer of a follow-up session or acceptance that the client will make contact if they feel the need. This offer is made without anxiety and in full confidence that clients will be conducting their own life process of psychological evolution. Practitioners may find this attitude harder to maintain if a client seems to have worked only in one of the earlier stages, and even this still seems incomplete. If trust is particularly difficult to incorporate, then a client may have worked only on one of the issues which belong to the preparation stage (see Table 2). To make some headway in sharing a present problem, and to accept a less self-damaging solution may be all that is necessary at present.

> At the last session, Judy felt trapped by the situation. Yes, of course she would miss this woman but surely she did not have to admit to this. She wanted to finish on a high note, feeling pleased with herself for getting out of the hospital, and finding some part-time work. Her extravagantly wrapped present lay on the table between them. The social worker opened it slowly, commenting on the care Judy had taken with the paper and the card, and finally, exclaiming with pleasure about the gift itself. Then she looked up at Judy. There was no escape. She had become used to being honest in this room, and she knew the counsellor could cope with her complicated mixture of feelings: sadness, anger and a strange sense of relief, almost like happiness. With this woman, Judy had faced her father's shameful weakness and his betrayals. She had admitted to her longing for her mother's arms. It would not be too difficult to blurt

out the truth about her present emotions. Perhaps she would, at last, use some of those ever-present paper tissues.

SUMMARY

In this chapter, the time-focused commitment has been described and illustrated. It should be remembered that this choice of commitment is made with the client's full agreement and, like the time-extended or time-expanded commitments, is always a continuation from the preliminary sessions of the mini-commitment. All the commitments described in this book rely upon a scrupulously conducted process of assessment and review, and the time-focused commitment will have been negotiated and mutually agreed at the first review (see Table 1). Once again, the six steps for every commitment delineated in Table 4 have been offered to the practitioner although, to some extent, each step worked through will have echoed and then deepened the work of the mini-commitment. The distinctive quality of this time-limited therapeutic engagement is the intensity with which the working alliance, already established, is now brought into direct confrontation with transference issues. Much use has been made of Mann's (1973) argument that this process is accelerated and made dynamic by the universally experienced 'horror of time' (Bonaparte 1940). As these repetitive patterns are brought into awareness, the focal theme, which has already been identified, can be addressed. Working with a clearly specified closing date, and to achieve a realistically limited agreed purpose, engenders optimism as well as conflict. This type of commitment demands of the practitioner a high level of sensitive, non-defensive understanding, most usually achieved through their own experiences of psychological therapy.

Chapter 7

The time-extended commitment
Maintaining the motivation

> I will never abandon you as long as you need me. In return for that, I
> want you to join me in a partnership to make me obsolete as soon as
> possible.
>
> (Cummings 1986: 430)

This proposition summarises the spirit in which the offer of a time-
extended commitment is made to a client. Both participants agree to a
therapeutic engagement which is open-ended, focused and goal-oriented.
The commitment is a continuation of the mini-commitment and has been
agreed at the first review. The ending date is not specified but is always in
view. The working alliance is one of mutual trust, symbolised by the
agreement that both participants will give each other sufficient notice of
termination. There is a full acknowledgement of the client's need for
personal change exerted by present psychological pain in the face of the
challenges of external life.

> At the present state of our knowledge, it is difficult to make precise
> predictions concerning the length of a treatment or the number of
> interviews required in any given case. Our task is to make the patient
> self-reliant by exerting a constant but not excessive pressure, blocking
> the patient's neurotic retreat into fantasy and into the past, and urging
> him toward the actual difficulties of his current life situation.
>
> (Alexander and French 1946: 37)

The authors of these words describe their approach as 'economical
psychotherapy'. The term could apply to most of the commitments outlined
in this book. Practitioners are urged to provide an optimal and minimal
intervention into a client's life process of psychological evolution. Full credit
is given to the importance and power of 'extra-therapeutic experiences'
(Alexander and French 1946: 37). The aim of the practitioner is to offer
their professionalism and a working alliance during this particular time of
intensive psychological change. It is always understood that this period,
while important, is only part of a client's life of psychological change and
development.

The time-extended commitment describes an open-ended arrangement where client and practitioner work together over an unspecified, but not interminable, period of time. Both participants have a clearly articulated agreement that a minimum of four sessions' notice will be given, by either party, before terminating this commitment to engage in psychological therapy. By making the offer of continuing commitment conditional upon this clear agreement, the practitioner is overtly addressing the temporary nature of professional assistance. The four sessions' notice is to be used, not merely for farewell purposes, but to ensure that this intense period of therapeutic work is defined, valued and rounded off in preparation for life outside psychological therapy (see Table 1). The practitioner will have used the mini-commitment to assess whether the client possesses enough motivation to adhere to a contractual arrangement which emphasises the curative properties of regularity, dedication and clear boundaries. Clients will also have had time, during the first few weeks, to decide how far they want to commit themselves to regular weekly sessions with this practitioner. Both parties have reached a clearly communicated arrangement. During the extended time, therapeutic work is punctuated by regular review sessions, usually linked to the 'natural breaks' provided by holidays, illnesses or unavoidable professional commitments.

Tim telephoned the organisational consultant a month later. He told her that he had enjoyed the two 'self-development' interviews arranged by personnel, but that he would now like to see her privately. Would that be possible? He sounded tense and shy, but determined. The consultant agreed to a series of meetings during which it became clear that Tim was experiencing considerable self-doubt. He had believed himself to have had a 'full analysis' and to be sufficiently sorted out. He had absorbed himself in his work as senior registrar in the teaching hospital and had accepted his occasional bouts of depression as normal. Now he had begun to question his social isolation and was subject to bouts of acute and lonely despair. The organisational consultant asked if he would like to work more psychotherapeutically with her. She could offer him an extended period of time, but suggested that they agreed very specific goals, related to a re-evaluation of his present lifestyle, and that they review progress in three months' time, just before Christmas. Tim found her approach somewhat brisk and pragmatic, but felt relieved that someone seemed to believe that any change was possible. He was weary of the bleak acceptance which seemed to permeate his life.

A time-extended commitment is not advisable as an arena for work with clients who have displayed ambivalence through chaotic time-keeping or constant cancellations, perhaps accompanied by requests for extra sessions in the same week. Occasionally these recurring incidents might be explained by contextual or cultural influences. Clients may not be aware of the importance attributed to punctuality in a Northern European setting or a badly organised appointment system may reflect the practices of an agency rather than the motivation of a client. Where there is evidence of an unspoken reluctance to maintain a contractual agreement as to time, duration and frequency, it is usually better to offer a time-focused commitment during which a more solidly based alliance can be built. The crucial test of motivation for time-extended psychological therapy is a freely given and authentic assent to the four-sessions closing agreement already outlined.

At the end of the college term, Peter's counsellor explained that he could continue to meet Peter on a regular weekly basis for the rest of the academic year. It would be possible to continue counselling sessions after this, provided that the counsellor was working in the same place. He paused at this point, and then, in genuine enquiry, asked if Peter himself was interested in continuing in such an open-ended agreement. Peter felt warm inside, pleased and somewhat flattered, but at the same time, his thoughts were racing. Did the counsellor think he was never going to get better, be a normal person who did not need counselling? Maybe he would get too fond of this pleasant man. In many ways, he would rather have him as a friend. Sometimes the sessions had been difficult, even painful. Peter began to talk of his need for constant support, almost as if he had not heard the counsellor's offer. Peter looked sad and ashamed as he said that he would always be a no-hoper, scared of being alone and yet uncomfortable with most people. The counsellor asked if he was feeling uncomfortable right now, and wondered if this was to do with the prospect of continuing counselling sessions. Peter began to mutter something about being very grateful but not wanting to be a nuisance. The counsellor asked Peter if he would be willing to agree that they should have four sessions before ending. Peter looked puzzled, and then alarmed. What did this ending business mean? The counsellor sounded confident as he predicted that a time would come when Peter would want to stop the sessions, at least for a time. Alternatively, either Peter or himself may move away. It was important that they make practical arrangements so that the work they had been doing together could be talked over before they said goodbye. His cheerful confidence was infectious. Peter relaxed. It all sounded quite straightforward, almost normal.

Within the parameters of the time-extended commitment, the six steps for every commitment can still be applied although they are worked through in a distinctively different manner.

Step 1: Making contact – the working alliance is an emotional bond

Who are you and where am I?

Having embarked on an open-ended commitment, both client and practitioner reconsider their impressions of each other. They are now pledged to meet on a regular weekly basis and, at some level, may even be dismayed by the prospect. The client is likely to be looking even more closely at this professional person, whose knowledge and expertise is to be their main resource during this difficult period of psychological changes. The practitioner returns the scrutiny, suddenly aware of their awesome responsibility to accompany another human being during a stressful and extended period of their life. This mutual reassessment is often unacknowledged, although it is essential that practitioners develop awareness of the awkward combination of relief, relaxation and dismay which is likely to operate at this time. There can be advantage in drawing attention to any renewed sense of encounter, and then inviting clients to share their experience of the situation. To be alert and alive to the essential mystery of another human being is not always easy when that other person becomes a part of a weekly routine. Gestalt therapy teaches and practices 'working with present awareness' (Clarkson and Mackewn 1993: 92), a series of self-statements about sensual impressions being received at any one moment in time. This exercise can be silently used to increase awareness and intensify observation at those moments when assumed familiarity obscures the constant shifts and risks of human encounter.

Do we like each other, and does it matter?

To work in an open-ended commitment without any enjoyment of the other person's presence would be a dismal prospect. As already discussed, in Chapter 5, a reasonable working alliance can be established during the preliminary weeks of the mini-commitment, even where there are initial reactions of like or dislike between client and practitioner. In this process, the real relationship elements of the interaction are differentiated from transference reactions and psychotherapeutic use made of the information. Working within the twelve to fifteen sessions of the time-focused commitment, with its intense focus on one particular core pattern of interaction, usually enables an early resolution of any remaining hostile feelings. Where the time of the commitment is extended, however, the far-reaching nature of this focal theme is explored extensively within the therapeutic relationship. Engaging with a client for a lengthier time-scale, practitioners need to have understood and set aside their own, more primitive, counter-transference reactions and to be feeling some 'non-possessive warmth' (Mearns and Thorne 1988: 59) towards their clients. Clients are likely to experience again the sense of demoralisation inherent in all psychological distress and will be quick to pick up any persistent attitude of dislike or distaste in the practitioner. Without some minimal level of 'unconditional positive regard' (Rogers 1961: 283) on the part of the practitioner, therapeutic work is unlikely to take place. This basic tenet of the person-centred humanist may not be sufficient for psychological therapy to take place, but it is certainly a necessary component. The offer of *any* continuation of commitment (see Table 1) should only be made to clients to whom the practitioner can extend this level of regard.

> During the Christmas break, Marion began to dread her next therapy session, which would be the first of what now seemed to be an endless series of painful meetings with someone whom she did not even like very much, and who probably disliked her too. Why had she been so eager to agree to this 'open-ended' arrangement? She wondered whether she could change her mind again. For a moment, she even speculated about cancelling the appointment by telephone. Not that this would solve anything. She would have to go back in the end, if only to fulfil the 'leaving contract'. Still ambivalent, feeling resentful and somewhat trapped, Marion found herself sitting again in that familiar room, faced by the other woman's enquiring gaze. She stared back, awkward and shy, yet determined not to pretend a warmth she did not feel. She began, abruptly, to describe her ambivalence about therapy. Surely there were other clients who would be more worthwhile than herself? The therapist smiled warmly as she said that this was not her own view, that she valued the sessions and respected the courage Marion had shown. Marion relaxed. This sounded genuine enough. It was good to feel accepted and respected, even though she struggled with the notion of herself being in any way 'valuable'. She began to talk about the ways she had put herself down during the break.

Do we trust each other enough?

It is not, however, necessary for clients to like practitioners, only to trust them enough to behave correctly in their role as practitioners. For many clients, especially those who have extensive traumatic experiences within interpersonal relationships, the issue of building basic trust may be the entire focus of therapeutic engagement. In Table 2, this is described as the main practitioner task during the preparation stage of a client's life process of psychological evolution. Even where a client's issues seem to fit into one of the later stages described, perhaps the self-care or even the empowerment stage, it is advisable to address again issues of mutual trust before embarking on the wider and deeper exploration of focal concerns typical of a time-extended commitment.

Now that they had agreed a commitment to 'psychotherapy', Tim became stiff and guarded in his responses to the therapist. His initial shy but eager courtesy hardened to a cold politeness accompanied by doubt and suspicion. He questioned her qualifications and experience several times, appearing to forget her answers between sessions. The therapist was patient and warm, reflecting openly upon his need for reassurance that she was professionally competent. At the third session, she asked him what he feared most about seeing a therapist. Tim hesitated, and then blurted out his anxiety that his colleagues should somehow find out about the sessions. He knew that she still had links with the head of the hospital personnel department and, here he began to stammer, it would be unfortunate if something slipped out, unintentionally. The therapist responded by acknowledging his discomfort, his fear of betrayal and asked what he would need from her to feel more confident regarding the confidentiality surrounding these sessions. She suggested that they make this issue central until he felt really safe. Tim relaxed slightly. He had expected her to be defensive and critical of his vulnerability.

Step 2: Testing the commitment – the working alliance is contractual

The more diffuse the time-boundaries of a commitment, the more important are the 'healing aspects of regularity, dedication and clear boundaries' (see Chapter 2: 22). These may need to be restated after a few sessions of an open-ended contractual commitment have taken place. Clients and practitioners are both at risk of forgetting professional agreements if they are engaging with a rich and confusing range of problematic issues.

What do you require of me, professionally?

At an obvious level, clients will expect practitioners who have offered an ongoing commitment to be available for a substantial period of time in the immediate future. This consideration is sometimes ignored by practitioners whose training has been based on an assumption of ongoing psychological therapy. Any offer of longer-term therapeutic engagement has to be balanced against the pressures and demands of external life. The promise to 'never abandon' (Cummings 1986: 430) a longer-term client is essentially a proposition of good intention. In reality, practitioners move, get ill or even die. These existential risks need to be considered when offering any form of time-extended or time-expanded commitment. Once engaged, clients may seek reassurance that there will not be any sudden breaks, that sufficient notice will be given of holidays and other absences, and that the time and place agreed is likely to remain stable. Other clients seem not to care about last-minute changes of venue, or a sudden appointment change. This can turn out to be a rationalisation or denial of a more primitive emotional response which, unless brought to the surface, can interrupt and undermine weeks of productive work. When cancellations or room changes are unavoidable, practitioners, whatever their orientation, can use the situation beneficially by remaining sensitive and open to all verbal and non-verbal responses. Working with a continuous focal theme, and with the completion of this particular therapeutic stage always in view, any clash between professional limitation and client expectation can be employed to illuminate and work through a focal theme.

Jane had been seeing the university student counsellor every Monday afternoon for two terms. They had agreed to continue until the end of the academic year when the counsellor would be finishing her one-year fixed-term contract. At the beginning of the summer term, Jane received a letter informing her that the counsellor would no longer be able to see her on Mondays, and offering her an appointment on a different day and in a different room. She felt outraged. Yes, she could manage this new appointment time as it was on her free afternoon, but she did not want to change. She had become used to preparing for the session at the weekend. She often went for long walks on Sunday afternoon, thinking about herself, the changes she had made since that terrible year of hospitalisation. On Wednesday she would be halfway through the week, preoccupied with lectures and assignments. She phoned up the counselling service and questioned the receptionist closely. What was the reason for the change of time? She even considered seeing another counsellor, but realised, just in time, that this was an even worse prospect. The first session of the term was difficult for both participants. Jane felt sullen and withdrawn, and her counsellor appeared to be harassed and tired. The hour seemed endless, and then Jane suddenly blurted out an angry question about the changed appointment. The counsellor was immediately alert, involved, and eager to explain that her employment contract had been altered. Jane felt mollified but still disturbed. The counsellor wondered if Jane had been reminded of all the disruption in her childhood, and accepted that this must seem like yet another experience where she was expected to give up her own needs for consistency and a steady routine.

What do I ask of you, as a client?

Where there is an extension of time, an agreed range of issues to work on and some optimism regarding outcome, what practitioners look for in their clients is continuing evidence of motivation. Initially, clients demonstrate their resolve by accepting the four-week closing agreement, as outlined above. Over time, this initial confidence is likely to wear thin, especially as more painful issues arise, and the relationship between practitioner and client begins to reflect the problematic patterns of external life. Practitioners can weather these fluctuations in motivation if their clients remain faithful to the contractual elements of the working alliance. Clients who fail to attend, or who continuously cancel their sessions at the last moment, are possibly demonstrating a more basic failure of motivation, particularly if they are unwilling to discuss these events. Often, these signs of discomfort are followed by a session during which the client declares a wish for immediate termination. Sometimes this situation can be retrieved by links to the focal issue, and a reminder of the original closing arrangement. Where this approach fails, clients cannot be held to a contractual agreement which has no legal standing. Failures in clients' commitment to longer-term psychological therapy can usually be ascribed to failures at assessment, an over-positive review at the end of the mini-commitment period, or a client's fundamental misunderstanding of ongoing psychological therapy. By reminding clients, at regular intervals, of the contractual parameters agreed, practitioners safeguard the work and make clear their own understanding of this therapeutic engagement.

Now that Marion had a manager's job at the centre she felt tired most evenings. Her son was being really difficult, staying out late, arguing about everything and even pushing her around. The therapy sessions did not seem to help her deal with any of the stress in her life, and even made things worse. She would come home all stirred up, feeling angry and distressed, after an apparently calm discussion about her childhood experiences. Marion had always taken pride in her punctuality. She hated being late for any appointment. Nevertheless, she found herself arriving later and later, first by only a few minutes and then as much as quarter of an hour after the start time. She felt trapped between guilt and resentment when the therapist continued to finish sessions on time. She decided to end the therapy sessions, and arrived resolute and on time for her next session. The therapist accepted her decision without question, only commenting that they had a four-sessions closing agreement. She reminded Marion that their agreed aim had been to understand better what childhood patterns were still being repeated. Was there something going on between the two of them now which had familiar echoes from the past? Marion sat quietly, accepting the suggestion that she close her eyes and focus on physical sensation rather than trying to remember a specific event. Almost immediately, Marion realised how tensely she was gritting her teeth, and she recognised a familiar sick feeling in her stomach. Filled with shame, she remembered the messy scenes going on at home, fearful that this competent woman would despise her. Once again she was letting things happen which she should be able to stop. Even though this time it was a fourteen-year-old boy and not her grandfather, there was still the same combination of secrecy and despair. She started cautiously to share this discovery, relieved and scared at the same time. The therapist accepted the powerful link, and then reflected on the real difficulty of being single mother to a boy already taller than herself. Now Marion began to weep. Why had she expected to be criticised and punished, rather than understood?

Step 3: Expectations and pitfalls

What do you hope to gain?

Motivation springs from hope of gain. Clients have demonstrated their trust in the therapeutic process by committing themselves to an open-ended time-scale. Although clients will have discussed their aims during preliminary sessions, and reaffirmed these when the choice of a time-extended commitment was made, these are likely to become increasingly elaborate or more diffuse as the range of issues explored becomes wider and deeper. Practitioners are responsible for reminding clients of their original aims and ensuring that these do not get lost, or become unrealistic. The overall purpose of the practitioner is to engage with the client on work appropriate to their particular stage of psychological growth and then to make themselves, at least temporarily, obsolete so that their clients can return to their external lives equipped with a wider range of strategies to tackle 'the business of being human' (Gilmore 1973: 5). As with a more time-limited therapeutic engagement, it is important to honour every significant gain in insight, emotional authenticity and behavioural change.

Tim was shocked by the brisk way in which his new therapist would interrupt his carefully considered descriptions of the thoughts he had entertained during the week. She would ask him what he had been doing at the time, or even what he wanted from her, right now, in response to these disclosures. Tim would pause, feeling offended and yet intrigued. She seemed to be insisting on some sort of immediate connection between them. He tried to avoid her bright gaze as he returned to his recent understanding that he fitted Jung's description of the intellect/ sensation type. 'So', the therapist asked, 'what is the practical problem you need to solve right now?' Tim felt immediately scornful. He remembered the respectful silence of his analytical sessions, punctuated only by statements which were often difficult to understand but which were full of wisdom. This woman seemed only to be interested in him making some small change in his social life. Impatiently, he agreed that he would have lunch with his colleagues at least twice during the following week. However, it was several weeks before Tim managed to meet this objective, by which time he was eager to hear the therapist acknowledge how difficult it must have been for him to cut through his habitual reserve.

What was your previous experience of psychological change?

Again, this subject is likely to have been explored already, during the preliminary weeks of assessment and the mini-commitment. Memories of previous practitioners, of educational experiences and of other developmental periods of their lives influence a client's response to this period of psychological change. If these memories are positive, clients are likely to expect a similar pattern of involvement, and be constantly comparing this practitioner with previous professional helpers. If there are negative aspects to the remembered time of change, clients will be on the alert for any recurrence.

> At the end of the college year, Peter realised that he had stopped thinking of himself as peculiar, a 'weirdo'. He had talked through some of his strangest fantasies with his counsellor. He had even described the time when he had imagined himself to be controlled by demons who watched him from a parallel universe. The counsellor seemed to hold a very firm opinion that Peter was an imaginative and intuitive person who was particularly susceptible to any form of mind-altering substance, legal or illegal. He said Peter had developed an unusually high level of awareness to his own physical state, and could alarm himself unnecessarily by attributing a normal reaction to some abnormal cause. The counsellor had been interested in this process, and had helped Peter to work through a series of self-addressed questions whenever he was beginning to feel stressed out. Peter himself had realised that he had been having strange experiences ever since the operation on his balls when he was about seven years old. Nobody had really explained to him what was going on. The doctors and nurses had made jokes. His parents had been embarrassed, insisting that he would forget all about it when he was older. He remembered lying in bed, sore and scared, wondering what he had done wrong. Talking this through with the counsellor, man to man, had begun to make sense of his painful adolescence, his fears about masturbation and his retreat from any possible sexual encounter. Why had none of the doctors and counsellors he had seen before realised what was going on? They had made him feel even more of a freak.

What do you fear?

Probably the most common fear expressed by clients in an open-ended therapeutic engagement is of becoming dependent on the practitioner, or on the regular weekly sessions. Where this fear is not acknowledged, or even denied, particular caution is needed. First, it is a reasonable apprehension for any adult to express. To need to be attended to, on a weekly basis, by a professional helper, with no clearly stated finishing date, is unusual in most cultures. The nearest parallels are probably found in religious procedures, *dharsan* in the East and *confession* in the West. The modern Western emphasis on individualism encourages and admires self-sufficiency, tough-minded coping and personal responsibility. More traditional cultures are likely to discourage talking to a stranger once an immediate problem, which affects the family group, has been resolved. Those clients who never express any misgivings about becoming dependent on ongoing psycho-therapy or counselling are likely to have become, in some way, habituated to the ritual of therapeutic interviews. They may have been institutionalised during their use of mental health services, perhaps as a psychiatric in-patient. Alternatively, they may have become 'therapy junkies', viewing their weekly sessions as a necessity without seemingly progressing in their stated wish for change or transformation. Encouraging exploration of this subject in the early weeks of a time-extended commitment can bring into the room a variety of hopes, fears and assumptions. Issues of power and authority can be faced head on, and practitioners alerted to their own professional needs and dependencies.

> As the end of the academic year approached, Jane became anxious. She had felt fine about their agreement that the counselling sessions would continue to the end of the year. Now she remembered how dreadful she had felt at the end of her time in hospital. She had suddenly found herself back at home with only the prospect of a six-monthly check-up meeting with the psychiatrist. She had not kept to this arrangement, ignoring the letter offering her a half-hour appointment. Then she had moved away, enrolled for a university course and tried to forget that whole disastrous episode. Seeing a counsellor was very different but what if the same thing happened? She could not bear to feel so powerless again. What if she started having the breathless panic attacks of the first term? She questioned the counsellor closely. Was she going away for the summer? Did the counselling service stay open? The counsellor confirmed that the service did stay open and then suggested they plan how to use the last few sessions. They could explore what had been achieved and look at what still remained to be worked on. She asked Jane how she felt about ending. She seemed fully to accept the mixture of fear, anger and relief which Jane described. She said she would herself feel both sad and glad as the ending approached; sad to be saying goodbye, but glad to have been witness to all the changes that Jane had made. Jane felt relieved. Apparently she did not come over as a helpless dependent, unable to manage without weekly counselling sessions.

How will you stop yourself getting what you want?

Ideally this question will have been explored extensively during the mini-commitment. The ways in which individuals can sabotage their own desires are varied, but almost always available to consciousness. This information is invaluable to the therapeutic process, as long as it is remembered and used to assist both client and practitioner during the inevitable period of time when failure seems to loom. One or both participants may feel stuck in terminal boredom or, conversely, the sessions may seem fraught with danger. Clients begin to feel trapped by their agreement to a four-week closing arrangement. Introducing this question again, perhaps referring back to the avoidances admitted to during intake sessions, can clarify what is going on, and avoid premature closure at the same time.

Marion's objective became clearer with every session. She wanted to say a final goodbye to the past. She was fed up with being seen as a victim, and with letting herself be treated as one. In sessions with the therapist, she would affirm her rights, her power and her adulthood. Yet she still experienced herself as small and powerless in certain circumstances. The therapist asked her to list these situations, to see if there was a link. Marion began to catalogue all the times she had recently lost her self-esteem. These ranged from a recent visit by the director of the charity she worked for to her attempts to sort out the milkman's bill. She realised that she was no longer daunted by conflicts with her work colleagues, all of whom were women. Marion looked up at the therapist, startled and dismayed. So that was it! She was still scared of men, and trying every which way to please them, whether they were bosses or tradesmen. The therapist asked Marion to imagine what stopped her treating these men in the same way as she would treat a woman. What was the risk? Marion was quiet for a time. Then, slowly, she began to admit that she often enjoyed feeling looked after by men, and one way of ensuring this was to play helpless and be admiring, even flirtatious.

Step 4: Telling 'the story' – entering the client's life process

What brought you here, now?

At a subtle level, this question needs to be renewed throughout any extended period of psychological therapy. It is very easy for the original problematic issue to be lost in the mass of material now being discussed. Has the presenting concern been resolved, or has it been replaced by more fundamental and searching issues? Without the spur of some form of psychological distress, engagement in psychological therapy becomes meaningless. This might not be acute or dysfunctional. Experiencing 'lives of quiet desperation' (Thoreau 1910: 5) or harbouring a nagging sense of personal dissatisfaction is often enough to keep clients coming to sessions, week after week.

Tim settled down to the routine of weekly psychotherapy sessions. They gave a point to the week, and he remembered how soothing he had found most of his analytic sessions. There had been great satisfaction in making careful and exact links between his childhood experiences and his recurring depressive moods. Lying on the couch, Tim had felt comforted, held and fully understood. He began to tell this new therapist about the discoveries he had made regarding the sterile loneliness of his parents' home, the complete absence of social life and his own sense of isolation at boarding school. The therapist listened carefully, commented on Tim's adaptation to his upbringing and then asked Tim what had been on his mind as he travelled towards her office this morning. Tim felt affronted. She seemed more interested in his trivial everyday concerns. He began, rather scornfully, to describe how angry he had felt about the noisy party held by his neighbours last night. She questioned him closely. How had he reacted, at the time? What had he done about it? Tim began to stammer again as he admitted to his sense of impotence as he had hovered outside his front door, trying to find the courage to go next door and complain. The therapist asked him to imagine that he had done so. What might have happened? Uncomfortably, Tim shared his picture of himself as a stiff spoilsport confronting a room full of laughing party-goers. She held his eyes with her own warm gaze. He felt tearful and angry.

Where have you been?

Where there is more time, clients often tell much more of their personal history. One of the main therapeutic advantages of longer-term psychological therapy is making available to clients enough space to tell and re-tell their stories. With each re-telling, clients understand more clearly the roots of the recurring pattern which now forms the focal theme for therapeutic work. This can engender compassion for the child or the younger self who once had to evolve this particular strategy for survival. At the same time, practitioners listen carefully to check the accuracy of any focal theme which has already been speculated upon and tentatively articulated. If the patterns emerging from a client's story seem to conflict with these explanatory notions, this new information can be used to reformulate another temporary hypothesis. Sometimes a client will produce completely new material as they re-tell their story. This can be illuminating and disturbing, testing any received opinions which a practitioner might be harbouring.

The therapist suggested to Marion that she imagine a man sitting in on the session. A chair was put to the side of the room, and Marion found herself glancing continuously in that direction. She became shy and excitable at the same time. Her voice rose to a childish pitch. She made jokes about herself, and wriggled about in her own comfortable chair. The therapist drew attention to all these activities. Marion suddenly started to re-tell the story of her grandfather. This time she focused upon her enjoyment of the afternoons she had spent with him. He had been so kind, had called her his 'little princess', and had made her feel clever as well as pretty. She paused, and looked down. A dark flush suffused her neck. In a low, pain-filled voice she wondered if she had even invited his furtive fondlings.

How was it for you, then?

As this question is explored, the emotional charge in a client's story becomes apparent. This process is particularly relevant if the client's stage in their life process of psychological evolution (see Table 2) is moving from disclosure to catharsis. Where time for therapeutic work is extended, this is likely to take place. Very often, it is to give time and space for re-experiencing painful emotions that clients will have chosen to work in an open-ended commitment. Even so, practitioners need to constantly check that a client has enough self and environmental support to maintain their external lives when working with distressing memories. The aim is to tell the story, re-experience the emotions and then move to questioning the past. If clients merely re-experience traumatic experiences without active enquiry and challenge, there is a risk that they will be confirmed in reactive and restricted attitudes which underlie their present distress. Very often, a practitioner's role is gently to initiate the questioning process, providing a view from outside the primary scene. This tentative exploration must not distort the client's truth, and can often be carried in the tone with which a practitioner reflects back the story.

On the first day of her exams, Jane's car broke down. Minutes ticked by as she tried to make the engine turn over. It was a busy ring-road and none of the passing cars stopped to help. Finally she managed to push the car to the side of the road, flagged down a taxi, and arrived in time to sit the exam. She appeared calm and efficient, finished the exam paper in good time, and walked out into the sunshine. Suddenly she began to shake and cry. She found a phone box, and sobbing, rang her husband. He arrived and took her home. The next morning she rang the counsellor and asked for an earlier meeting. By the afternoon, Jane was waiting outside the counsellor's room, still shaken but excited. She wanted to tell the counsellor what she had remembered during the night. She had been only four years old when her mother had run away from home. She remembered being wrapped up in a blanket and sitting terrified in the back seat of a car. Her mother had been driving, but now there was no-one around. Other cars rushed by. She was alone and nobody was going to come and get her. Here Jane paused. 'So you had to look after yourself, and you were only four', said the counsellor, gently, 'and you were far too young to do that.' Jane agreed with anger and energy. Suddenly it seemed so clear. No wonder she had been scared of every new challenge, and yet could never ask anybody to help. She had been a little girl who grew up too fast, who had to look after her mother as well as herself. It all made sense.

This reframing of the past is also the main work of the next two life process stages, self-care and renunciation. Where clients have re-engaged in psychological therapy to work with these issues, there is likely to be a recurrence of cathartic feelings within the container of the working alliance.

Step 5: Working with the focal theme for this stage

What keeps happening again and again?

As a client reflects on their story, the practitioner continues to point out the repetitions. In these lie the main clue to a focal theme, the central issue which underlies a client's strategies for survival. Where there is enough time, the same patterns will inevitably begin to emerge within the therapeutic relationship, and affect the working alliance. The practitioner's basic therapeutic orientation is likely to influence the speed with which attention is drawn to this development. Psychoanalytic practitioners will allow more time for the incongruence between the reality of a firmly established helping relationship and the unreal transference which is operating. In due course, an interpretive link may be offered, although the full reparative experience relies on a client's own recognition of incongruity. Cognitive-behavioural practitioners are likely to make swift and articulate interventions with the aim of encouraging interpersonal change in the therapy room and so encouraging clients to question their current constructs or beliefs. The more active humanist practitioners will use a very similar methodology although with more concentrated attention to the emotional change which accompanies these behavioural experiments. Practitioners who follow Rogerian principles are more likely to trust in the unconditional warmth and respect operating within the therapeutic relationship. With this support, client and practitioner together may be able to explore and challenge the lack of authenticity in the present situation. The approach delineated in this book allows for a variety of theoretical integrations. Above all, the task of the practitioner is to maintain a clear and steady focus on the central issue, taking only as much time as is appropriate to the commitment agreed, and bearing always in mind the stage of psychological evolution which this client appears to be working through.

Tim often spent much of the therapy session gazing out of the window. It was the only way in which he could avoid the therapist's eyes. She seemed to be insisting on constant encounter. She always sat immediately opposite him, and would lean towards him enquiringly with every question. He began to know intimately the shape of the tree outside her window. One day she asked him to describe what qualities he would ascribe to the tree. Tim felt embarrassed, but tried gamely to respond to this bizarre request. The tree was large, quiet, firmly rooted; it had survived its city environment, and seemed to make no demands. The therapist leaned forward again. She asked him to compare the tree with herself. Tim wanted to refuse, but his natural politeness propelled him into an embarrassing account of his experience of her as lively, questioning, small and persistent. He realised he was also leaning forward. He felt uncomfortable and yet excited. The therapist asked him to stay in contact with her a little longer. For a moment Tim felt terrified and then he began to laugh. How could this small woman be such a threat?

If this is the pattern, how was it learnt?

This question arises naturally as a client begins to realise the strength and tenacity of a survival strategy which has now become an habitual, though often inappropriate, response in a wide range of situations. Even in the absence of obvious difficulty or stress, the same collection of thoughts and feelings suddenly materialise, usually followed by a characteristic behaviour. Almost everybody can, on reflection, identify their own habitual response by completing the *'When in doubt . . .'* sentence. When in doubt, people may habitually react by *withdrawing* or by *having a crisis* or by *taking control*.

So what do you need to re-learn?

Powerful internal injunctions will have been shaped by more than one earlier experience, no matter how traumatic. There will have been reinforcements and these are likely still to be operating. The focal theme is often symbolised by a 'pivotal metaphor' (Stern 1985: 260).

> The fact is that most experienced clinicians keep their developmental theories well in the background during active practice. They search with the patient through his or her remembered history to find the potent life-experience that provides the key therapeutic metaphor for understanding and changing the patient's life. This experience can be called the *narrative point of origin* of the pathology, regardless of when it occurred in actual developmental time.
>
> (Stern 1985: 257)

One particular 'narrative point of origin' (Stern 1985: 257) is likely to be produced by a client to explain, satisfactorily enough, why they have developed the set of script-like responses which are now restricting their choices. To some extent, the factual truth of this event is not important to the therapeutic process. It is however, important that clients produce and affirm this 'therapeutic metaphor' themselves, and do not have it, in any way, induced or imposed by the practitioner. There is a particular risk of this happening where a practitioner holds to a narrow theoretical base, and attempts to fit their clients into their own notions of cause and effect. At all times, focus needs to be tempered with flexibility and some degree of scepticism. Clients can be encouraged to widen their understanding of the past, make their own links to the present and question their own assumptions. With extended time, clients can expand their own belief systems, supported in their new learning by a non-invasive therapeutic alliance.

Marion spent the next week in a nightmare of shame and confusion. She wished she had never become involved in any form of therapy. At least she had known where she was when she was just getting on with her life, without thinking much about the past. She had got rid of all those destructive men, had made a good life for herself and her son and had even been able to help other women change from victims to survivors. She had almost forgotten about the business with her grandfather. Now Marion could think of nothing else. It had all been her own fault. She had been a dirty little seductress, and she was still at it, going all soft and flirtatious as soon as a man was around. Angrily she poured out her disillusion and self-contempt as soon as she was sitting opposite the therapist again. The therapist seemed sad and worried. She commented on Marion's strength, her determination to survive and her constant self-appraisal. How did these qualities fit the present picture? Marion was suspicious. This sounded like flattery. She wanted to be punished and released from this corrosion of guilt and shame. Slowly she began to tell the therapist about her enjoyment of being controlled sexually. She realised now that she had chosen hard violent men when she was younger, longing to be released into passion by domination. It had never worked because they had always displayed some weakness, had become dependent on her in some way. She had not wanted to be hurt physically, just held firmly and given what she needed. Marion paused, she listened to the therapist pointing out that this sounded like what a small child would long for. For weeks now they had been exploring the wishes of what her therapist called her 'inner child'. She knew already that she carried inside herself, in her core, an unloved little girl, longing for acceptance and approval. Slowly, her impulse towards self-punishment started to dissolve.

So, what work is needed now?

More than insight is necessary to generate new learning. In the time-extended commitment, there is the opportunity for a series of calculated and conscious experiments with alternative ways of responding, first in the therapy room and then in external life. Wherever possible, these experiments should initially be carried out in settings and with individuals of minor significance to the client. If clients try out some new, although perhaps more authentic, ways of doing and being with people and in settings crucial to their well-being and self-esteem, the endeavour becomes too risky and loses its experimental freedom. The more crystallised the client's repetitive patterns, the more likely the disruption caused in established relationships.

> After her exams, Jane seemed dispirited and low. She told the counsellor how she seemed trapped by her own decisions. She was stuck with this punishing routine of college work and housework. It was all very well realising that she had always fulfilled the anxious carer role. Who was going to take care of her, if she stopped rushing around? Jane was angry with her husband. He said he cared about her and yet, night after night, it was Jane who rushed into the kitchen and prepared supper, set the table, washed up and then did the ironing. Why could he not see what was needed? He only seemed to want a meal in front of the TV and then perhaps some sex. She had given him an ultimatum. Either he changed or she would take the children away and set up a different home. There were plenty of single mothers on her course, and they managed fine. She paused, breathless, looking scared and defiant. The counsellor asked Jane what changes of behaviour she would like from the counsellor. Jane was embarrassed and then surprised by the flood of ideas that came into her mind. She would like the counsellor to speak up more, to swap chairs, to wear brighter colours and to change the pictures on the wall of the counselling room, perhaps even change their meeting place altogether, back to the warm quiet space where they used to meet. She stopped breathless and alarmed by her apparent impudence. The counsellor laughed. Would Jane be happy for her to fulfil the easiest of these requests or did she want everything at once? Perhaps they could negotiate. Later the counsellor suggested that Jane listed all the changes which she wanted her husband to make, in his behaviour. She suggested Jane include everything, from the tiniest alteration to a major transformation. Jane grumbled over the task but began to enjoy it, even giggling at some of her more outrageous wishes.

Step 6: Reviewing the commitment – past and future

A key element of time-extended work with clients is the use of several review sessions. To an extent, practitioners will be constantly conducting some form of internal review, possibly before and after every session. Once outside the intensity of therapeutic interaction, notes are made or audiotapes played. With the help of these aids, an overview can be maintained and made of use to clients, especially when engaging in a more formal review process. It has already been emphasised that these review sessions punctuate the time-extended commitment, and would usually take place before or after the natural breaks provided by holidays and other responsibilities. Where illness interrupts the therapeutic process, it is advisable to carry out a review as soon as psychological therapy recommences.

> Peter's counsellor was ill. He had turned up for his usual session at the beginning of the autumn term and the receptionist had told him that they had written a letter cancelling the appointment. She did not know when the counsellor would be back and said he could see somebody else instead. Peter did not want this. He wanted to ask what was wrong with the friendly Irishman but she did not look as if she would answer his questions. He felt angry and tearful as he walked away. The next week Peter returned at his usual time, hoping against hope that the counsellor would be there. The receptionist was patient but seemed to be hiding irritation. They would be in touch with him as soon as the counsellor returned. Once again Peter turned down the offer of another counsellor. It was four weeks before the letter arrived. Peter was relieved and yet frightened to see how much thinner the counsellor's smiling face had become. The Irishman was frank about the recent operation 'on his waterworks'. He answered all Peter's shy enquiries and then moved briskly on. He enquired closely into Peter's experience of his absence, accepting as normal that Peter had felt let down and angry, as well as anxious. He suggested they re-cap where Peter had got to all those weeks ago, and make sure they both knew what he wanted to work on next. Once again, he managed to make the situation seem normal.

Shall we continue?

Once involved in an open-ended therapeutic commitment, many practitioners shrink from asking this question. It is thought to imply rejection or lack of motivation. At the same time, clients may also find it difficult to query their need for continuation. Generally, the difficulty lies more with the manner in which the subject is introduced. An open and relaxed invitation to discuss the pros and cons of continuation is unlikely to alarm clients. A tense and anxious series of questions about the benefits experienced so far, accompanied by any hint of time-rationing, is likely to alarm and irritate clients who have freely entered into an extended therapeutic engagement. Full attention needs to be paid to the focal theme itself. Is rejection an issue for this client? Has this client always avoided close relationships or is there a tendency to cling to or merge with authority figures? These patterns will already have been discussed between client and practitioner, and will almost certainly have manifested in the therapeutic relationship. Discussions about continuation will bring any hidden or ambivalent feelings into the open. This is an opportunity to employ the working alliance to the full so that practitioner and client can ensure that any continuation is based on renewed motivation, and that the client has a freedom of choice regarding future commitment.

After approximately three months, Tim's new therapist suggested a review of what she preferred to call their 'contract'. Tim found the commercial overtones of the term somewhat distasteful, and felt both irritated and apprehensive. It was like being given an end of term report. He supposed that he would have to list all his 'achievements', another of her favourite words, in order to justify continuing. Yet he did want to continue. He had not felt really depressed since the weekly sessions had begun. He was enjoying lunching with his work team. Recently he had gone for a drink after work with one of the registrars. They had played a light-hearted game of pool instead of talking shop. He listed all these 'achievements' eagerly, keeping an anxious eye upon the therapist. Did she look pleased? Would she let him continue? The therapist was warm and affirming. She asked Tim about his earlier fears that colleagues would be critical of his seeing a psychotherapist. Tim grinned. The registrar had told him that he was in therapy himself, and that the psychologist did some weird form of bioenergetics. So would Tim like to continue with their weekly meetings, or would he like to fix a closing date? The therapist was watching Tim closely. He muttered something about having no other option, it was up to her. The therapist looked sad as she commented on the lack of choice he must have experienced in the past whenever he was sent off to boarding school. She would like to offer him as full a choice as possible now. He could continue the weekly sessions, or take a short break, or even start having two sessions a week. She said she enjoyed working with him and was prepared to be flexible, although she appreciated that he might want to 'practice' his new 'skills'. Tim winced at her language while savouring this new sense of being valued and powerful. He asked if she was sure that he could take a short break. He would like to start again in the autumn. He always felt better in the spring and summer, and he had planned a couple of holidays. They agreed to continue for another month, and then temporarily 'close down' just before Easter. Tim wondered if he would ever find the courage to criticise her use of jargon.

At one of these review sessions, the decision whether to finish, or complete, this particular time-extended commitment will be discussed in earnest. Using the term completion rather than the more usually used word, termination, conveys the spirit in which this ongoing therapeutic engagement has been entered. Clients have been accompanied through a significant stage in their own process of psychological evolution, and may even have progressed through several of the stages as delineated in Table 2. Now is the moment to conduct a full and final review (see Table 1) and to use the last four sessions to look back, to celebrate achievements, to acknowledge the unfinished business and to plan the immediate future. Above all, these final sessions allow for feelings of rejection to be fully expressed. At this time, the universal 'horror of time' described by Mann (1973) is likely to manifest, allowing client and practitioner to reflect on the impermanence of all human experience. The difficulty for all practitioners, working in an open-ended commitment, is to distinguish between a client's normal need to recycle previous experiences of endings and separations and a genuine recognition that this is not, after all, the time to close down therapeutic work. Paradoxically, this is more likely to be the case if a client has sought premature closure, and has questioned the need for the final four sessions. Here the more objective guidance offered by good consultative supervision is invaluable. While encouraging practitioners to remain flexible for as long as possible, it is advisable to resolve any consideration regarding a return to the time-extended commitment well before the fourth and last session.

> Marion realised that she had been seeing the therapist for nearly a year. Now it was autumn again, the time when she usually started a new project of some kind. Last year the project had been herself. She would ask the therapist if it was time for her to stop. Surely she must have other clients wanting the space. The therapist began to talk about all the painful ways in which Marion had experienced the termination of relationships. She had fled from two violent partners, run away from her parents' home, and been forced to leave the one foster home where she had been reasonably happy. Marion insisted that this was very different. She wanted to do some evening classes and get on with her life. She had a good home now, lots of friends and even her son had shaped up a bit. The therapist looked dubious but agreed that they make a tentative plan to finish in the next few weeks. At the next session, Marion said she had been thinking. Perhaps it was a bit soon to stop. She would continue to make therapy her project for the moment, if that was still all right with the therapist. Marion paused, ready to defend her apparent lack of decisiveness but the other woman seemed happy enough to agree to her plan.

What are the alternatives?

This subject will, inevitably, be addressed at the completion stage. However, if clients express disappointment and dissatisfaction during an earlier review, it is advisable to raise the possibility of other therapeutic options. If clients are empowered with choice, then their freely given assent to continue is likely to benefit future sessions. Alternative options are always available,

and practitioners are well advised to demonstrate a non-defensive acceptance of the benefits of groupwork, family therapy, co-counselling and
finally, returning to life outside psychological therapy (see Table 1).

The benefit of 'viewing psychotherapy as an episodic service rather than as a
"one shot" deal in which relapse is equated with failure' (Culverwell *et al.*
1994) is not generally promoted. Peake, Borduin and Archer (1988: 13)
describe the psychotherapist as 'a healer who makes interventions at sympto-
matic junctures in the life cycles of individuals and families'. This relaxed
and modest conception of the practice of psychological therapy was pres-
aged by Franz Alexander in 1946, against the background of a rigid
psychoanalytic orthodoxy within which the superior efficacy of long-term
and frequent analysis was not questioned.

> During an interruption the patient learns which of his previous difficulties
> he still retains, and the following interviews usually center around those
> emotional problems in which he needs further help. The author of this
> section has used the method of one or more preparatory interruptions
> almost exclusively during the last twelve years (the interruptions varying
> in length from one to eighteen months) and has found that the analysis
> after interruption has, without exception, become much more intensive,
> accomplishing more in the following few weeks [of once-a-week psycho-
> therapy] than had been achieved in months before.
>
> (Alexander and French 1946: 36)

One of the alternative options to be discussed on completion of the time-
extended commitment is that clients may indeed be taking a break to
engage with their lives, and test out their new learning and any self-transformation which has been achieved. The offer of follow-up sessions, after a
reasonable length of time, is nearly always attractive to clients, and offers
the practitioner an opportunity to evaluate the previous work.

> Jane arrived five minutes late for her last session with the counsellor. She
> had never been late before although this punctuality had been paid for
> by anxious clock-watching during lectures. She was surprised to find
> herself so calm as she explained that she had been obliged to stay until
> the end of the seminar because it had been her presentation. The
> counsellor smiled and said that, for some people, arriving late might
> almost be seen as some sort of cure! Jane realised that she was indeed
> less obsessionally punctual, just as she had learnt to tolerate a less than
> perfectly tidy home. She told the counsellor that she would miss her and
> handed over the carefully chosen thank-you present she had prepared.
> They discussed what Jane would miss most, and how she could support
> herself during the next year. Jane sounded wistful as she described being
> confident that she would be all right, most of the time. She would miss
> the feedback. The counsellor asked if she would like to book in for a

'check-up' session, in about four months' time. Jane was delighted with this suggestion. She had assumed that there was no alternative to a complete goodbye. Once again the counsellor seemed to be demonstrating that rules could be bent.

How shall we work together now?

Whether a client is leaving with a plan to return to the same practitioner, or continuing after the review session, this question can be explored fully within the setting of an ongoing and mutual commitment. It is a reminder that the process of therapeutic sessions is as important as the content. Practitioners of psychological therapy will have been trained to observe process but the acuteness of clients' observations, with regard to what has been going on in the therapeutic relationship, can still be a surprise. This is well demonstrated by the experiment in mutual record-keeping carried out by Yalom with his client, Ginny Elkin (Yalom and Elkin 1974). Too often reviews are concentrated upon *what* has been the focus of the work rather than *how* that focus has been applied. Practitioners can obtain valuable feedback regarding the methodology they are using, and may be encouraged to expand their approach or even to question the limitations imposed by their theoretical orientation. 'The greater the number of approaches that the therapist can handle the wider the range of patients he or she will be able to help'.   (Frank 1985: 74).

Have the goalposts changed?

As weeks, or months, pass by, there is a danger that any achievements made have become so much part of a client's self-image that they are discounted. Some clients lose sight of their original wish to complete, while others may be limiting their progress to the resolution of an unrealistic desire for complete self-actualisation. To some extent, working within a goal-oriented and focused approach to psychological therapy may have induced these unrealistic expectations. Review sessions, during a continuing therapeutic engagement, provide an occasion to record, and even celebrate, progress made, as well as to accept the imperfect and unfinished nature of all self-development. Clients can be encouraged towards a more generous acknowledgement of seemingly small shifts in the way they view their worlds and interact within their social network. From this base they can plan further extensions of their personal strengths and look forward cautiously to an increased sense of well-being.

During the second college year, Peter started going out with another student, a lively young woman who was also a member of the Students Union fell-walking club. She was warm and loving, determined to get

Peter 'out of his shell'. He enjoyed all the attention she gave him, and felt comfortable in her arms, but he disliked the constant evenings out with her friends which seemed so important to her. The counsellor pointed out that Peter had made a considerable shift in letting himself enjoy a close sexual relationship. He reminded Peter that a year ago he had been timid with all women. He suggested that they concentrate now on the difficulty of competing with male rivals. Peter looked alarmed. He had been trying to ignore his jealous fantasies.

The four closing sessions offer an extended opportunity to prepare for the vicissitudes of life without psychological therapy. The prospect of future re-engagement in formal psychological therapy can be discussed and or a follow-up appointment can be agreed. All this should not detract from a relaxed acceptance that, both inside and outside the psychotherapeutic frame, clients will be, at some level, engaging in 'psychological growth toward a socialised maturity' (Rogers and Stevens 1967: 103). Client and practitioner have worked together on this endeavour for a time-extended but finite period. Hopefully, the client has made some progress and the practitioner has learnt from their place on the sidelines. Now the client will continue their life process of psychological evolution (see Table 2) in other settings, perhaps working through the next stage without professional help or possibly returning to the working alliance in some form.

It was Tim's last session before the planned break. He told the psycho-therapist that he felt as if he was going on holiday. He had expected her to laugh and encourage him in this cheerful fantasy so he was taken aback when she asked him about his attitude to psychotherapy. Was it like going back to school? Did he have to 'qualify' in some way? They discussed Tim's underlying anxiety about getting it right for his father. Tim decided he would spend the summer without trying to please anybody. This turned out to be more difficult than he had expected. He became fascinated by how difficult it was for him to know what he really wanted for himself, when there was anybody else around. He looked forward to the autumn. It would be good to 'work on' this issue. He missed the small lively woman with the gentle eyes in spite of her use of psychobabble.

SUMMARY

In this chapter, the time-extended commitment has been differentiated from the other ways of working within a time-conscious and focused approach to psychological therapy. Always a continuation of the preliminary sessions of the mini-commitment, this level of commitment is agreed between practi-tioner and client through a process of assessment and review culminating in the first review (see Table 1). The need for four sessions to close down an ongoing commitment forms part of the explicit agreement to work together without a fixed closing date. Throughout the chapter, the six steps for every commitment (see Table 4) have been considered in the light of this more open-ended approach to psychological therapy. Advantages, disadvantages and complexities have been delineated. Working over an extended time with a motivated client offers particular opportunities for a fuller exploration of their personal history and current problematic issues.

As with the time-focused commitment, practitioners are urged to define and then refine their clients' insight into a 'central issue' (Mann 1973, 1981), so that clients can understand and work through the 'present and chronically endured pain' (Mann 1981: 36) which brought them to psychological therapy. This focal theme is likely to be encapsulated within the specific stage or stages of the client's life process of psychological evolution (see Table 2). Some clients are able, within the extended time of the commitment, to progress through more than one of these life process stages. Others may use the time to disclose their story in full, to work gradually through a deeply cathartic experience, or to use the therapeutic relationship as a reparative experience leading to responsible self-care and eventual renunciation of survival strategies which have become dysfunctional.

Constant reviews culminating in a second major review (see Table 1) are advised for those working in this open-ended commitment. Practitioners have been reminded of the benefits to clients of time out from psychological therapy. Within these parameters, the time-extended commitment is of service to clients with whom the working alliance is firmly established and who possess enough motivation and insight to stay with difficulties that arise, if only for four closing sessions.

Chapter 8

The time-expanded commitment
'A direction, not a destination'

> Trials never end, of course. Unhappiness and misfortune are bound to occur as long as people live, but there is a feeling now, that was not here before, and is not just on the surface of things, but penetrates all the way through: We've won it. It's going to get better now. You can sort of tell these things.
>
> (Pirsig 1976: 403)

So Pirsig concludes his account of the transformative journey on a motorcycle he undertook with his son. While not intended as a description of the outcome of a time-expanded commitment, this passage conveys well enough the open, flexible and realistic optimism towards which client and practitioner travel together in this particular therapeutic journey. Indeed it is likely to be as replete with risk and uncertainty as any motorcycle ride. Appropriate only for a minority among those seeking psychological therapy, this level of commitment is chosen by those clients who have demonstrated, both during the intake process and during the mini-commitment sessions, their wish 'to be that self which one truly is' (Kierkegaard 1941: 29). They realise that this will mean working through profound levels of dis-ease and discomfort. They may already have used psychological therapy, and other forms of self-development, and are often functioning more than adequately in their external lives. Some are involved in a helping profession, perhaps themselves using some form of psychological therapy in the service of others. Others are successful careerists who have become aware of a fundamental emptiness, a basic dissatisfaction with their lives. This latter group have often experienced a recent crisis in their lives which has been worked through but has shaken their self-image. To some degree, they have begun to question their *being* in relation to their *doing*.

The precepts of Carl Rogers (1961), Rollo May (1989) and Martin Buber (1970) are particularly appropriate for practitioners working within a time-expanded commitment. They have translated the hard realism of European existentialist philosophy into a practice of psychological therapy which is idealistic, optimistic and appropriate for clients aspiring to 'the good life' of the 'fully functioning person' (Rogers 1961: 183). However, to work with clients questioning their own hard-won ego strength, practitioners need to be able to discern, without flinching, hidden areas of shame, rage, desire and dependency, as they erupt into the therapeutic relationship. For this the more empathic and non-defensive transformations of psychoanalytic theory and methodology are necessary. One of the most clearly delineated integrations of these two theoretical orientations can be found in the work of Michael Kahn (1991), which has informed this chapter:

> they have introduced a hugely important middle way between the schools of warm support and those of neutral transference analysis, a middle way that combines the advantages of warm engagement with the advantages of working actively with the relationship itself.
>
> (Kahn 1991: 14–15)

The time-expanded commitment has been defined as an agreement, between client and practitioner, to meet, at least once a week, for up to four to five years, with regular reviews and with a clear understanding that at least two months will be needed to come to a mutually agreed conclusion (see Table 1). On both sides, this is a somewhat momentous commitment, although the implications are not always fully discussed at the beginning. The preliminary sessions of the mini-commitment offer practitioners an opportunity to think ahead as far as possible. Are they likely to be practising in the same place, or within the same agency, for the next few years? What verbal agreements need to be put in place with regard to absences, holidays and cancellations? How realistic and durable are the financial obligations entered into? These clients are engaging in a therapeutic engagement which may outlast the practitioner's present employment in an agency, or which may be affected by increases in private practice fees. In considering carefully these pragmatic resource constraints on an offer of time-expanded engagement, practitioners may find themselves reshaping their offer of psychological therapy into an offer to work in a time-extended format.

The differences between an *expanded* and an *extended* commitment are as follows:

1 The self-transformative aims of this therapeutic commitment are clearly but tentatively formulated and may be re-visioned and expanded at any time. (In an extended commitment, goals are specific.)
2 The expanded duration of therapeutic commitment is addressed only with regard to the closing agreement. This is seen as a safeguard against premature closure, and as a signal of respect for the expansive nature of the transformatory work envisaged. (In an extended commitment, the question of closure is regularly revisited, and linked to the achievement of specified goals.)

3 Clients have previously worked through the three earlier stages of an expanded life process of psychological evolution (see Table 2), usually with another practitioner. Both practitioners and clients are aware that elements of preparation, disclosure and catharsis may be recycled in the service of the focal themes appropriate to the final stages of self-care, renunciation and empowerment. (In an extended commitment, only one stage, or a part of one stage may be worked on intensively, so as to enable a return to external life for further self-development.)

4 External pressure for clients to change their behaviours has been replaced by internal stress arising from feelings of painful dissatisfaction and inauthenticity. These can sometimes border on despair, although there is genuine optimism regarding self-transformation and *expansion*. (In an extended commitment, clients are likely to be focused upon the interpersonal challenges of external life.)

Once launched into a time-expanded commitment, regular reviews are necessary to maintain and renew the initial sense of direction. It is at these times that the focal theme is reinstated, examined for relevance and perhaps itself transformed into a more global interpretation of underlying patterns of thought, feeling and behaviour. This revised 'central issue' (Mann 1973) will be closely linked to that previously formulated, but will increasingly be revealed in all its subtlety as a personalised version of the universal human predicament, described succinctly by Rollo May:

> That person needs to find his or her true self, and this is accomplished by arriving at some degree of unity of consciousness with the unconscious levels of childhood experience, the deeper levels of the collective unconscious and ultimately with that source of his mind which is in the very structure of the universe.
>
> (May 1989: 27)

The client who enters a time-expanded psychotherapeutic venture may have plumbed the depths of personal degradation and/or scaled the heights of successful social integration. Now they seek, in Rogers's words, to 'achieve a spontaneous, existential and creative inner freedom' (Rogers and Stevens 1967). Once again, the six steps for every commitment can be used to track and monitor the course of this process.

Step 1: Making contact – the working alliance is an emotional bond

Not only does the full emotional engagement of a working alliance have to be maintained throughout time-expanded psychological therapy, but it will need to become more profound in order to withstand the darker reaches of terror, rage and despair of an ego under threat. Emphasis is on what Rogers (Rogers and Stevens 1967: 89) describes as 'the *quality* of the interpersonal encounter with the client which is the most significant element in determining effectiveness'. In this same passage, Rogers is, as in most of his influential writings, referring to 'professional work involving relationships with people'. Rogers himself does not specify different modalities of the 'interpersonal encounter' or therapeutic relationship. Nevertheless, these 'attitudinal or experiential elements' which Rogers believed were necessary in order to 'make a relationship a growth-promoting climate' (Rogers and Stevens 1967: 90) fit the working alliance rather than the real relationship (See Chapter 3, Table 2 and Gelso and Carter 1985), as far as the practice of psychological therapy is concerned. Where there is no distinction made between professional partnership and person-to-person contact, the potentially therapeutic conditions of empathy, congruence and non-possessive warmth can become confused with personal friendship.

> Ayesha had enjoyed her first few sessions with this therapist. She liked and respected the quiet little woman with her sharp sense of humour. Ayesha told her new partner how relieved she was to find a psychoanalytical therapist who appeared relaxed and tolerant about lesbianism. She had expected to defend her newly found sexual orientation but the therapist seemed totally unsurprised, interested but in no way questioning Ayesha's celebration of her own and her partner's bodies. Ayesha began to imagine asking the therapist to dinner. She pictured a cosy candle-lit scene, with the intrusive tensions between her partner and herself dissolving away under the wise blessing of the older woman. At the next session, she introduced this idea as a semi-humorous suggestion, her joking words negated by the tautness of her body. The therapist said, firmly and calmly, that she appreciated the invitation but did not feel it would be helpful to Ayesha's work with her. She paused as Ayesha swallowed back the tears in her throat and agreed, hastily and angrily, that it had been a daft idea. Of course she had not really meant it seriously. She began to describe the latest quarrel between Jane and herself. She blamed herself completely. She would never get it right, and maybe they should split up right now. The therapist asked if she noticed the similarity between the two situations. Ayesha had so much love to offer and found every boundary set up by her partner and by her therapist threatening and life-denying. Ayesha's stiff formal posture changed as she curled into the armchair sobbing like a rejected child.

Who are you, and where am I?

While Rogers includes, as one of these optimal conditions for psychotherapeutic growth, the positive attitudes and accurate perceptions of clients themselves, he nevertheless places most emphasis on the practitioner's level of awareness. In specifying the overriding importance of quality in a therapeutic relationship between client and practitioner, he had, in Kahn's view, 'placed no particular importance on encouraging the client to attend to and discuss the relationship with the therapist, nor had he given any weight to consideration of the unconscious' (Kahn 1991: 14). It is this deliberate and active use of the ebb and flow of feelings and thoughts as they influence the quality of interpersonal contact which informs the best of psychoanalytic psychotherapy. Working with a time-expanded relationship, the practitioner's awareness of subtle shifts in recognition and perception between the two participants becomes crucial. There is a danger that the prospect of a lengthy therapeutic engagement might encourage client as well as practitioner to adopt the 'tendency towards passivity' (Malan 1975: 8) already cited in Chapter 2. Asking this question of 'Who are you, and where am I?' at first silently, and then sharing their tentatively formulated impressions, practitioners engage their clients in active and immediate understanding of repetitive transference patterns.

> Duncan was pleased that he had decided to continue with therapy. He could relax now, knowing that the therapist would provide him with insights into his unhappiness. He even looked forward to these being painful to hear. He needed to be whipped into shape. He knew he had always been a weak and selfish bastard. His first wife had told him that. He was surprised to find the first session of their new arrangement to be so unsatisfactory. The male therapist was quiet and alert, but said very little. He seemed to be watching Duncan closely, and be content to confirm whatever Duncan said. Duncan began to feel indignant. He did not wish to pay out good money, even though he could well afford it, just to be echoed. His tones became more clipped. He told the therapist about his heavy work schedule and his need to keep his colleagues off his back. The therapist suddenly asked if Duncan felt threatened at this very moment. Duncan started to deny the other man's insight, and then fell silent. He gazed miserably at the therapist. Yes, he felt competitive and discounted, determined not to be outwitted by the man opposite. As he admitted this, he noticed again how warm the therapist's eyes seemed to be. He felt attracted and yet scared. He realised that it was easier to keep other men at bay by competing with them.

Do we like each other, and does it matter?

As with the time-extended commitment, for a practitioner to enter an open-ended therapeutic engagement without feeling some positive feelings of warmth and acceptance would be to risk re-traumatisation of the client and failure of the working alliance. Increasingly, writers (Peck 1978; Lomas 1987) have suggested that any substantial psychotherapeutic work needs to be supported by 'love as equivalent to the theologian's term *agape*, and not in its usual romantic and possessive meanings . . . a kind of liking which has strength and which is not demanding' (Rogers and Stevens 1967: 94). Should we, with Lomas (1987: 146) 'take it for granted that practitioners will hope to act towards their patients with honour and love and not make an issue of it (lesser words, such as caring, liking, warmth, compassion, may be substituted for love but this does not alter the argument)'? The danger is that this assumption can become soft and sentimental, too easily adopted as a credo. If they genuinely feel this enduring degree of positive regard, practitioners are able to weather periods of weariness, discomfort and distaste.

> At the next session, Ayesha used the time almost exclusively to complain about her work setting. She described her boss as an impatient critical woman, who seemed only to be interested in the power politics of the institution and not to care about the clients. The therapist made links to Ayesha's own experiences of institutional politics, since her childhood in the children's home. Ayesha appeared to discount any possibility of a personal pattern, returning again and again to her manager's lack of sensitivity and abrasive relationships with the office staff. The therapist suddenly yawned. Ayesha stopped speaking and looked down at her feet. She felt humiliated and panicky. She was boring the other woman with office politics instead of getting on with the therapy. Maybe the therapist would really like to get rid of her. The therapist apologised, frankly admitting that she had lost concentration. She said that she realised how painful it must be for Ayesha to have to deal with mistakes in her therapist as well as her boss. Ayesha looked up. The other woman looked warm, gentle and sad. She had expected the brisk defensiveness and bright false smile with which her boss met Ayesha's criticisms. Once again, she allowed herself to imagine that this woman really cared for her, even when she was being an unrewarding client.

It helps to be aware of the difference between *doing* and *being*, and to be clear that psychotherapeutic love is directed towards a client's essential nature rather than towards their behaviours. Whether there needs to be a mutuality of this form of love for psychological therapy to be most successful, as posited by Lomas (1987: 146), is more doubtful. It has been suggested by Brazier (1993: 89) that a client's 'need to love' is even more fundamental than their need to be loved, hence the extraordinary forbearance shown by many mistreated children towards their parents. For such clients to prematurely display a similar unconditional love to their therapists may be to extend their early confusion between loyalty and justice. Probably such shared warmth and respect belongs only to the final stages of a long-term therapeutic engagement, and is a manifestation of a real relationship, and of the client's generally increased ability 'to love and to work' (Freud 1964).

Do we trust each other enough?

In contrast, the continuing existence of mutual trust between client and practitioner is a crucial component of all successful psychological therapy. Clients who choose, in full awareness, a time-expanded commitment are already demonstrating trust in the therapeutic process. This will be tested and is likely to veer between dependency and apprehension as the fundamental nature of the transformation attempted is revealed.

> Duncan told the therapist about his most disturbing repetitive dream. These always involved a group of dark figures beneath a fire escape. They were absorbed in some private ritual, centring upon someone who lay prone and motionless on the ground. In his dream, Duncan would creep up, peering between their shoulders, dreading to see the face of their victim. He would wake up, cold and sweating, knowing that it was probably himself laid out for sacrifice. He hesitated for a long time. Then he blurted out the most shameful thing about the dream. He would always be sexually aroused as well as scared, with an urgent desire to relieve himself by masturbating. Duncan prepared himself for the therapist's distaste and contempt. He looked forward to it. He despised this side of himself. Strangely, the therapist seemed to understand both his self-disgust and his erotic enjoyment of the murky nightmare. He found it hard to believe that this shameful fantasy should be acceptable and even begin to make sense as a part of his inner life.

Practitioners need, above all, to trust in their long-term client's ability to survive profound depression and searing anxiety. This means holding to a fundamental optimism, containing their own misgivings and retaining a basic belief in the psychotherapeutic process.

Step 2: Testing the commitment – the working alliance is contractual

The emphasis on a warmly positive, empathic and authentic relationship should not be read to imply that the time-expanded commitment is any less in need of clear professional boundaries. If anything, the journey embarked upon depends upon the vehicle of consistent and clear arrangements regarding time, place, duration and, where appropriate, cost, just as Pirsig's journey (1974) was dependent upon a well-maintained motorcycle.

What do you require of me professionally?

Working over a time-expanded period, clients need to remain very clear about their professional rights as a consumer of a psychological service. They have entered into an agreement by which the practitioner has promised to remain professionally available, as far as possible, for a considerable length of time. Reasonable arrangements have been put in place for any breaks in the therapeutic engagement whether planned or unplanned. Over time, and particularly when working through a powerful primitive transference reaction to the authority figures of early childhood, clients may lose their own sense of authority within the professional engagement. They can become 'client' upon the practitioner in the more ancient definitions of the word, as 'hanger-on, led-captain, parasite, satellite, camp-follower' or even 'protégé(e), ward, charge, nursling, foster-child' (*Roget's Thesaurus*). At these times, exploration of this theme can be used as a gentle reminder of a client's autonomy and of the practitioner's role as ally and consultant. Changes of venue, appointment times and sudden cancellations are all issues which need careful discussion and which are opportunities for practitioners to display the *non-defensiveness* which Kahn (1991: 15) has described as the *sine qua non*, the crucial component without which nothing is likely to be accomplished.

Initially, it had been difficult for the therapist to find a space in her clinical caseload for Ayesha. She was well known in the area, especially to other psychotherapists and counsellors, and Ayesha had to wait several weeks for a permanent space in the week to be made available to her. Now she was embarked on an agreed period of long-term psychotherapy with one of the most respected therapists in the city. Unfortunately her appointment time was the last one of the day for the therapist, and this meant Ayesha staying on late at her office at the end of her own busiest day. She would drive back to the suburbs after her session, usually feeling emotional, hungry and physically drained. For several months she endured this pattern, telling herself, and her worried partner, how fortunate she was to have found such a good therapist. What did one stressful evening a week matter? She and Jane began to have arguments about this. Jane suggested that she come into town by bus that evening so that she could drive Ayesha home. Ayesha felt her privacy was being invaded and her ability to cope questioned. She explained this to the therapist as an example of her long-term resistance to any form of dependency. She remembered how deskilled and childlike she had been in her marriage, and the ways she had used alcohol to desensitise herself, only to find herself even more incompetent and incoherent. Ayesha was surprised that the therapist seemed initially more concerned with the immediate problem. She got out her diary and began to search through the crowded pages. She offered Ayesha another appointment time, which would become available in three weeks' time. It was at the end of the afternoon, and would fit in well with Ayesha's work schedule. In the meantime, she suggested that Ayesha take up Jane's offer. They could still work on the therapeutic implications of doing so. She reminded Ayesha that this important work needed her health and energy. Ayesha felt embarrassed and pleased by the careful consideration she was being shown.

What do I ask of you as a client?

In offering an expanded commitment to a client, practitioners have been advised to practice some form of selection, even if their theoretical background influences them otherwise. These criteria have already been spelt out in the introduction to this chapter. Clients entering upon this journey towards self-realisation are likely to possess enough stability in their external lives to fulfil their side of the professional bargain. They expect to be able to attend sessions on a regular basis, and to give several weeks', or months', notice of their wish or need to end therapeutic engagement. During the first months, occasional discussion about these arrangements is useful both as a reminder and as an opportunity to monitor how clients are experiencing this level of commitment. These practical components of a long-term therapy relationship demonstrate a client's high investment in psychological evolution. If this begins to fade then the professional contractual agreement is also likely to falter. Nevertheless, practitioners must hold a balance between sensitivity to possible hidden motives for altering appointments and realistic acceptance of the external demands of a client's life.

Step 3: Expectations and pitfalls

Since self-transformation is a process of becoming rather than an end in itself, any discussion about outcome, desirable or undesirable, of this expanded engagement in psychological therapy is transformed into a contemplation of the journey so far.

What do you hope to gain?

Over time the answer to this question is likely to shift back and forth. Consistently, clients, exploring themselves with this intensity, demonstrate a profound and universal human wish to know themselves and to experience true peace in mind and spirit. At other times, clients seem to be concerned only to achieve a trouble-free domestic life, or more career satisfaction. The continuum between psychotherapy and spiritual search has been questioned by many. Needleman describes the wish for evolution in the form of self-knowledge as follows:

> Thus it is not a question of acquiring strength, independence, self-esteem, security, 'meaningful relationships,' or any of the other goods upon which the social order is based and which have been identified as the components of psychological health. It is solely a matter of digesting

deep impressions of myself as I actually am from moment to moment: a disconnected, helpless collection of impulses and reactions, a being of disharmonized mind, feeling and instinct.

(Needleman 1983: 15)

At this interface between personal stability and what can be experienced as almost total disintegration of identity, practitioners can assist clients by reminding them that psychological therapy exists to assist them in establishing a more real sense of self through 'an *expanded* sense of what they can feel or do' (Welwood 1983: 46). When this search reaches beyond the work of psychotherapy, which is to integrate and 'to heal the self-defeating splits between different parts *within ourselves'*, then it may be better for a client to seek, within an overtly spiritual teaching, a way to 'dissolve the fortress of "I", and heal *our split from life as a whole'* (Welwood 1983: 47).

> Joanna started visiting the alternative book shop in the covered mall every Saturday. She had wandered in there one morning, bored with shopping and entranced with the casual unhurried atmosphere of the shop. There was a little restaurant at the back and most of the customers seemed to consider it perfectly normal to take a book to browse through as they had their coffees or herbal teas. There was a big notice-board which advertised local events including the meetings of a thriving Buddhist society. Joanna went to one or two, finding them interesting but somewhat naive. She was critical of their view of emotion as something to be perceived and let go rather than expressed fully. Her own experience of therapy had led to her being more open and expressive with her friends, and she valued her increased sense of authenticity. Talking to other members of the Buddhist group, she realised that they were actually questioning the value of having a strong sense of self. This was intriguing.

What was your previous experience of psychological change?

The trouble with making any neat distinction between psychotherapy and spiritual search is that, once out of immediate psychological pain, it is easy to imagine being en route to the distant peaks of spiritual realisation. Looking back on previous times of crisis and distress can illuminate ways in which repetitive patterns still hold sway over responses to stressful situations. It is still possible to fall down the same 'hole in the sidewalk' (Nelson 1985), particularly where clients believe themselves to have achieved some sort of final and permanent psychotherapeutic cure, or consider themselves to be fully analysed. Looking back at previous work also offers clients an opportunity to acknowledge real changes that have taken place in their external lives, and to accept continuing areas of dissatisfaction. The concrete challenges of everyday life can then be used as part of the development of heightened self-awareness rather than being split off and disowned in a narcissistic search for personal salvation (Lasch 1978).

What do you fear?

A distinguishing characteristic of many clients committed to a longer-term search for self-realisation is that they are often more wary of the dangerous side-effects of psychological therapy. They have already worked on themselves and have realised how painful it is to re-experience the raw immediacy of primitive emotions. They realise how their friends, families and partners may feel excluded and threatened by their commitment to a private process of intensive self-examination. Some will have been disappointed in their previous experiences of psychotherapy or counselling. Practitioners can themselves feel threatened by the expertise of previous professional helpers and may be tempted to collude with these criticisms. Only if there has been a clear breach of professional ethics should any response beyond a warm empathic interest in the client's subjective experience be necessary. Whatever the fears expressed, these can be brought back to the surface during the regular review sessions recommended for this level of commitment.

> As time went by Duncan began to question his allegiance to Alcoholics Anonymous. The groups seemed less supportive and he was tired of the constant demand to tell his story. He wanted to move on. He told the therapist that he had been shouted at by three women in the group, accused of being a male abuser because he had questioned the motivation of one of them. He had felt lonely and unjustly accused. Nobody had come to his defence. He wondered now if he should complain to somebody. The therapist agreed that it must have been a painful and isolating experience. Once again, he must have felt scapegoated, just as he had experienced in his schooldays. The therapist asked what ground rules had been established for the group. Could Duncan have referred to these? Duncan remembered that there was a 'no blame' rule. He wondered why he had not invoked this. He realised that his long experience as a respected member of AA had broken down in the pain of being thrust back into the outsider role of his childhood. He knew very well how to approach the women in the group next week. Perhaps he had been checking that the therapist was on his side, unlike his schoolmaster father.

How will you stop yourself getting what you want?

Once again, clients with experience of previous psychological therapy are likely to know their own tricks of avoidance and denial. These will have been explored at intake and during the mini-commitment sessions. However, as clients move into a different stage in the life process of psychological evolution the strategy for avoidance is likely to change. A client may have disclosed, and re-experienced in emotional catharsis, their previous formative experiences. They no longer avoid discussing the past and can express their feelings, but they may now be adopting a victim position, continuously recycling their genuinely sad story and blaming the past for present difficulties. In this way they are stopping themselves from taking responsibility for their lives, being alert for script-like patterns of interaction and, where possible, changing their responses. Working over an expanded time-span, practitioners need to develop a sharp awareness of what is not being addressed in the way of psychological development.

> Ayesha had been using the couch with her therapist for most of the year. This had been satisfying at the beginning. She had revisited her experiences at the children's home, with new understanding of her continuing vulnerability to any hint of abandonment. She had realised for the first time that she had never questioned her parents' lack of contact. Now she knew that they probably could have visited her, but had never chosen to do so. She realised how eager she had been to forgive them. She became obsessed with their betrayal. She talked of herself as 'an abandoned child' and used this in her arguments with Jane. Her partner was accused of being cruel to this 'inner child' whenever she questioned Ayesha's wish to control all their domestic arrangements. Ayesha told the therapist that she had decided never again to let herself be hurt. She had told Jane this, she declared triumphantly. The therapist remarked quietly that Ayesha seemed to have decided to opt out of a real relationship. Ayesha was shocked into shrill dismay. What did the therapist mean? She was only looking after herself. The therapist said calmly that all adult love involved risk and pain as well as pleasure. Maybe Ayesha was hoping that Jane would become a second mother to her. Ayesha felt angry and exposed. She had not wanted to admit to her longing to be mothered.

Step 4: Telling 'the story' – entering into the client's life process

To revisit the past in order to relinquish its grip, reframe the present and move into a more authentic future is the massive transformation sought by most clients committing themselves to an expanded period of psychological therapy. Practitioners working with these clients can assist by finding a focal theme which runs through from past to present and which is influencing their aims for the future.

What brought you here?

When pressure to change is internally motivated, clients are less likely to present clear-cut problematic situations which they wish to resolve. More usual is a gradual buildup of dissatisfaction and frustration with the way they themselves are responding to everyday events. Very often, these self-criticisms are not echoed by their friends, families or partners. At most, other people will comment on some evidence of tension or irritability. These clients have learnt to cope, well enough, with the difficult business of living, and may lead an enjoyable life for much of the time. What they bring to the therapy sessions are their hidden tensions, the moments when they feel cut off from their loved ones, and their uneasy perceptions of their own inauthenticity. These confessions can only emerge when clients sense practitioners to be fully accepting and non-judgemental.

> Ayesha and her partner returned from a long summer holiday. They had reached a new plateau of understanding and commitment to each other. Ayesha was brown and relaxed as she lay on the therapist's couch. She mused about her good fortune, the way she was surrounded by friends, had a loving partner and a reasonable relationship with her adult children. How had all this happened? She did not feel that she had the right to so much when there were people in the world with nothing, not even food and shelter. The therapist commented on Ayesha's unease, her need to examine everything, including her own happiness. Ayesha agreed. It made her feel safer not to take anything for granted. The therapist said that perhaps Ayesha would always need to be watchful, ready in case her security was suddenly removed, as it had been in the past. She sounded calm and matter of fact. Ayesha felt the rebellious despair rise up for a moment. She had raged so often against the way she seemed trapped by the past. The therapist's voice had been warm and affirmative. Ayesha relaxed again. She talked about the wise person she wanted to become. The therapist remarked that Ayesha had already developed a 'wise child' who had learnt from the past and who seemed to be protecting her in the present. Ayesha was silent, sad for the premature wisdom thrust upon herself when she had been young, trusting and optimistic, and yet grateful for the reformulation offered her. She left the session feeling more substantial, grounded and ready for the next part of her life.

Where have you been?

As clients become more aware of the masks, the facades behind which they seem to be trapped, so they seek to discover the origins of these false selves. If childhood stories are retold, now with a more acute understanding of the messages behind the history, clients can begin to understand the power of the early conditioning. Complex and subtle patterns of response were formed at a pre-verbal stage of development and are now firmly attached to a self-concept seemingly impervious to any rational decision to be otherwise.

Rogers (1959) has described the gradual replacement of the real self with the false self as a child attempts to meet the conditions of worth attached to their caretakers' love and respect. Kohut (1971) describes how the repression and frustration, in infancy, of normal needs for enough praise and recognition for their uniqueness can lead individuals, in adulthood, into an uneasy sense of failure and despair.

> The person then is likely to suffer from insecurity and feelings of worthlessness, interrupted on occasion by surges of unrealistic grandiosity and, in some cases, maladaptive boasting when these powerful needs for mirroring burst momentarily through the barrier of repression and futilely strive for some crumbs of gratification. Thus a necessary structure of the *self* is stunted.
>
> (Kahn 1991: 86)

How was it for you then?

This explanation of present patterns of emotional distress based on a reconstruction of the past could become a purely intellectual exercise for many clients. For others it could lead to a futile and powerless attempt to sit in judgement on those early caretakers. By demonstrating compassion and empathy for the impressionable children their clients once were, practitioners can encourage clients to become increasingly in touch with the elementary longings and impulses they experienced in infancy. Once acknowledged within the therapeutic relationship and setting, these can be expressed in all their unrefined vigour. Over time, the release of energy experienced may begin to influence external relationships as clients become more aware, genuine and spontaneous in their inter-personal exchanges. For some clients, this level of personal transformation may be highly disruptive to the lifestyle they have built up. As they work through the life process stage of empowerment, they will need support in restructuring their relationships and recontracting with the external social system (see Table 2). The quiet background presence of their long-term therapist or counsellor can provide continuing validation for this process.

> Duncan had started challenging other members of the AA group and had even had an angry quarrel with his mentor. He realised that he had been accepting other people's views of himself even when they did not ring true. He was seen by his friends as a helpful man, always available at the end of the telephone. At work he was seen as a willing workhorse, not a high flyer but worth his substantial salary because he was so reliable. Until recently, he had accepted his role as a permanent bachelor, useful to his many women friends as a shoulder to cry on, an occasional partner to some social event. Duncan raged about all these roles to the

therapist. He demanded that he be loved for himself, and be accepted as a potent and creative man. Duncan stopped, looking longingly at the man opposite. The therapist suggested he stand up and repeat his demands loudly and assertively. Duncan hesitated, his hands began to shake and he looked down at his feet. The therapist asked whose gaze he was avoiding. Duncan mumbled something about not making a fool of himself in front of another man. Slowly he looked up. The therapist's eyes were warm, accepting and attentive. Duncan stood up.

Step 5: Working with the focal theme for this stage

It has already been suggested that clients engaged in the expanded commitment are likely to have worked through several of the life process stages described in Table 2. The task of the practitioner working over time with a client, whose aim is to achieve some fundamental personal transformation, is to remain in touch with the focal theme appropriate to the work in hand. This does not mean that there will be a different strategy for survival revealed at every stage, but that the concerns being addressed may present a different facet of what has been the central issue. External events or the distressing memories aroused may require some recycling of issues appropriate to an earlier stage. Returning regularly to the questions listed below will clarify and re-focus client and practitioner.

What keeps happening again and again?

As with the more time-conscious commitments, the repetitive pattern will have been identified as a central issue for therapeutic work during the mini-commitment sessions. Clients engaged in a time-expanded commitment may have become fully aware of these recurring situations during previous periods of personal development. However, over a lengthy period of therapeutic engagement, the focal theme, the continuously repeated attempt to survive stressful situations using an outdated strategy, can become blurred. Meanwhile, as the relationship between client and practitioner increases in significance over time, it will provide ideal conditions for the repetition of 'strategies for survival' formed with past significant figures.

> At the moment of the existential encounter between therapist and client, the client's whole world is present. All of the clients' significant past relationships, all their most basic hopes and fears, are there and are focused upon the therapist. If we can make it possible for them to become aware of their world coming to rest in us, and if we can be there, fully there, to receive their awareness and respond to it, the relationship cannot help but become therapeutic.
>
> (Kahn 1991: 160)

Here Kahn is referring to the healing effect of re-experiencing an intense emotion, which has been painfully repressed until this moment, and which now can be released in the presence of an interested, non-defensive and benevolent practitioner.

> Ayesha had resigned from her job. She had decided to take up an offer of part-time teaching work at the local college and had agreed to supervise the voluntary workers for a drug and alcohol advisory service. At first she was euphoric, arriving at the therapist's door with flushed cheeks and shining eyes. She looked forward to being at home more, able to enjoy her home with Jane and to see her friends for coffee whenever she wanted. Gradually, her enthusiasm died. She began to feel unsure and scared. The therapist was even more silent than usual. Ayesha stared at the ceiling. She would have to be practical now. Would she be able to afford these sessions? She began to talk about terminating the therapy. The therapist commented on Ayesha's dismal tone of voice and the tension in her shoulders. She seemed to be bracing herself against something. Was it the prospect of a lonely and unsupported future? Ayesha did not have to be reminded that this was a familiar experience for her. She had left her marital home with nothing. She had fought for her children's custody. She had been homeless for a time. The therapist gently asked her if she needed to recreate a desert landscape again so as to affirm her undoubted courage and independence. Ayesha sat up on the couch, and swung round towards the therapist. Then she spoke slowly and clearly. She did not have to do it alone any longer.

If this is the pattern, how was it learnt?

Once again, there may be clients who already realise that these distressful patterns of interaction were learnt as strategies for survival, either in infancy, or during a traumatic period of their lives. Other clients may not have such a clear picture of the logic behind a pattern which is a source of pain and dissatisfaction in their present lives. In either case, there is now time to elaborate this understanding, to increase compassion for their earlier selves and, in due course, to move from judgement towards insightful acceptance of the past. This latter task belongs to the stage of renunciation described in Table 2, and should be approached carefully. Acceptance and forgiveness belong first to the 'inner child'. Only when there is a protective adult in place and any punitive inner monitor, or superego, silenced should it be extended to those who originally caused the pain.

> Duncan struggled with his recognition that his father had failed him when he was a boy. He had a reasonable relationship with his father now, visiting him at weekends in the retirement home. His father seemed

weak and old, almost pathetically grateful for Duncan's attention. It was surely wrong to blame him for the past. His AA re-education had emphasised his own weakness and his need to seek help from a 'higher power'. The therapist nodded. He suggested that, as a vulnerable little boy, Duncan had learnt to blame himself rather than question the way his much admired human father had used 'higher power'. Duncan felt confused. Maybe he would have to reconsider his present belief system as well as his understanding of the past. This was going to take a long time.

What do you need to re-learn?

It is often when sufficient behavioural change has taken place to ensure a reasonable level of coexistence in society that the pervasive influence of early learning experiences becomes sickeningly apparent. Clients may be enjoying more satisfying working lives and healthier interpersonal relationships. However, under stress, the original self-protective patterns re-emerge, now in the form of suppressed thoughts and feelings. What started as an conscious wish to express warmth towards another person is mysteriously converted into a complex struggle for control or a manipulative attempt to achieve praise. It is these intra-psychic experiences which clients bring to the time-expanded setting, seeking to extend their internal psychological health, without risking their external well-being. This may mean questioning more deeply their fundamental belief system, formed within the original powerful influences of family, culture and social system.

Ayesha had been born into an Anglo-Indian family. Even after she had been placed in the children's home by her parents, her aunts and uncles had continued to send her cards and presents on her birthday, at Easter and at Christmas. Their insistence on elaborate family parties with all the best china and cutlery laid out on a damask tablecloth was enshrined in Ayesha's memory. She approached each Christmas as an arduous undertaking for which she was solely responsible. Even though her children were now adults, with their own partners and families, Ayesha agonised about the size of the new flat she shared with Jane. Surely they would all have come over for Christmas if she had still lived in the large shabby house where she had spent most of her life as a single mother. She was angry with Jane for gleefully planning an elegant Christmas meal for two, with smoked salmon and pheasant rather than an over-large and unnecessary turkey meal. The therapist commented that Ayesha had been brought up to believe that Christmas should be for others. Ayesha argued that surely this was right. It was a time for unselfishness, for giving to others. Her voice was shrill and defensive. The therapist agreed that this was a highly principled way of viewing Christmas.

Ayesha hesitated. Her indignant moral stance began to fade. She closed her eyes and tried to listen to herself. She realised that she was scared of being lonely without her family around her. Why had she not explained this to Jane? Her elder daughter had asked them both to stay, but Ayesha had dismissed this invitation at once. Once again she had chosen loneliness rather than any hint of dependency.

So what work is needed now?

Having discovered an almost unconsciously held set of beliefs, clients may feel helpless. They perceive themselves to be 'driven' by compulsions to 'Please People', to be 'Strong' or 'Perfect', to 'Hurry Up' or to 'Try Hard' (Lapworth, Sills and Fish 1993: 95). These positive reinforcements are often harder to dismiss than all the harshest of early criticisms or threats. Other people praise their ability to achieve, to persist and to nurture. It is left to the practitioner to offer an expanded opportunity for clients to allow full awareness of their real needs to surface. By allowing these to arise and be expressed in the presence of this trusted, and yet peripheral, *other person*, clients can re-examine their lives and consider areas which might still need changing. More importantly, they can begin to reclaim the energy used to suppress these disowned and shadowy aspects of their characters.

Duncan had been away on a business trip. He returned triumphant. He had attended a conference and given the keynote speech. He had been controversial, amusing and passionate. His colleagues had crowded round him afterwards, asking questions and obviously surprised into admiration. He had met a woman who found him attractive and they had slept together. As Duncan described these events, his voice began to waver. He avoided the therapist's eyes and seemed not to be aware of the other man's interest and pleasure. When the therapist remarked that Duncan had changed his role with his colleagues as well as breaching the years of celibacy, Duncan looked alarmed. He protested that he still had a long way to go. He knew he would always be an alcoholic and he still found it difficult to say no to others. He was basically weak and easily influenced. The therapist commented that Duncan seemed scared of his own strength and power. Duncan laughed and relaxed as he described himself as a reluctant rival.

Step 6: Reviewing the commitment – past and future

As with all the commitments outlined in this book, regular reviews are useful to clients engaged in a time-expanded period of psychological therapy. Each natural break provided by a holiday, a time of sickness, or any other absence, provides an opportunity to discuss what is being achieved by the weeks and months of regular meetings, and to examine what is being missed.

Shall we continue?

Within the increased security of long-term psychological therapy, this question may, paradoxically, be perceived as a threat. The major disadvantage of having no closing date to work towards is that the wish to 'restore infantile omnipotence and, with it, timelessness' already cited (Mann 1973: 9) may seem realistic. Yet, at an adult level, clients will be aware that this therapeutic engagement is not eternal. By questioning the purpose of continuing, client and practitioner can revisit and reformulate the broad aims sketched out during preliminary sessions. If these have become unrealistic, this is an opportunity to recognise the fact and reshape aspirations.

> During the fourth year of therapy, Duncan began writing a book for children. He was excited and inspired. He attended a writing workshop and then joined a writers' group. They met once a month to discuss their work. He was introduced to a woman who illustrated children's books. She agreed to do some work for this book, and they became friends and then lovers. Duncan struggled with his fear that he would make another disastrous relationship. He talked through every nuance with the therapist. He had just decided that they could move in together when she became pregnant. Duncan was angry. He felt tricked and trapped. He asked the therapist to tell him what to do, and became even more angry because the other man responded with agreement that these events were forcing Duncan to make some difficult decisions. He reminded Duncan that they had decided to continue for another year in order to work on Duncan's newly found autonomy. Now he was asking his therapist to make choices for him. It seemed that it would be some time before Duncan could be comfortable with his newly realised potency. Duncan frowned and then grinned. This was true, on all counts. He began to discuss his fear of failing as a father. He did not want his own son to feel neglected and unloved.

For some clients, the question of continuation may be even more relevant. These are those who have realised that such a long-term commitment is not really what they want. Here the two months' notice may need to be invoked, or even reconsidered. Clients who change their minds after a few months will appreciate serious consideration of their change of direction. Any exploration of their reluctance to continue must be combined with respectful acceptance of their right to close down this period of self-development over a period of weeks rather than months.

What are the alternatives?

At some point, even the most rewarding and long-lasting of healing relationships must draw to a close. Otherwise there is a danger that the professional encounter becomes too central in a client's life. Time is needed to discuss, well in advance of completion, how clients plan to replace the sessions and find their self-support and environmental supports (see Table 2) in their external lives. Have they achieved and restructured their external relationships and partnerships? Have they confronted and recontracted with their external social system? Will they now move on to use other forms of therapy, or peer support, or a sustaining social network? All these focal tasks belong to the final empowerment stage of the life process of psychological evolution described in Table 2. Not all clients engaged in a time-expanded commitment will have reached this stage. Some will have worked intensively on the focal tasks of an earlier stage of this life process over a lengthy period of time, and are now ready for a break. They may return for a more time-limited period in the future, or they may wish to continue their personal development elsewhere.

Ayesha had entered her third year of therapy. Looking back, she mused upon the difference between her three therapists. Her first counsellor had been the same age as herself, a practical and insightful woman whose challenges had shocked her out of a slide into alcoholism and self-damaging violence. The group therapist had been a quiet and authoritative man, who had encouraged her to recognise her own potential as a sensitive and imaginative person with the ability to help others. Only with this present therapist had she been able to bring together her vulnerability with her strength. Now she was able to allow herself to accept some care from others without losing her precious sense of self-reliance. She still felt driven, at times, by her need to prove herself to others, but this was less of a problem. She wondered if the time had come for a break.

Up to this point, there has been an assumption that these clients are ending a reasonably successful period of time-expanded psychological therapy, for which they were accurately assessed to be suitable. Of course there may be other clients with whom practitioners have worked over a long period of time because of the considerable amount of stress and disturbance in their clients' lives. These external pressures have made it difficult for clear arrangements to be made as to length of commitment, and psychological therapy may now need to be extended into another setting. In these situations, group therapy, as an alternative to individual work, should be introduced as early as possible.

Many humanist and psychodynamic approaches to psychotherapy or counselling foster a progression to groupwork, or the use of groupwork in conjunction with individual therapy. Hans Cohn (1986) uses with his clients a carefully structured, and theoretically sound, developmental progression from the one-to-one re-working of early dyadic relationships to the sibling or peer relationships offered by a combination of group and individual therapy. Cohn (1986: 329) works long term but 'except in a few special cases' suggests to his clients that they join one of his own therapy groups 'after no less than six months of individual therapy and no more than eighteen months'. In due course, individual sessions are reduced and then closed down while group therapy continues, with the whole process lasting 'between four to five years'. This model of psychoanalytically oriented therapy, 'concerned with certain existential aspects of psychotherapy' (Cohn 1986: 328) is a model of well-thought-out long-term psychological therapy. In settings where a cognitive-behavioural approach is employed, clients are unlikely to be offered such long-term involvement as is described by the time-expanded commitment. However, when a distressed and traumatised individual has, by default, remained in virtually unbroken therapeutic contact, practitioners might consider using groupwork in combination with a more clearly time-focused individual therapy.

> Ayesha's therapist had offered her a place in her own therapy group. Ayesha was torn between feeling pleased and doubtful. She did not relish sharing this wise little woman with other people. In many ways she would prefer to do without therapy altogether. On the other hand, she knew that she had a history of leaving situations abruptly and suffering traumatic feelings of rejection and abandonment. The cost of the weekly group would be less, and she had recently been struggling with the financial problems inherent in being self-employed. Ayesha decided she would accept the offer of a place in the group. The therapist had said something about a chance to re-examine her feelings about her younger sister. She knew now how jealous she had been that her little sister had stayed at home with her parents. Ayesha winced away from the knowledge that she might now want feel like the therapist's favourite child.

How shall we work together now?

An important function of any review session is that an opportunity is given to step outside of the therapeutic process in order to examine its nature. While practitioners will have been making observations of non-verbal interactions throughout, in this working alliance mode, clients can be given an opportunity to become more aware of the interactional patterns which may have built up. The lengthier the period of therapeutic engagement, the further both participants are likely to be from the first fresh observations of their early contact. Renewing the freshness of encounter, permitting critical feedback and extending mutual awareness are essential to maintain the momentum of continuing therapeutic engagement. If, on the other hand, the review process has led to a decision to discontinue the expanded commitment, then even more attention to process will be needed during the weeks of disengagement and closure. Clients are likely to re-experience problematic thoughts and feelings which appeared to have been worked through long ago. It is as if they need, out of awareness, to test out their new understanding against old strategies for survival, while still in the therapeutic frame. By remaining calm, containing and, when necessary, challenging these outdated patterns, a practitioner demonstrates faith in their client's increased authenticity.

> Now that the individual sessions were definitely coming to an end, Ayesha became increasingly critical of the therapist. The little woman could be irritatingly passive and quiet. She did not seem interested in Ayesha's recent quarrels with the other lecturers at the college. When the therapist did comment on Ayesha's complaints about the head of department and her cronies, she seemed always to emphasise Ayesha's tendency to suspect all authority figures and to suppress her own feelings of rivalry and ambition. She stormed at the therapist that she was fed up with being pathologised. Surely this was a time to offer Ayesha some support rather than to criticise her and accuse her of childish jealousy and envy. The therapist said she was aware that Ayesha was very angry. She asked if Ayesha was feeling scared and lonely as well. Ayesha stopped shouting and sat back in her chair. She felt exposed, vulnerable and understood. She began to describe how much she hated new situations, and how anxious she was about joining the group.

Have the goalposts changed?

For clients who seek to become a 'more fully functioning person' (Rogers 1961: 191–2), impending completion brings into question the realistic likelihood of ever achieving this aim. While accepting that psychological evolution is always an ongoing journey, some recognition of achievements and lasting changes is necessary for nearly all clients, and satisfying to most practitioners. Clients realise how ways of being and doing which once seemed unobtainable are now part of their normal functioning selves. The nature of their *real selves* may still be mysterious but they possess an increased awareness of their responses to the people and situations they encounter. This heightened sensitivity may be uncomfortable at times but it has been allowed and fully accepted within the therapeutic alliance. They will already have experimented with this new sense of self in their external life situations. Now they will be on their own, without the regular therapeutic sessions. During the last weeks of psychological therapy, practitioners can encourage a realistic reframing of the future, checking that environmental supports are in place and that external relationships are reasonably healthy.

> It was Duncan's last session with the therapist. He felt pleased with himself, and only a little sad. He gave the therapist a book of Auden's poems. He said he realised that he would have hesitated to do this a year ago because reading poetry written by a known homosexual might not be considered a manly thing to do. Now he wanted to share his favourite poems with the other man. He had marked the ones he particularly liked. He felt hopeful about the future but realised that it would some-times be tough. He asked if he could return for a session in six months' time, to report on progress. He would be a father himself then. He might need some advice. The therapist smiled warmly. He would always be very interested to hear how Duncan was getting on. Duncan's eyes filled with tears. He knew this was true and he also knew how much he had longed for his father to say those words when he was a boy. He had left home long ago, but this felt like the real thing.

SUMMARY

In this chapter, a fourth and final choice of commitment to psychological therapy has been examined. The time-expanded commitment has been described as an agreement between client and practitioner to engage, for an unspecified length of time, in a searching and wide-ranging process of facilitated psychological evolution. To commit themselves to this work, clients and practitioners must be highly motivated, and be reasonably confident that they can realistically offer such an investment of time and energy. For clients, or for agencies, there will also be financial considera-tions. It has been suggested that this choice of commitment is likely to benefit only that minority of clients who seek a profound and life-changing therapeutic experience. They will have demonstrated their determination and expressed their hopes, comparatively clearly, during assessment and mini-commitment sessions.

Although brought into the psychotherapeutic setting by at least one 'serious and meaningful problem' (Rogers 1961: 282), these clients are likely to be functioning adequately enough, from an external point of view, to maintain such a longstanding therapeutic engagement. Their main motiva-tion is based on a deeply personal sense of internal unease even where external changes are sought. The expanded time needed is represented by an agreement that at least two months will be needed to close down and complete the work. Clients engaging in this form of psychotherapeutic commitment are likely to reformulate their aims as time passes. Regular reviews are encouraged and it is probable that clients will work through the three later stages in a life process of psychological evolution, as proposed in

Table 2. The overlap between this type of psychological therapy and spiritual search has been tentatively explored and practitioners recommended to refer their clients to a more overtly spiritual practice and teaching when an authentic enough level of self-awareness has been established.

Chapter 9

Nine clients in search of psychological evolution

Overarching issues for practitioners using a time-conscious approach

Any attempt to provide a relatively clear and integrative approach to psychological therapy is likely to be incomplete. In the preceding chapters practitioners have been introduced to a process of structured commitment-making in the form of a flexible 'flow-chart' progression of negotiated agreements regarding the length of time and possible outcome (see Table 1). The emphasis throughout has been on accurate initial assessment and continuous reviews for which a checklist has been provided in Table 3a. An emphatic argument has been made for the episodic nature of all forms of psychological therapy which highlights the peripheral position of all practitioners of psychological therapy. Each client's life process of psychological evolution has been conceptualised as inevitable, central and independent of any particular practitioner's expertise. Practitioners are required to judge, with humility and sensitivity, where and how to enter this lifelong process.

To aid them in their search for a correct entry point, a stage model has been proposed to demonstrate the progression in psychological change and personal development applicable to a wide range of psychotherapy and counselling clients (see Table 2). Central to this process is the gradual discovery and elaboration of a focal theme, or 'central issue' (Mann 1973) arising from survival strategies, now outdated and largely dysfunctional. Linked into the model is the mode of therapeutic relationship likely to assist and inform the practitioner's understanding of the focal task relevant to the client's stage of psychological evolution. Assessment and review have been envisioned as a shared process between client and practitioner, at the initial intake interview and at regular intervals or choice points throughout the therapeutic engagement. The four major categories of commitment delineated in Table 1 have been elaborated at length and illustrated by fictional case examples which extend throughout the book.

In this chapter, the reader is invited to consider some of the implications and meta-considerations which span the terrain explored through this approach. There are concerns which seem to go beyond these four main

themes of assessment, contractual commitment, stages of personal development and therapeutic relationship. Also incomplete are the *stories* of the
fictional clients whose encounters with practitioners have been used as
illustrative scenarios throughout the previous chapters. In an attempt to
tackle both types of 'unfinished business' (Perls, Hefferline and Goodman
1951: 140), these overarching issues are now discussed through the stories
of these nine fictional consumers of psychological therapy. Although none
of these characters represent any one real person, they are, of course,
based on a very large group of courageous individuals who have
sought out and used some form of psychological therapy, and whose
experiences, together with those of their practitioners, has led to this
book being written. Inevitably, some of the opinions expressed in this
chapter, and throughout the book, are also based on personal experience
and observation, gained during a reasonably wide-ranging experience
within the profession of psychological therapy, as provider and consumer.

LIFE PROCESS OR THERAPEUTIC PROCESS? – JOANNA'S STORY

Although the centrality of the client's life is emphasised throughout this
book, it is the practitioner's encounter with their client's process of
psychological evolution that is highlighted. Inevitably there has been an
under-emphasis on ways in which clients move through stages of personal
development during the times when they are not working with a practitioner
of psychological therapy. Any of the 'stages' outlined in Table 2 could be
worked through by clients as they experience the challenges provided by
their external lives.

Joanna is an example of a client whose encounter with psychological
therapy is brief and, initially, unsatisfactory. In Chapter 3, Joanna encounters a male practitioner whose theoretical orientation and training seems to
have been broadly humanistic. He tries to work with her in an open and
friendly manner, relying on the warmth and congruence of his approach to
establish a therapeutic relationship which he believes to be sufficient to
effect healing. He does not establish a clearly structured working alliance,
nor does he become aware of the rapid development of transference as
Joanna attaches to the therapist all the dependency, anger and disappointed
love that she feels towards her dead father. In the context of Chapter 3,
these scenarios are used to support the argument that all competent practitioners need to be aware of the three components of the therapeutic
relationship likely to be influencing what is going on between client and
practitioner at all times. Gelso and Carter (1985: 192) hold that most
'therapeutic failures can be accounted for by under-attention to a given
component in a particular case'. In this case too much attention was given

to a warm and friendly real relationship and too little to the burgeoning transference relationship which could have been contained by establishing a strong and clear working alliance. Within this container, the male therapist could have followed his humanistic orientation by gently challenging the transference and thus more overtly 'providing a climate' within which Joanna could move naturally towards discovering 'the utmost freedom to become herself' (Rogers 1961: 185). As for the stages categorised in Table 2, Joanna begins to trust this therapist and to do some preparation stage work on current problem areas, but this tentative exploration is halted by the breakdown of the therapeutic relationship.

Joanna moves from over-idealisation to disillusionment in quite a short time, and has no inclination to take up the proffered referral to a woman counsellor. She lives 'for several years' (p. 87) with her feelings of grief and rejection, gradually increasing her self-understanding through applying to herself some of the ideas she finds in books about psychology. No doubt she moves through experiences in her external life which validate her insights about herself and which enable her to independently prepare herself for the disclosure and catharsis stages (see Table 2). It is several years before she tries again to make use of psychological therapy through contacting a woman practitioner with 'letters after her name' (p. 87). Joanna has become discriminating and cautious, much more of an informed consumer of psychotherapy.

With this second therapist, Joanna moves rapidly to a broader understanding of the roots of her depressive episodes, especially with her realisation of her denied experience of being motherless. The therapist shows awareness of transference issues from the beginning, tackling first her own clumsiness in suggesting a male therapist and ignoring Joanna's sensitivity to rejection (see Chapter 5). She responds to Joanna's fear of dependency by offering brief focused therapy (see Chapter 6), and then proceeds by consistently highlighting the central issue of Joanna's repeated experience of abandonment through her mother's absence, haphazard and inconsistent caretaking by her father and his mistresses, followed by her father's early death. After rapid work on the disclosure stage, Joanna appears to have enough ego-strength to benefit from an intense but brief catharsis experience, and to return to her external life with increased energy and emotional awareness to engage in less formal forms of personal development.

Joanna's story illustrates the episodic nature of much psychological therapy. She found a practitioner who was prepared to enter into a businesslike agreement to make herself 'obsolete as soon as possible' (Cummings 1986: 430). This reasonably satisfactory encounter with the practice of psychological therapy is likely to encourage Joanna to make use of this resource again, if and when she perceives a need. She already has developed close and confiding friendships which are likely to provide enough therapeutic support for her in the future. Within this friendship circle, and possibly through her experiences of romantic love and her working life, Joanna will have opportunities to complete her own self-care and renunciation tasks. She has some interest in joining a therapy group, but this is likely to remain a somewhat distant option unless her present supportive network breaks down or her abandonment issues become restimulated in some way. When she does become interested in joining a group of some kind, it may be one involved with spiritual search rather than purely self-empowerment.

DOES THEORETICAL ORIENTATION MATTER? JANE'S STORY

Throughout this book, a case is made for practitioners using a focused, committed and time-conscious approach whatever theoretical orientation they espouse. The major theories all use different languages to demonstrate the roots of human unhappiness, the nature of psychological evolution and the manner in which psychological therapy can provide healing. A considerable body of research has demonstrated that effective and competent psychological therapy does not belong to one particular orientation (Luborsky *et al.* 1975, Sloane *et al.* 1975, Smith and Glass 1977, Lambert 1986). However, theoretical explanations are better understood as powerful myths by which practitioners derive meaning for their work. Practitioners operate best if they are working within a theoretical understanding which matches their own fundamental belief systems and their cultural backgrounds.

Jane's therapeutic experience with her counsellor does not depend on the counsellor's own theory of psychological change but on her persistent efforts to maintain a clear and warm working relationship throughout Jane's first year at university. Jane herself has experienced a more analytic type of psychotherapy during her hospital admission. Although this had been a disappointing experience, she is initially suspicious of engaging with a counsellor from a non-medical background. The counsellor is encouraged by her supervisor to offer a trust-inspiring and clearly articulated working alliance (see Chapter 2). Once engaged, Jane enjoys the novelty of the counsellor's practical approach to problem-solving which she realises is very different from the preoccupations of the analytic psychotherapist. The difference turns out to be in emphasis because the counsellor also encourages Jane to discover the childhood roots of her anxious and obsessional coping strategies. Although her relationship with her mother is constantly attended to by Jane and her counsellor, the transference relationship is never overtly unpacked. This particular practitioner seems more comfortable with helping Jane to recognise the way her childhood experiences are being transferred on to the stresses of her present lifestyle. It is possible to speculate that, if the time-extended commitment offered to Jane (see Chapter 7) had become more time-expanded, the neurotic elements of the transference might have had an impact on the relationship between counsellor and client. Certainly, it seems likely that Jane would continue to be suspicious of people who were not as rule-bound as herself. In this area she appears, by the last session, to be considering her counsellor's flexibility as a possible model for her future self-development.

The overall message from Jane's story is that she was helped by being offered a contractual commitment within which she could negotiate a therapeutic engagement that offered her security without making her feel dependent. She appears to benefit from the steady focus on survival strategies arising from her childhood experiences, and from freedom to discuss and negotiate the closing date. This final meeting becomes, for Jane, a symbol of completion to work towards, and the last four sessions are fully used to prepare for a break from therapeutic engagement. Together, practitioner and client have progressed through the stages of preparation, disclosure, catharsis and self-care. The counsellor would have been deriving meaning and support from her own theoretical persuasion but this remains peripheral in importance to Jane at this stage. Since Jane is studying the social sciences, it is reasonable to speculate that she will spend some of her second year at university reading about some aspect of applied psychology. This might lead her to reflect upon the theoretical explanation for her own process of change, or even lead her back into another episode of psychological therapy.

The theorists quoted in support of this approach are affiliated to a wide range of orientations, from cognitive behavioural (Peake, Borduin and Archer 1988, de Shazer 1988, Talmon 1990, Cade and O'Hanlon 1993) to psychoanalytic reformists (Alexander and French 1946, Mann 1973) and modern integrationists of existential humanism, ego psychology and object relations theory (Ryle 1990, Kahn 1991). It should be possible for a practitioner to remain loyal to their own theoretical affiliation, to think and talk about their work within their usual parameters, and still to use the structures proposed by this approach, and encapsulated in Tables 1–4. For instance, Jane's counsellor might have limited her interventions to cognitive-behavioural problem-solving, translating the central issue into an irrational belief arising from childhood conditioning and reinforced by Jane's present lifestyle and the demands of an academic setting. Instead she uses an approach indicative of an integration of cognitive-behavioural and psychoanalytic understandings which are cogently framed by the way she uses contractual commitment and a focal theme within a curative relationship.

ASSESSMENT OR SELECTION? PETER'S STORY

Throughout this book the importance of sensitive and accurate assessment by the practitioner has been emphasised. This is a continuing process with each review session providing another opportunity of assessing the usefulness of the therapeutic engagement, revisiting and revising aims and the agreed terms of the contractual commitment. Wherever possible, clients are invited to share in this review process, although the major responsibility lies with practitioners. Assessment is very often presumed to be synonymous with selection. It is this aspect of an initial interview which can alienate prospective clients and be seen as an unpleasant responsibility by many practitioners, to be avoided if possible.

In Chapter 2, practitioners are guided through a series of progressive choice points (see Table 1) whereby selection is broadened. At each point, practitioners are urged to consider which therapeutic engagement is appropriate, available and acceptable to this client at this particular point in time. At the initial intake interview, practitioners strive to judge accurately whether a potential client is, on the one hand, in crisis or 'visiting', or, on the other, willing to engage in some form of contractual commitment. Whatever the outcome of this decision-making process, practitioners can proceed by making some sort of offer. People who are in crisis are given straightforward support and advice about available resources, and then invited to return for one or two follow-up sessions in the near future. People who seem to be, at this point in time, only speculatively interested in utilising psychological therapy for themselves, can also be offered one or two sessions, probably on a weekly basis, to explore the reality of therapeutic engagement and inspire any latent motivation to continue. Those individuals who are clearly willing to engage in psychological therapy, if only temporarily, are offered the ubiquitous mini-commitment, to be followed by an offer of further engagement, selected from the three main types of commitment. The practitioner is, therefore, working to select the most fitting contractual offer for this client at this time, rather than seeking to select out, or exclude, clients as unsuitable for treatment. A refinement of this initial assessment process, described and demonstrated by the more radical revisions of Talmon (1990), is the offer of the *single-session therapy*, made at the outset of the initial interview. The keynote of Talmon's approach, as with the contractual process outlined throughout this book, is flexibility and openness to adaptation and to any change in opinion of client or practitioner.

Peter's initial encounter with psychological therapy is delineated in Chapter 4 (p. 50) as an example of a badly conducted assessment interview. The woman counsellor he meets is set upon making a therapeutic contract. She misses, or misreads, Peter's rapidly escalating sense of crisis and imminent psychotic breakdown. She presumes him to be defensive and controlling, rather than perceiving his panicky need for containment and advice. Peter leaves the session early, alarmed and increasingly losing touch with reality. He lands up in the casualty ward of a hospital where he is fortunate in encountering a sympathetic and pragmatic young doctor who gives him the temporary sanctuary he needs. Psychiatry is kind to Peter, and he progresses through to attendance at a day centre and enrolment in higher education. There he is once again assessed, this time by a shrewd but informal male counsellor, the 'friendly Irishman' (see Chapters 4 and 7), who takes him on as a client.

The counsellor shows great sensitivity in his relaxed acceptance of Peter's recent psychotic experiences, choosing initially to offer practical befriending to the lonely young man. He realises that Peter needs to re-enter the world of consensual normality and to shed the stigma of his recent involvement with psychiatry. When Peter responds to the counsellor's warmth and steady interest, which includes a value-free acceptance of his recent hallucinatory experiences, the counsellor offers him a time-extended therapeutic commitment. Peter and his counsellor are shown engaging in a subtle process of ongoing assessment and selection. Peter decides that he feels safe enough with this counsellor, and is able to reframe the counselling process as supportive of his autonomy as well as his need. The counsellor decides that Peter will be able to benefit from gentle exploration of the historical reasons for his recent psychosis, and for his continuing experience of psychological distress. He combines this with some stress management training which helps Peter to control his panic attacks. A less experienced or a more cautious practitioner might have offered Peter a more time-limited commitment with specific focus on coping strategies. He would probably have benefited from such an offer, although not so profoundly, and would initially have enjoyed a break from being a mental health service user.

Peter continues into a second year of counselling, surviving the disruption of his counsellor's unexpected sick leave. He is consistently reminded of the contractual boundaries of the arrangement, and knows that he can always call a halt to the process by invoking the four-sessions closing agreement. This closing session is not described in Chapter 7 but it is likely that, as Peter's social life becomes more settled and he can manage his sexual relationships without too much alarm, he will decide to finish with the counselling sessions. In any case, his time at college will draw to a close and his counsellor will encourage him to move on in his life as a reasonably normal young adult with unusual gifts of imagination and imagery. If conventional selection criteria had been rigidly applied, Peter might have been excluded from any offer of counselling or of insight-based psychotherapy. He could have been considered 'too fragile' for the latter and too much of a psychiatric out-patient for the former. Counsellors working with clients like Peter need to keep in close touch with their medical advisors, so that their use of medication can be monitored and gradually terminated, where appropriate.

CLIENT OR CULTURE, WHICH NEEDS TO BE HEALED? MARION'S STORY

A consistent criticism made by the critics of psychological therapy (see Chapter 1) is that reforming energy is deflected from social ills to individual discomfort. This can become a way of blaming and stigmatising individuals for lack of self-responsibility, deviance and weakness. It has been suggested that the project of the self has been enshrined by the modern cult of individualism and given a spurious reality (Foucault 1976, Giddens 1991) which conceals the real nature of modern industrial society. By extolling a fragile independence and attacking the family and thence, the cultural, religious and tribal traditions which have sustained communities in the past, psychological therapists increase the alienation and hypocrisy of an unjust society. In particular, psychotherapy stands accused of pathologising the individual by seeking out causes for human distress in childhood experiences rather than tackling the real traumas of adult life. Another milder criticism is that the vast majority of psychological therapy is carried out with individuals, and does not attempt to engage with the complex series of contexts within which the therapeutic engagement is taking place.

In the approach outlined in this book, practitioners are consistently advised to understand their work with clients as peripheral to the realities of life outside psychological therapy. Individual users of psychotherapy or counselling are portrayed as being engaged in a temporary project whereby they hope to understand better how to tackle the difficult 'business of being human' (Gilmore 1973), and from which they emerge not changed but with more effective strategies for survival. The existence and persistence of real injustice, prejudice and inhumanity is seen as the background within which individuals who seek out psychological therapy have grown up, been wounded and are now surviving. If, as Masson (1989) argues, ordinary human friendship were enough to help fight an unjust society, then it would be better to invest all the energy of psychological knowledge in community projects, peer groups and the development of some form of co-counselling (Heron 1979).

This argument founders on what seems to be a persistent demand for some sort of personal re-education through psychological therapy by some individuals, albeit a minority. They recognise that their present struggle to live co-operatively and authentically with their fellow human beings is experienced as unsatisfactory and unsuccessful. While this may be true of many others, these individuals have reached a point of critical transition, often expressed through some external crisis or problematic situation. At some level, they seek another opportunity, a second chance, to form or re-form their identity through interpersonal contact, moving through the dyadic developmental experience before returning to the larger group. This self-educative experience requires the neutrality of professionalism to contain the vulnerability and necessary regression attached to most episodes of mature learning. The difficulty is for the professional partner in this dyad to maintain humility and respect for the other person involved in this project. There is a temptation to adopt a permanent parentalism, to defend against personal inadequacy and to over-inflate the importance of the practitioner, the theory or the methodology.

Marion's story is of a woman who has experienced much of the injustice in human society. She was brought up in a working-class home where the pressures of economic inequity contributed to the inarticulate violence of her father and the dependency of her mother. While very young, Marion learns quickly that survival depends on pleasing and appeasing males, and that females, of which she is one, are weak, despicable and disposable. To be a female child in this family was to be used and blamed. Her encounter with middle-class morality was equally humiliating. For a short time she was questioned by male doctors and social workers about her sexual experience with her grandfather. She sensed, correctly, their embarrassment and distaste, which she attributed entirely to her own culpability. At 14 Marion rebels against this social conditioning by leaving home early only to repeat the learnt pattern of subservience to male domination. She is used and abused by several men, only breaking with this cycle when her child is put at risk.

At this point, Marion seeks out psychological therapy (see Chapter 2). As she has been taught from childhood, she ascribes blame to herself. She wants to change herself, not the social world in which she lives. To engage her in psychological therapy at this stage would be to engage in the victim-blaming and useless introspection cited by many critics of psychotherapy (Pilgrim 1992). The practitioner she encounters does not fall into this trap. Marion is given useful information and referred to a supportive and consciousness-raising peer group of women who had survived similar injustices. When Marion next searches for psychological therapy, some years later, it is because she is finding her internal lack of self-esteem is blocking her from accepting a management post within the community centre where she works. This is a centre for women who, like Marion, have suffered abuse within a male-dominated society. Marion has moved from being a survivor within a hostile culture to being a reformer and a champion of other former victims. She understands fully that the obstacles to her progress lie in her own habitual attitudes. She is now ready to work with a therapist to explore, understand, challenge and develop her self-image within a therapeutic relationship.

In spite of her undoubted motivation, Marion finds psychological therapy a struggle from the very beginning. She dislikes the woman therapist to whom she has been referred and, at first, this antipathy is mutual (see Chapter 3). There are issues arising from the real relationship, differences in class and culture, which are probably intensified by Marion's memories of middle-class doctors and social workers, and even by a re-activation of her understandable distrust of and disappointment in her unprotective mother. The therapist is a quiet restrained woman who is abstinent in her expression of emotion while Marion's depressed and defeated mother was unable to speak up for herself. However, their professional relationship survives, with the support of good supervision. Marion and the therapist achieve a reasonable enough working alliance to move through the trust building stage of preparation. While still engaged in the preliminary sessions of mini-commitment (see Chapter 5) Marion battles through disclosure to the emotional re-experiencing of the catharsis stage (see Table 2). This rapid progress might have persuaded another practitioner to offer Marion a brief time-focused commitment. This would have been a mistake. Marion's toughness hides her vulnerability to rejection and criticism. The offer of any form of time-limited contractual agreement, so soon after revealing her deepest feeling of grief and rage, would have damaged the grudging trust and respect she had developed towards the practitioner whom she still 'did not really like' (p. 88) and endangered her aim of achieving intrapsychic levels of self-care (see Table 2).

Throughout the therapeutic process, the different social experiences of client and practitioner are evident. The woman therapist displays several failures in empathy very typical of the precarious position of a practitioner working with clients whose problematic issues lie on the margin between social reform and self-development. It could reasonably be argued that Marion would have made better and faster progress with a woman whose life story had been similar to her own. Certainly there would have been easier rapport and more shared warmth in the therapeutic relationship. The disadvantage of too closely shared a background might, however, have led to a comfortable series of sessions where the enemy outside became focal rather than Marion's own inner sabotage. With time, the active insistence of the therapist on exploring the dynamic behind Marion's interpersonal behaviour pays off. Marion makes crucial contact with the core issue which underlies her continuing lack of self-esteem and undermines her social relationships.

In Chapter 7, the time-extended commitment between Marion and her therapist is shown as persisting in spite of Marion's impulses towards a different type of self-improvement project. The therapist seems to be guarding against any premature exit although she remains consistent in using the closing agreement to structure her management of Marion's proposed departures. Marion is a fast worker and has enough independence of spirit to insist upon completion when she is sure that she has had enough therapy. She will, by that time, have released enough energy and personal strength to provide the leadership needed for her external work and emerging political ambitions.

SHORT-TERM OR SHORT-CHANGED? JUDY'S STORY

The most frequently asserted criticism of a structured and time-conscious approach to psychological therapy is that it is unsuitable for the 'fragile' individuals who present psychological distress in the form of 'addictions, psychosis, severe personality disorders and suicidal acting out' (Butler and Low 1993). Even one of these characteristics would be cited as a sufficient criterion for exclusion by many practitioners, including some who specialise in brief psychotherapy (Crits-Christoph and Barber 1991). These clients usually have a longstanding history of critical incidents culminating in some form of hospitalisation or medical intervention. The received and popular wisdom among most psychotherapists and counsellors is that for these 'damaged' individuals only the offer of long-term and open-ended psycho-analytic therapy is appropriate. Some even argue that to offer any form of time-limited commitment is in itself abusive of clients who have experienced traumatic events and whose ego-strength is demonstrably lacking.

This belief runs counter to the pragmatic realities which these clients face when they are at their most distressed and dysfunctional. They are depen-dent upon the limited resources of the mental health services which they encounter. Their current level of dysfunctional behaviour means that they are unlikely to be supported by their own funding, and any funding provided by their relatives may well be hedged with less than therapeutic conditions. In Britain, this mismatch between the recommended long-term treatment with psychoanalytic psychotherapy and its availability has led to the National Health Service (NHS) preferring to fund brief behavioural and cognitive interventions to enable clients to cope better with their lives. Until recently, this pragmatic solution often concealed a weary acceptance that this was a second-best resolution of the situation. The development of Cognitive Analytic Therapy (CAT) by Ryle (1990) has boldly challenged this belief by arguing that, in working with personality-disordered and disruptive patients, 'the time limit represents a safety net for both patient and therapist' and that after 'rapidly establishing an effective working alliance . . . these severely damaged individuals usually have the capacity to observe and reflect upon themselves' (Ryle 1990: 123) within the sixteen weeks of a CAT contract. This structured and assisted reflection within a supportive therapeutic relationship leads towards changes in behaviour and emotional distress which may enable these clients to become functional within their social environment. Once socially and financially independent, these short-term clients may choose to return for longer-term psychological therapy.

Judy is a young woman with self-damaging and suicidal behaviours who has been assessed as unsuitable by the psychoanalytically oriented psycho-therapy department of the hospital to which she has been admitted. She is referred to a psychiatric social worker 'for informal befriending' (see Chapter 2). This practitioner has not been given the powerful integrative tools developed by Ryle (1990) and his colleagues, but she steadily and swiftly engages Judy in a highly structured but flexible commitment to psychological therapy. In Chapter 4, the social worker's use of structured assessment and review is given as a working example of the checklist approach to assessment and review demonstrated in Table 3a. The fact that her work is labelled as 'counselling', and perceived by the social worker herself as preparation for longer-term psychotherapy, does not detract from the profound nature of Judy's self-development during this period. The counsellor works with empathy and sensitivity, although always keeping to the agreed structure within which goals are articulated and a focal theme uncovered (see Chapter 5). She shows flexibility and understanding in offering six preliminary sessions, the equivalent of a mini-commitment, to give Judy time to agree to a more demanding commitment to relinquish all her self-damaging behaviours in return for a continuation with psychological therapy. Judy struggles within this container, but responds with increased trust and motivation.

Within the agreed number of time-focused sessions, Judy develops a clear understanding of how her childhood and adolescence had led her into a dependent and collusive relationship with her parents (see Chapter 6). She struggles to establish a separate identity and to discard her role as the 'identified patient' within her family. The existence of a clearly articulated commitment and a fixed closing date provides her with a safeguard against further dependency, and bolsters her tentative self-confidence as she establishes a new friendship network as a reasonably healthy young adult. Although a re-referral to the hospital psychotherapy department is considered by Judy as well as the social worker, she is unlikely to take up this option. Clients like Judy typically long to be valuable and are often attracted into some branch of the 'caring professions', where, for several years, they sublimate their wish to heal themselves and their families by working on behalf of other casualties from dysfunctional families. Only when she is faced with another period of crisis, typically a feeling of 'burn out', is Judy likely to seek out another episode of psychological therapy. In this she would be assisted by her memories of the psychiatric social worker whose gentle and appropriately time-structured interventions provided her with a model for assisted psychological evolution. Motivated by her previous good experience of one-to-one therapeutic engagement, and having achieved a reasonable level of external stability, Judy would eventually be a candidate for either a time-extended or time-expanded commitment. She would still need a clearly articulated exit structure as well as a practitioner who could contain within the therapeutic relationship all the banked-up rage and grief which Judy used to act out in multi-impulsive and self-destructive behaviours.

PROFOUND ANALYSIS OR PERMANENT PATIENT? TIM'S STORY

In Chapter 1, the prevailing opinion that 'in the best of all possible worlds, longer-term psychotherapy would be the response of choice' (p. 6) is challenged. The tendency to conflate profundity with the length of time spent engaged in psychological therapy is particularly prevalent within the exclusive but influential world of psychoanalytically trained practitioners. In Britain there is still a grudging awe for 'analysis' even amongst those practitioners whose training has been within a humanistic or cognitive-behavioural orientation. This is concealed behind the shrill, and often misinformed, criticisms and cynicisms expressed during workshops and training sessions about the 'abuses' of analytic abstinence and the Freudian tradition in general. As their training progresses and they become experienced practitioners, these erstwhile critics often turn towards one of the psychoanalytic schools, whether Jungian or Freudian, for their own prolonged experience of psychological therapy. This conversion is usually gradual and demonstrates the practitioners' own search to extend and expand their psychological evolution. However appropriate for the professional, as well as personal, development of some psychotherapists and counsellors, this deepening of understanding through long-term therapeutic commitment is not necessarily beneficial. For some individuals this becomes long-term avoidance of the core and crucial issues which cripple their interpersonal and social relationships.

Tim's story is used, in Chapters 2 and 3, to illustrate the subtle ways in which long-term psychotherapy can become a box instead of a channel towards change. Initially, Tim seeks out 'analysis' for somewhat dubious motives. Although spurred on by genuine pain arising from a recent failure in a romantic relationship, he prefers to explain away his twice a week psychotherapy sessions as a part of his professional development. He finds a psychoanalytically trained practitioner who facilitates Tim in a very rapid discovery of his core issue, 'a painful pattern of unexpressed emotional need leading to continual avoidance of intimacy and subsequent relationship failures' (p. 25). This remains a purely intellectual discovery for the next two years while Tim enjoys the status of being a mental health professional with the expensive privilege of analysis and the comforting collusion of mutual admiration provided by his twice-weekly sessions. His analyst is a warm and caring man, able to provide accurate and insightful interpretations within a supportive relationship. However, he does not effectively challenge Tim's fear of sexual intimacy and preference for social isolation, nor unpack the twinning transference which develops. This is manifested in the therapy session where Tim's description of his military father is met with apparent mutuality of experience and calm discussion rather than a possible catalyst for Tim's grief and anger. Later, Tim joins a training group led by the same analyst and the twin-like relationship is compounded by his fostering Tim's special role as a colleague within a non-medical group. This failure to challenge the comfortable aspects of their relationship leads to Tim's increased isolation even in a group setting.

Tim returns to psychological therapy only when his social isolation and depressive mood states are uncovered by his encounter with a practitioner who combines organisational consultancy with psychotherapy. Once again he is offered an extended period of therapeutic engagement but, this time, the offer is structured by explicit goals and behaviour-based experiments, to take place between sessions (see Chapter 7). The practitioner insists on explicit and immediate engagement with the problematic issues which Tim has been accustomed to discussing and understanding rather than tackling. This is uncomfortable for Tim, and he defends himself by remaining critical and disdainful about her training and her use of informal skills-based language. He has learnt to avoid contact with other human beings by retreating into abstract intellectualisations. This is now being challenged, and Tim is faced with his fear of and his longing for other human beings. Given a free rein by the practitioner, he exercises his choice to take a break from psychological therapy in order to explore the risky business of living more authentically in a social environment.

He returns with a clearer understanding of the direction in which he needs to move, and to a reluctant admission of his attachment to the practitioner. Tim will rapidly develop an erotic transference towards this lively woman, whom he finds both disturbing and irritating. Working through and disclosing these feelings within the container of a professional relationship, Tim will learn to risk and survive passionate emotions. His need to be special and different from normal mortals will fade and with it his tendency to idealise authority figures. It will be more possible for him to engage in the messy fluctuations of ordinary sexual encounters and amorous relationships. He may even be able to take a chance on romantic love and partnership.

CLIENT AS CONSUMER OR PREMATURE EXIT? GUY'S STORY

Throughout this book, the advantage of a clear exit structure has been asserted and extolled. Practitioners have been advised to consider most of their clients as likely to benefit from a reasonably brief episode of formal involvement in psychological therapy. Research has been quoted to substantiate this notion (Budman 1981, Koss and Butcher 1986, Talmon 1990, Kopta *et al.* 1992) and it has been baldly stated that only a minority of individuals really want, or need, any form of extended or expanded commitment. In particular, the advantage of a clearly defined closing date has been celebrated. This theoretical position has been supported by Mann's (1973)

argument that there is a universal desire to recreate the timelessness of
infancy and avoid facing the real problems of a finite human existence. This
'horror of time' (Mann 1973: 9) is as prevalent in practitioners as clients,
and, combined with a wish to be compassionate, can increase their difficulty
in maintaining an agreed closing date. Since psychological therapy is
usually equated, by non-practitioners, with a breakdown in normal functioning, many clients will be attracted to the notion of achieving change by a
specific date. Practitioners critical of time-limited psychological therapy are
likely to cite this rapid progression towards completion as indicative of
premature exit.

Guy is one of these clients. A child of the 1980s, he sees counselling as a
resource to be used in his life-long search for self-improvement and in his
battle to be accepted into a competitive white society. Pragmatic, intelligent
and sophisticated, he engages rapidly with the concept that his childhood
experiences were likely to be influencing his present behaviours (see Chapter
2). He is, initially, less aware that his emotions are going to be so deeply
touched. He moves precipitately to the catharsis stage and it seems likely, at
this stage, that the time-focused commitment may result in a superficial
'flight into health' (Greenson 1967: 276). However, his counsellor encourages him to restrict his more painful feelings to the therapy room by leaving
them there, written down on a piece of paper (see Chapter 5). From the
outset, Guy is in touch with the repetitive patterns occurring within the
therapeutic relationship itself. His suspicion of benevolent authority in the
form of white middle-class females and his more archaic anger with mother
figures in general becomes focal, but only after he has experienced the
counsellor as considerate and aware of his hard-won self-respect. The
transference elements of his interactions with the counsellor are compounded by her age, her gender and by their racial differences.

To work with such intensity within a short time, the counsellor has to
return Guy continually to the central issue, whether his stated difficulties
are with her, his fiancée or his future mother-in-law. The therapeutic
engagement moves from the mini-commitment to the time-focused agreement (see Chapter 7). The counsellor makes use of a missed session and the
impending closing date to make clear links to Guy's complex feelings of
rage, suspicion and longing which fuel his resistance to emotional attach-
ments, especially with women. Finally, she gently unpacks his wish to adopt
herself as 'a replacement ideal parent', encouraging him to move from self-
care to the renunciation stage (see Table 2). So, with his attention re-
focused on his real-life relationships, Guy and the counsellor are described
as reaching a satisfactory completion of a time-limited and brief psychotherapeutic commitment.

In some ways this may seem too neat a conclusion. The counsellor has
respected Guy's role as a customer, and stayed faithful to his original aims
which were to use the limited time to prepare himself for his planned

marriage to a young middle-class white woman. The more profound issues of his fanatical fear of engulfment and his flight from his own racial heritage may have been ignored and even colluded with by the use of such short-term therapy. However, for practitioners to insist upon longer-term psychological therapy, no matter how insightful the reason, is to claim a position of superior knowledge and to discount the natural evolutionary progress of their clients. Guy has sought and experienced a successful experience with a skilled practitioner. When he encounters emotional discomfort again, perhaps through his children's experience of racial prejudice, he will turn again towards some form of psychological understanding. He may even take up the counsellor's suggested referral to a black or Asian male psychotherapist.

THE MONEY QUESTION: CAN PSYCHOLOGICAL THERAPISTS AFFORD TO WORK WITHIN THIS MODEL? AYESHA'S STORY

Talmon (1990) is one of the few writers describing a brief model of psychological therapy who tackles the difficult question of the practitioner's need for monetary remuneration. His promotion of single-session therapy (SST) brings this issue into stark relief. He suggests that therapists may be resisting or ignoring the possibility of using SST deliberately in their practices because the single session does not provide enough opportunity for knowledge about clients, intimacy with clients or financial reward from clients.

> Money, knowledge and intimacy are powerful forces in therapy, as they are in most aspects of life, and cannot be ignored when a therapist needs to decide whether to offer a patient more therapy. Therapists must take good care of their own needs if they are to take good care of the needs of their patients.
>
> (Talmon 1990: 129)

This straightforward and sympathetic acknowledgement of the dilemma is encouraging. Talmon (1990: 129–32) goes on to recommend two solutions. For therapists who work for a third-party provider, whether this is a salary-providing organisation or through an insurance scheme, he recommends negotiating higher financial remuneration for shorter-term work. He argues that all practitioners will increasingly have to explain the cost-effectiveness of their treatments to all purchasers. For practitioners providing a 'direct service (with no third-party payments)' Talmon (1990: 131) suggests that they might consider two ways forward. They could stagger their fees so that deliberately structured short-term work commands a much higher fee. In addition, they could offer a 'flat fee per treatment' which would entail accurate assessment as well as considerable confidence in one's own proficiency. These solutions are very much based on clearly established and agreed outcome criteria. The more subtle changes and unexpected areas of self-development would be difficult to predict or to describe in advance.

These recommendations might seem bold and somewhat alien to the more reticent UK practitioner, brought up in a climate where a public health service, charitable endeavours and volunteer guidance workers have traditionally provided the bulk of psychotherapeutic support to the general population. The majority of UK practitioners receive their initial training within these settings, and their attitudes towards direct financial negotiation can be influenced by an ethos which deplores the need to charge people who are psychologically distressed. This argument is put forward boldly by Pilgrim (1993: 157) who argues that, since Thatcher's rise to power in 1979, 'the wider political context has ... legitimized the notion that the cash nexus is honourable, rather than corrupting and discriminatory'. Pilgrim links this general argument against clinical private practice with an assertion that the practice of psychological therapy is a form of assisted 'personal learning' which is 'of dubious efficacy' and 'marginal utility', with clients likely to experience three possible outcomes: 'substantial personal help, or it might be a waste of time and money, or they might feel worse after the contact than before' (Pilgrim 1993: 159). He dismisses completely the arguments that people are more likely to value a service for which they pay a fee, and to enter into increased levels of dynamic communication within the therapeutic relationship. Pilgrim (1993: 158) points out the sparsity of evidence for these arguments and suggests that there is a large area of 'associated guilt' felt by the psychotherapeutic profession about charging fees for their services.

While, in an ideally benevolent and all-providing society, all forms of professional help in coping with the difficult 'business of being human' (Gilmore 1973: 5) might be provided by centrally funded public services, this is certainly not the case in most societies at the end of the twentieth century. Lawyers, accountants and other consultants provide help for people who are faced with personal and interpersonal difficulties, only a small amount of whom qualify for any form of free service. Their approach to charging fees is considerably less tinged with guilt and is based on a professional belief in their services as necessary and useful, for a limited and specific length of time. Their charges vary according to expertise and reputation. If practitioners of psychological therapy could adopt a similar pragmatic approach, then they may be able to offer, to private individuals as well as to organisations, a service which is clearly defined in purpose and in duration. This transformation might entail a loss of mystique and an increased attention to generally accepted and well researched methodologies rather than to arguments about theoretical orientation.

Ayesha is an example of a convinced consumer of the psychological therapies. She has three consecutive experiences of being a client, one of which was within group therapy. It is possible that the first of these encounters, at a time of increasing crisis and dysfunctional behaviour, was provided by a public service, or within the voluntary sector. When we first meet Ayesha, in Chapter 2, she has decided to re-enter the field. She seeks out an experienced and much sought-after practitioner, a woman much older than herself who seems wise and well-grounded in her approach. Ayesha has quite clear aims at first, related to her own observation that she was repeating the relationship patterns of her disastrous marriage with her new partner, a woman. She expects and accepts an offer of ongoing, or time-expanded, psychological therapy. The contractual commitment entered into does not seem to include considerations of a time limit or of specific outcome criteria. The elderly practitioner does not overtly suggest a preliminary mini-commitment or conduct structured reviews. She appears to be comfortable with her own tradition which we can imagine to be originally psychoanalytic. Presumably this practitioner now makes her living from private practice as a psychotherapist. She is fortunate in that she is popular and receives more referrals than she needs (see Chapter 8).

Ayesha does not seem to begrudge the considerable investment she is making in her own psychological therapy over the next three years. Even so, for Ayesha, as with most clients, paying for the sessions is an extra expense which she probably worries about from time to time. Significantly, financial considerations influence her decision about ending individual therapy and moving into her therapist's group (see Chapter 8). At this time, Ayesha has herself become self-employed and is setting up her own private practice as a counsellor. She is likely to use her own experience of being a client as a model for her own practice. It could come as a surprise to her that many of her clients will not have the same accepting attitude to unstructured long-term engagement in psychological therapy. They may leave unexpectedly and without discussing the real reasons for their departure. If financial considerations are not included in any discussion of expectations and desired outcomes, then there is a danger that this becomes a hidden but major influence. Ayesha will be limiting her practice to clients who are wealthy enough not to worry about money or who are themselves practitioners and accept therapeutic engagement as a legitimate expense. In this way, many practitioners are likely to continue the self-perpetuating avoidance of this crucial issue, adopting a slightly guilty acknowledgement that they rely upon their long-term clients for their basic financial security.

Most practitioners of psychological therapy are highly principled and ethically aware individuals. Surely it is worth their considering some of Talmon's (1990) solutions as described above. For those who develop a high level of skills in accurate assessment and flexible reviews, clearly defined offers of contractual commitments and precision in finding a focal theme, it is surely appropriate to match fee to expertise rather than to length of time. This could mean offering clients, after a preliminary period of assessment, a limited amount of sessions at a higher fee per session with the option of a longer term of psychological therapy at a lower fee per session. This interpretation of Talmon's rather cut and dried, outcome-based recommendations allows for more flexibility and for subtle areas of motivation to be addressed as they are allowed into awareness. To enter into such an agreement, clients would be operating from a position of choice rather than being the recipients of a traditional procedure. It has been argued throughout that longer-term psychological therapy is an option to be considered only by clients with enough stability and ego-strength to consider themselves as discerning customers. Decisions about cost or length of therapeutic engagement are not appropriate in situations of crisis or disorganised thinking. For clients in these situations some form of holding arrangement, preferably provided through a third party of some sort, is indicated. Only when there is some relaxation of pressure to seek help can prospective clients make an informed choice.

CONTRACTUAL CLARITY OR FLEXIBILITY IN COMMITMENT? DUNCAN'S STORY

Throughout this book there has been an emphasis on both clarity and flexibility. These can seem to be contradictory aspirations and they are certainly held in tension by most thoughtful practitioners. The flow-chart of decision-making encapsulated in Table 1 describes three major choice points, preceded by an initial instantaneous assessment as to whether a client is in crisis, 'visiting' or willing to engage. Very little credit may seem to be given to a more relaxed wait-and-see engagement with the client. Practitioners are urged to offer a clearly defined contractual commitment and then to move briskly into discerning the entry point needed at this stage of a client's life process of psychological evolution (see Table 2). In addition, practitioners are offered, in Table 3a, a checklist to aid continuous assessment and review of the therapeutic process. Even when settled into one of the four major types of commitment, practitioners are asked to consider working through a series of questions as they progress through the six steps for every commitment described in Table 4. Provided with such a wealth of prescriptive guidelines, practitioners might be tempted either to transform the ideas offered in this book into a rigid framework or to dismiss them entirely as impractical and inappropriate for real clients consulting real practitioners. If this latter judgement is made, then the book has failed to emphasise the crucial importance of retaining a flexible and open mind, using these tables as aids to a continuing and uncertain process.

Duncan is a client whose engagement in psychological therapy can be described through the model proposed in this book, and yet demands both flexibility and structure from the practitioner who takes him on as a client. His initial encounter with this male psychotherapist is at a time of crisis (see

Chapter 2). His marriage has just collapsed and he is behaving chaotically, drinking heavily and losing support from his friendship circle. He insists that he needs long-term psychotherapy while violently accusing his mother-in-law of ruining his wife's childhood. The practitioner makes an immediate judgement that this man needs holding with a crisis intervention. He provides a reality-based problem-solving session in which he assesses the risk factors involved and offers another appointment during the same week. This may have been kept but Duncan does not return for the more structured assessment interview which he has been offered. The practitioner has been open and honest with Duncan, recognising the value of using the real relationship and postponing any discussion of a working alliance and completely eschewing any reference to the paternal transference which almost immediately emerged (see Chapter 3). At this point, it could be inferred that Duncan's motivation to use psychological therapy has been mishandled, and a potentially insightful client has been given a few coping strategies to make him reasonably functional again.

However Duncan does return to investigate psychological therapy, two years later. In the meantime, he has continued his process of psychological evolution in his own way by becoming a member of Alcoholics Anonymous. It could be argued that he has found the perfect setting for his transferential issues in the benevolent and effective parentalism of this organisation. He seems to have worked through several of the stages outlined in Table 2, in a very different order from that listed. He has worked on some of the self-care issues, choosing to link this with a somewhat premature renunciation of the anger and grief experienced in childhood. Without too much preparation, he has entered willingly into intense levels of disclosure, within the AA group setting. To a certain extent he has put in place the self-support and environmental support associated with the final stage of empowerment. The practitioner has to work his way carefully into Duncan's own developmental process, focusing upon the areas which have been neglected or avoided.

For this reason, and in opposition to much of the guidance given at the beginning of Chapter 8, Duncan is accepted as a client within the time-expanded commitment. He is offered some preparatory sessions which he uses with energy and dedication, entering rapidly into catharsis and working through painful childhood experiences with authenticity and insight. Only when he is embarked upon a long-term commitment does Duncan display real difficulties with regard to trust and issues of power normally associated with the preparation stage. He tests the therapist's patience and dedication as if he had only just encountered psychological therapy. He continually tempts the other man into parenting him and indulging his masochistic longings, while remaining competitive and distrustful. To work with Duncan, the practitioner using the approach outlined in this book, would need to continually monitor all the stages described in Table 2 as well as every step outlined in Table 4, in order to discover which facet of the focal theme was becoming apparent. He would need to match his timing and pacing to Duncan's own readiness for change. Above all he would need to remain alert and totally flexible, ready to work within the spirit of focus and commitment while using whatever parts of this structured approach were, at this time, useful and necessary. Given this backing, Duncan is able to continue the process of self-development through insight initiated at his very first crisis management session. His last session with the practitioner is replete with satisfaction as well as a realistic acceptance that life still has much to teach him.

CONCLUSION AND COMPLETION

In this chapter, as in the book as a whole, the thread of the clients' fictional stories has been woven through the theoretical integration offered by the use of focus and commitment as a baseline for the practice of time-conscious psychological therapy. Wherever possible the client's life experience has been made central and practitioners encouraged to develop their professional expertise in order to provide a peripheral but essential service when needed. Above all excellence in discernment of focal issues, combined with strategic assessment of each individual client's present and ongoing requirements, is presented as an impossible but worthwhile goal. This pursuit of excellence requires humility, value-free acceptance of clients as experts in their own lives, and awareness of the wider context within which all psychological therapy takes place.

BIBLIOGRAPHY

Alexander, F. and French, T.M. (1946) *Psychoanalytic Therapy: Principles and applications*, New York: Ronald Press.

American Psychiatric Association (APA) (1987) *Diagnostic and Statistical Manual of Mental Disorders*, 3rd edn, revised, Washington, DC: American Psychiatric Association.

Argyle, M. and Trower, P. (1980) *Person to Person: Ways of communicating*, London: Harper and Row.

Barkham, M. and Shapiro, D.A. (1989) 'Towards resolving the problem of waiting lists: psychotherapy in two-plus-one sessions', *Clinical Psychology Forum* 23: 15–19.

Beck, A.T. (1976) *Cognitive Therapy and the Emotional Disorders*, New York: International University Press.

Beveridge, W. (1942) *The Beveridge Report: Social Insurance and Allied Services*. London: House of Commons.

Bloom, B.L. (1981) 'Focused single-session therapy: initial development and evaluation', in S.H. Budman (ed.) *Forms of Brief Therapy*, New York: Guilford Press.

Bonaparte, M. (1940) 'Time and the unconscious', *International Journal of Psychoanalysis* 21: 427.

Brazier, D. (ed.) (1993) *Beyond Carl Rogers*, London: Constable.

Breuer, J. and Freud, S. (1955) 'Studies on hysteria', in J. Strachey (ed.) *The Standard Edition of the Complete Psychological Works of Sigmund Freud*, vol. 2, London: Hogarth Press (first published 1895).

British Association for Counselling (BAC) (1992) *Code of Ethics and Practice for Counsellors*, Rugby: BAC.

Buber, M. (1970) *I and Thou*, trans. W. Kaufmann, Edinburgh: T. and T. Clark (first published 1923).

Budman, S.H. (ed.) (1981) *Forms of Brief Therapy*, New York: Guilford Press.

Butler, G. and Low, J. (1994) 'Short-term psychotherapy', in P. Clarkson and M. Pokorny (eds) *The Handbook of Psychotherapy*, London: Routledge.

Cade, B. and O'Hanlon, W.H. (1993) *A Brief Guide to Brief Therapy*, London: Norton.

Cardinale, M. (1984) *The Words to Say It*, London: Pan Books.

Casement, P. (1985) *On Learning from the Patient*, London: Routledge.

Clarkson, P. (1989) *Gestalt Counselling in Action*, London: Sage.

Clarkson, P. (1990) 'A multiplicity of psychotherapeutic relationships', *British Journal of Psychotherapy* 7 (2): 148–63.

Clarkson, P. (1994) 'The nature and range of psychotherapy', in P. Clarkson and M. Pokorny (eds) *The Handbook of Psychotherapy*, London: Routledge.

Clarkson, P. and Mackewn, J. (1993) *Fritz Perls*, London: Sage.

Cohn, H.W. (1986) 'The double context: on combining individual and group therapy', *Group Analysis* 19: 327–39.

Crits-Christoph, P. and Barber, J. (eds) (1991) *Handbook of Short-term Dynamic Therapies*, New York: Basic Books.

Culverwell, A., Agnew, R., Barkham, M., Hardy, G.E., Rees, A., Shapiro, D.A., Reynolds, S., Halstead, J., Stiles, W.B. and Harrington, M.G. (1994) 'The Second Sheffield Psychotherapy Project and Collaborative Psychotherapy Project: some initial findings and their clinical implications', *Clinical Psychology Forum* 72: 5–9.

Cummings, N.A. (1986) 'The dismantling of our health system: strategies for the survival of psychological practice', *American Psychologist* 41: 426–31.

Dahlberg, C.C. (1970) 'Sexual contact between client and therapist', *Contemporary Psychoanalysis* 5: 107–24.

Davanloo, H. (1980) *Current Trends in Short-term Dynamic Therapy*, New York: Aronson.

de Shazer, S. (1985) *Keys to Solution in Brief Therapy*, New York: W.W. Norton.

de Shazer, S. (1988) *Clues: Investigating solutions in brief therapy*, New York: W.W. Norton.

Dinnage, R. (1989) *One to One: Experiences of psychotherapy*, London: Penguin Books.

Dryden, W. (1991) *A Dialogue with John Norcross. Toward Integration*, Milton Keynes: Open University Press.

Ellis, A. (1970) *The Essence of Rational Psychotherapy: A comprehensive approach to treatment*, New York: Institute for Rational Living.

Elton Wilson, J. and Barkham, M. (1994) 'A practitioner-scientist approach to psychotherapy process and outcome research', in P. Clarkson and M. Pokorny (eds) *The Handbook of Psychotherapy*, pp. 49–72, London: Routledge.

Erikson, M.H. and Rossi, E.L. (1979) *Hypnotherapy: An exploratory casebook*, New York: Irvington.

Evans, R.E. (1987) 'The First Meeting', Paper prepared for psychology undergraduates (unpublished).

Eysenck, H.J. (1952) 'The effects of psychotherapy: an evaluation', *Journal of Consulting Psychology* 16: 319–21.

Foucault, M. (1976) *Madness and Civilization*, London: Tavistock.

France, A. (1988) *Consuming Psychotherapy*, London: Free Association Books.

Frank, J. (1985) 'Therapeutic components shared by all psychotherapies', in M.J. Mahoney and A. Freeman (eds) *Cognition and Psychotherapy*, New York: Plenum.

Freud, S. (1964) *New Introductory Lectures on Psychoanalysis*, London: Hogarth.

Gelso, C.J. and Carter, J.A. (1985) 'The relationship in counseling and psychotherapy: components, consequences and theoretical antecedents', *Counseling Psychologist* 13 (2): 155–243.

Giddens, A. (1991) *Modernity and Self-identity*, Cambridge: Polity Press.

Gilmore, S.K. (1973) *The Counselor-in-Training*, New Jersey: Prentice-Hall Inc.

Greenson, R.R. (1967) *The Techniques and Practice of Psychoanalysis*, vol. 1, New York: International Universities Press.

Haley, J. (1976) *Problem-solving Therapy*, San Francisco: Jossey-Bass.

Hartley, D.E. and Strupp, H.H. (1982) 'The therapeutic alliance: its relationship to outcome in brief psychotherapy', in J. Masline (ed.) *Empirical Studies of Psychoanalytical Theories*, vol. 1, pp. 1–37, Hillsdale, NJ: Erlbaum.

Heron, J. (1979) *Co-counselling*, revised edn, Human Potential Research Project, University of Surrey, Guildford.

Hillman, J. and Ventura, M. (1993) *We've Had 100 Years of Psychotherapy and the World's Getting Worse*, Harper: New York.

Horvarth, A. and Greenberg, L. (1985) 'The development of the Working Alliance Inventory', in L. Greenberg and W. Pinsoff (eds) *The Psychotherapeutic Process: A research handbook*, New York: Guilford.

Howard, G.S. (1986) 'The scientist-practitioner in counseling psychology: toward a deeper integration of theory, research and practice', *The Counseling Psychologist* 14: 61–105.

Howard, K.I., Kopta, S.M., Krause, M.S. and Orlinsky, D.E. (1986) 'The dose-effect relationship in psychotherapy', *American Psychologist* 41: 159–64.

Howe, D. (1993) *On Being a Client*, London: Sage.

Kahler, T. (1978) *Transactional Analysis Revisited*, Little Rock: Human Development Publications.

Kahn, M. (1991) *Between Therapist and Client: The new relationship*, New York: Freeman and Co.

Kierkegaard, S. (1941) *The Sickness unto Death*, Princeton: Princeton University Press.

Kohut, H. (1971) *The Analysis of the Self*, New York: International Universities Press.

Kopta, S.M., Howard, K.I., Lowry, J.L. and Beutler, L.E. (1992) 'The psychotherapy dosage model and clinical significance: estimating how much is enough for psychological symptoms', paper presented at the Annual Meeting of the Society for Psychotherapy Research, Berkeley, California, June.

Koss, M.P. and Butcher, J.N. (1986) 'Research on brief psychotherapy', in S.L. Garfield and A.E. Bergin (eds) *Handbook of Psychotherapy and Behavior Change*, New York: John Wiley.

Koss, M.P. and Shiang, J. (1994) 'Research on brief psychotherapy', in S.L. Garfield and A.E. Bergin (eds) *Handbook of Psychotherapy and Behavior Change*, New York: John Wiley.

Kosviner, A. (1994) 'Psychotherapies within the NHS', in P. Clarkson and M. Pokorny (eds) *The Handbook of Psychotherapy*, London: Routledge.

Lambert, M.J. (1986) 'Implications of psychotherapy outcome for eclectic psychotherapy', in J.C. Norcross (ed.) *Handbook of Eclectic Psychotherapy*, New York: Brunner/Mazel.

Lapworth, P., Sills, C. and Fish, S. (1993) *Transactional Analysis Counselling*. Bicester, Oxon: Winslow Press.

Lasch, C. (1978) *The Culture of Narcissism*, New York: Norton.

Lomas, P. (1987) *The Limits of Interpretation: What's wrong with psychoanalysis?* London: Penguin.

Luborsky, L., Singer, B. and Luborsky, L. (1975) 'Comparative studies of psychotherapy: is it true that everyone has won and all must have prizes?', *Archives of General Psychiatry* 32: 995–1008.

Luborsky L., Crits-Christoph, P., Alexander, L., Margolis, M. and Cohen, M. (1983) 'Two helping alliance methods for predicting outcome of psychotherapy', *Journal of Nervous and Mental Disease* 171: 480–91.

Luborsky L., Crits-Christoph, P., Mintz, J. and Auerbach, A. (1988) *Who Will Benefit from Psychotherapy? Predicting therapeutic outcomes*, New York: Basic Books.

McLeod, J. (1990a) 'The client's experience of counselling and psychotherapy: a review of the research literature', in D. Mearns and W. Dryden (eds) *Experiences of Counselling in Action*, London: Sage.

McLeod, J. (1990b) 'The practitioner's experience of counselling and psychotherapy:

a review of the research literature', in D. Mearns and W. Dryden (eds) *Experiences of Counselling in Action*, London: Sage.

Mair, M. (1989) *Between Psychology and Psychotherapy: A poetics of experience*, London: Routledge.

Malan, D.H. (1975) *A Study of Brief Psychotherapy*, London: Plenum Press.

Malan, D.H. (1979) *Individual Psychotherapy and the Science of Psychodynamics*, New York: Plenum.

Mann, J. (1973) *Time-limited Psychotherapy*, Cambridge, MA: Harvard University Press.

Mann, J. (1981) 'The core of time-limited psychotherapy: time and the central issue', in S. Budman (ed.) *Forms of Brief Therapy*, pp. 25–43. New York: Guilford.

Masson, J.M. (1985) *The Assault on Truth: Freud's suppression of the seduction theory*, Harmondsworth: Penguin.

Masson, J.M. (1989) *Against Therapy*, London: Collins.

May, R. (1989) *The Art of Counselling*, New York: Gardner Press.

Mearns, D. and Dryden, W. (1990) *Experiences of Counselling in Action*, London: Sage.

Mearns, D. and Thorne, B. (1988) *Person-centred Counselling in Action*, London: Sage.

Meltzoff, J. and Kornreich, M. (1970) *Research in Psychotherapy*, New York: Atherton.

Miller, A. (1985) *Thou Shalt not Be Aware: Society's betrayal of the child*, trans. H. Hannum and H. Hannum, London: Pluto Press (first published 1980).

Miller A. (1987) *The Drama of Being a Child and the Search for the True Self*, London: Virago.

Minuchin, S. (1974) *Families and Family Therapy*, Cambridge, MA: Harvard University Press.

Needleman, J. (1983) 'Psychiatry and the sacred', in J. Welwood (ed.) *Awakening the Heart: East/West approaches to psychotherapy and the healing relationship*, London: Shambhala. 5.

Nelson, P. (1985) 'Autobiography in five short chapters', in C. Black (ed.) *Repeat After Me*, Denver: MAC Printing and Publications.

Oldfield, S. (1983) *The Counselling Relationship: A study of the client's experience*, London: Routledge and Kegan Paul.

Orlinsky, D.E. and Howard, K.I. (1977) 'The therapist's experience of psychotherapy', in A. Gurman and A. Razin (eds) *Effective Psychotherapy: A handbook of research*, pp. 566–89, Oxford: Pergamon.

Peake, T.H., Borduin, C.M. and Archer, R.P. (1988) *Brief Psychotherapies: Changing frames of mind*, London: Sage.

Peck, S. (1978) *The Road Less Travelled: A new psychology of love, traditional values and spiritual growth*, New York: Simon and Schuster.

Perls, F., Hefferline, R.F. and Goodman, P. (1951) *Gestalt Therapy: Excitement and growth in the human personality*, London: Souvenir Press.

Pilgrim, D. (1992) 'Psychotherapy and its political evasions', in W. Dryden and C. Feltham (eds) *Psychotherapy and its Discontents*, Buckingham: Open University Press.

Pilgrim, D. (1993) 'Objections to private practice', in W. Dryden (ed.) *Questions and Answers on Counselling in Action*, London: Sage.

Pirsig, R. M. (1976) *Zen and the Art of Motor Cycle Maintenance*, London: Corgi.

Polster, E. (1987) *Every Person's Life Is Worth a Story*, London: Norton.

Pope, K.S., Sonne, J.L. and Holroyd, J. (1993) *Sexual Feeling in Psychotherapy*, Washington, DC: American Psychological Association.

Rogers, C.R. (1959) 'A theory of therapy, personality, and interpersonal relationships as developed in the client-centred framework', in S. Koch (ed.) *Psychology: A study of science*, pp. 209–10, New York: McGraw-Hill.

Rogers, C.R. (1961) *On Becoming a Person: A therapist's view of psychotherapy*, London: Constable.

Rogers, C.R. and Stevens, B. (1967) *Person to Person: The problem of being human*, London: Souvenir Press.

Rutter, P. (1990) *Sex in the Forbidden Zone*, London: Unwin.

Ryle, A. (1990) *Cognitive-Analytic Therapy: Active participation in change*, Chichester: Wiley.

Selvini-Palazzoli, M., Boscolo, L., Cecchin, G. and Prata, G. (1980) 'Hypothesising – circularity – neutrality: three guidelines for the conductor of the session', *Family Process* 19: 445–53.

Shostrom, E. (ed.) (1965) *Three Approaches to Psychotherapy: Client-centered Therapy*, film production, Orange, CA: Psychological Films.

Sloane, R.B., Staples, F.R., Cristol, A.H., Yorkston, N.J. and Whipple, K. (1975) *Psychotherapy Versus Behavior Therapy*, Cambridge, MA: Harvard University Press.

Smail, D. (1987) *Taking Care: An alternative to therapy*, London: Dent.

Smith, M.L. and Glass, G.V. (1977) 'Meta-analysis of psychotherapy outcome studies', *American Psychologist* 32: 752–60.

Smith, M.G., Glass, G.V. and Miller, T.I. (1980) *The Benefits of Psychotherapy*, Baltimore: Johns Hopkins University Press.

Stern, D. (1985) *The Interpersonal World of the Infant*, New York: Basic Books.

Stettbacher, J.K. (1991) *Making Sense of Suffering: The healing confrontation with our own past*, New York: Dutton Penguin USA.

Storr, A. (1979) *The Art of Psychotherapy*, London: Secker and Warburg.

Talmon, M. (1990) *Single-session Therapy*, San Francisco: Jossey Bass.

Thoreau, H.D. (1910) *Walden*, London: Everymans Library (first published 1854).

Vidaver, R.M., Archer, R.P. and Peake, T.H. (1988) 'Fiscal realities: observations, speculations, and suggestions', in T.H. Peake, C.M. Borduin and R.P. Archer (eds) *Brief Psychotherapies: Changing frames of mind*, London: Sage.

Ware, P. (1983) 'Personality adaptations', *Transactional Analysis Journal* 3.

Watzlawick, P. (1983) *The Situation is Hopeless, But Not Serious*, New York: Norton.

Weldon, F. (1993) *Affliction*, London: Harper Collins.

Welwood, J. (1993) 'On psychotherapy and meditation', in J. Welwood (ed.) *Awakening the Heart: East/West approaches to psychotherapy and the healing relationship*, London: Shambhala. 5.

Whitfield, C.L. (1987) *Healing the Child Within*, Florida: Health Communications Inc.

Yalom, I.D. and Elkin, G. (1974) *Every Day Gets a Little Closer*, USA: Basic Books.

Yontef, G.M. (1980) 'Gestalt therapy: a dialogic method', unpublished manuscript.

Index

Table 1 Focused and contractual commitments

ASSESSMENT/INTAKE INTERVIEW		
Either – **in crisis** – (not seeking psychological change)	*or* – **'visiting'** – (testing psychological therapy)	*or* – **willing to engage** – (take personal responsibility for psychological change)

FIRST CHOICE POINT	
'Holding' arrangement – 1–3 sessions (may be more than weekly)	*or* **mini-commitment** – 4–6 regular weekly sessions

SECOND CHOICE POINT
FIRST REVIEW

Life without psych. therapy:	*or*	**continuation** – Choice of three possible commitments: *time-focused, time-extended or time-expanded*	*or*	**referral** possibly to a **group**
STOP				*STOP*

time-focused: 10–13 sessions *including* mini-c. Clearly stated aims leading up to firmly agreed end date	*or*	**time-extended:** 4 sessions' notice of finishing. 12-plus sessions with final date in view. Several reviews	*or*	**time-expanded:** 2 months' notice of finishing. Up to 4–5 years. Regular reviews. End mutually agreed

STOP

THIRD CHOICE POINT
SECOND MAJOR REVIEW

life outside therapy	**lateral transfer** Focused- > Extended- > Expanded	**referral** or **group therapy**

Table 2 Working with a client's life process of psychological evolution

STAGE *Possible point of entry/area of focus (after intake)*	FOCAL TASK *Issues relevant to this stage tied into a focal theme based on earlier experiences*	FOCAL RELATIONSHIP *Working Alliance (WA) Real Relationship (RR) or Transference Relationship (TA)*
PREPARATION *Build trust*	Work on present problems. Defences/symptoms understood as strategies. Re-education about power issues and child devt.	WA — main mode and essential focus. RR — explore factual/cultural components; and put aside. TR — note clues.
DISCLOSURE *Respect and listen as the 'story' is told objectively by the adult survivor*	Experiences named/labelled. Description of situations and sensations with associated self-image. Original strategies for survival described and validated.	WA — essential to cushion vulnerability of disclosure and insights. TR — noted but not made focal: counter-transference contained. RR — only needed if modelling required or for cultural enquiry.
CATHARSIS *Facilitate contact with client's early emotional reality*	Re-experiences as child did. Queries and, with practitioner as witness, ally and advocate, reframes experience. Natural needs expressed versus adapted needs/reactive patterns.	TR — likely to be central for both participants. WA — in background and used to maintain coping strategies outside sessions. RR — cautiously contain.
SELF-CARE *Share in the 'corrective' emotional experience (Alexander and French 1946)*	Punitive and critical internal monitors replaced by insightful acceptance. Identity and related needs affirmed and restructured within cultural and social parameters.	TR — central; practitioner used to replace authority figures and previous models. RR — can be introduced to balance idealistic transference. WA — must be restated and used overtly.
RENUNCIATION *Encourage grieving, raging and letting go*	Sorrow and anger for lost ideals of childhood and parenthood. Acceptance of reality in past events. Allowing practitioner to step down from being the replacement ideal parent.	RR — can become more focal to replace idealisation. WA — maintained and wound down. TR — unpacked and worked with overtly, especially by client.
EMPOWERMENT *Observe the client getting on with existential issues of life*	Self-support and environmental support in place. Restructured relationships/partnerships. Confrontation/re-contracting with external social system. Use of groups/other networks/future therapy.	WA — available if required. Offer follow-ups/reviews. TR — likely to remain operational. Avoid intimate or financial connections. RR — contacts may be possible if abstinence maintained.

Table 3a Ongoing assessment and review

Client's name/no.	Intake/review/last session notes

....

GP info. .... Drugs/diet, etc. ....

Previous psych. therapy: ....

(1) Description of client and of process/personal and interpersonal
(present focus)

(2) Problems/concerns/themes/issues
(present focus)

(3) History: family/social/losses/gains/survivals
(past focus)

(4) Aims and goals/obstacles visualised
(future focus)

(5) Unfinished business
(present and future focus)

(6) Therapeutic alliance concerns/themes
(past and present focus)

(7) Transference issues to be considered
(past and present focus)

(8) Life process stage (use Table 2).
(Any diagnostic considerations?)

(9) Commitment agreed: Continuation?/Referral?/Close?
(use Table 1)

© 1996 by J. Elton Wilson

Table 4 Six steps for every commitment

Step 1: Making contact — the working alliance is an emotional bond
Who are you and where am I?
Do we like each other, and does it matter?
Do we trust each other enough?

Step 2: Testing the commitment — the working alliance is contractual
What do you require of me, professionally?
What do I ask of you, as a client?

Step 3: Expectations and pitfalls
What do you hope to gain?
What was your previous experience of psychological change?
What do you fear?
How will you stop yourself getting what you want?

Step 4: Telling 'the story' — entering the client's life process
What brought you here, now?
Where have you been?
How was it for you, then?

Step 5: Working with the focal theme for this stage
What keeps happening again and again?
If this is the pattern, how was it learnt?
What do you need to re-learn?
So, what work is needed now?

Step 6: Reviewing the commitment — past and future
Shall we continue?
What are the alternatives?
How shall we work together now?
Have the goalposts changed?
